Photographing

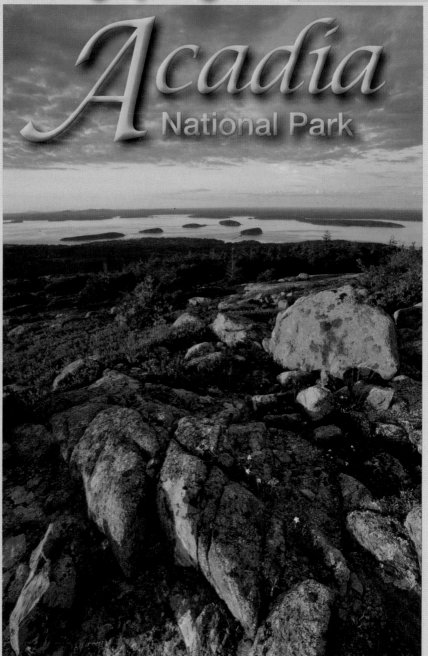

Acadia
National Park

The Essential Guide to When, Where, and How

ANALEMMA
PRESS

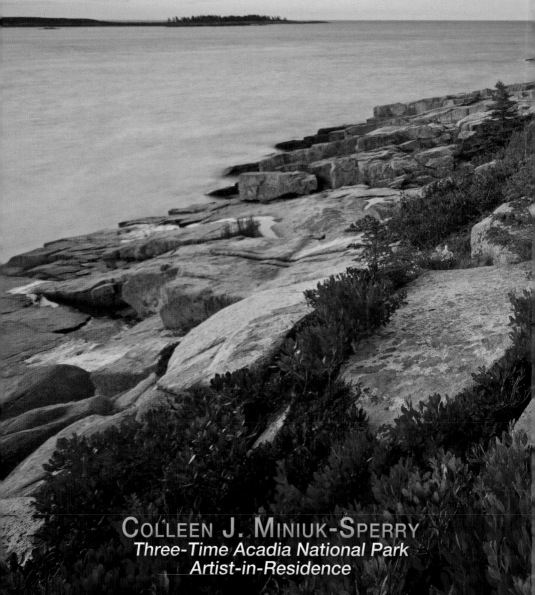

Photographing
Acadia
National Park
The Essential Guide to When, Where, and How

COLLEEN J. MINIUK-SPERRY
Three-Time Acadia National Park
Artist-in-Residence

To Kate Petrie, for her generosity, boundless knowledge of Acadia, and unmatched dedication to education.

To my loving husband, Craig, for always encouraging me to "go big or go home."

To the Miniuk and Sperry families for faithfully supporting me no matter the journey.

In loving memory of Craig's mother, Mercedes Ann Boos Sperry, who spent her final vacation on Earth enjoying the beauty and serenity within Acadia National Park.

Photographing Acadia National Park: The Essential Guide to When, Where, and How

Author & photographer: Colleen J. Miniuk-Sperry
Editor: Erik Berg
Graphic design: Paul Gill/Gill Photo Graphic

ISBN: 978-0-9833804-7-4
Library of Congress Control Number: 2013914867

Disclaimer:
Enjoying the outdoors is not without risk. Because no guidebook can adequately disclose all potential hazards or risks involved, all readers and participants must assume full responsibility for their own safety and actions while visiting the locations and engaging in the activities referred to in this book. The author and publisher disclaim any liability for any injury, suffering, or any other damage caused by traveling to and from a location, visiting a listed area, or performing any other act implicitly or explicitly suggested in this guide.

The author and publisher have conscientiously tried to include the most accurate and up-to-date information at publication time. However, since names, roads, places, conditions, access, and the like may change over time, please adequate research and prepare for your trip prior to your outing.

COVER PHOTO: *Waves swirl below Bass Harbor Head Lighthouse near Bass Harbor. Canon 5D, 24-105mm at 24mm, ISO 50, f/20 at 6 sec., polarizer, three-stop graduated neutral density filter.*

TITLE PAGE PHOTO: *View of the Porcupine Islands and Frenchman Bay from the Cadillac Mountain North Ridge Trail at sunset. Canon 5DMII, 16-35mm at 16mm, ISO 100, f/20 at 1.3 sec., three-stop graduated neutral density filter.*

OVERLEAF PHOTO: *Low sweet blueberry turns lipstick red in autumn along the eastern side of the Schoodic Peninsula. Canon 5DMII, 16-35mm at 16mm, ISO 100, f/8 at 10 sec., four-stop graduated neutral density filter.*

Acknowledgements

*T*hough my name is solely listed on the front cover, a project of this magnitude does not happen alone. Words can hardly express just how grateful I am to those who contributed to creation of this book.

Thank you, Kate Petrie, the Acadia Artist-in-Residence Coordinator, for giving me the honor of being an Artist-in-Residence three times. I could have never imagined the doors you and this opportunity would open for me when I first applied in 2009. If it were not for you, this book would have never existed.

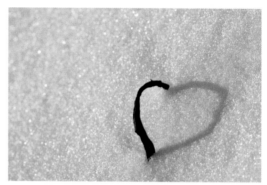

Nature shows its love along the Wonderland Trail. Canon 5DMII, 100mm, ISO 200, f/18 at 1/250th sec., two 12mm extension tubes stacked.

Special thanks to Acadia National Park and the Schoodic Education and Research Center (SERC) for hosting me during my residencies. So many employees and volunteers helped to make my stays unforgettable. I especially am appreciative of JoAnn and Ron Pippen, who, along with Kate, helped establish the Photojournalism program for the Schoodic Education Adventure (SEA)—a highlight of my photography career!

Endless thanks to my mom, Jacque, and husband, Craig, for serving as ruthless editors, reading and rereading this manuscript countless times. Thank you also to my dad, Bob, for his patience and persistence in securing sponsor partnerships and for his invaluable sales and marketing expertise.

I greatly appreciate the financial and equipment support, as well as the opportunity to collaborate with our gracious book sponsors: Arizona Highways Photography Workshops, Bar Harbor Inn, Gary Fong, Hunts Photo & Video, Hoodman Corporation, Manfrotto, Scenic Flights of Acadia, Wimberley, and Winter Harbor 5 & 10.

I am forever indebted to my "Virtual Focus Group," who offered much needed honest feedback and direction early in the project. A heartfelt thank you to Ambika Balasubramaniyan, Erik Berg, Jacque Miniuk, Bianca Antinore Miniuk, Denise Schultz, Kerry Smith, and Floris van Breugel for their help.

I am equally thankful to my friend, fellow photographer, and this book's graphic designer, Paul Gill, who in co-authoring my first book, *Wild in Arizona: Photographing Arizona's Wildflowers, A Guide to When, Where, & How* (**www.wildinarizona.com**), exposed me to a whole new set of skills which I needed to create a cohesive written and photographic piece. Now that I have ventured on my own for this guidebook, I truly appreciate the enormous amount of skill, time, and effort that goes into producing a book.

I am especially grateful for my unbelievably keen editor, Erik Berg, who has taught me more about verb tenses, comma splices, and compound modifiers than I ever wanted to know! Thank you, Erik, for always encouraging me to share my voice.

Finally, thanks to YOU for your support! With the purchase of this book, you are making a difference as 10% of this book's profit will go to the SEA program— an unsurpassed educational opportunity for children to learn about science and nature in Acadia National Park. Also, because of you, I have the fortunate chance to do what I love most every day: photograph and write about the Great Outdoors to help others enjoy it!

Table of Contents

Location Listing 8

Introduction 10

How to Use This Book 12

History of Acadia National Park 14

Seasons of Acadia 18

Preparing for Your Outing 22

Practicing "Leave No Trace" 23

Cautions 24

Photography Basics 26

Mount Desert Island Locations 44

Schoodic Peninsula Locations 148

Isle au Haut Locations 184

Additional Resources 203

Shoot Calendar 204

Top Experiences 208

Sponsors and Valued Individual Contributors ... 210

Index 216

About the Author 224

Low sweet blueberry flashes striking colors in October and November along the Schoodic Peninsula. Canon 5DMII, 100-400mm at 275mm, ISO 400, f/5.6 at 1/250th sec., polarizer.

"Making the Photo" Stories Listing

The author photographing a mushroom along the Witch Hole Pond Carriage Road. See the resulting image on page 40. Photo by Craig Sperry.

*I*n addition to the fifty selected locations, throughout this book, you will find 12 "Making the Photo" stories from my own numerous experiences and photographic learnings in the park. By sharing insights into my personal connection with the given subject matter, my photographic approach, and the results, I hope to inspire you to create your own photographs and stories during your visit.

1. Psychedelic Skypools 52

2. The Ocean is Like the Desert 80

3. Expecting the Unexpected 92

4. Flying High 104

5. Chasing the Stars 120

6. Ride With Me 134

7. Turning the Tide 140

8. Fish Sandwiches 154

9. Season for Change 168

10. Nemo Leaves its Mark 174

11. Chasing Light on Little Moose Island 180

12. Looking for Answers 190

I am proudly donating 10% of the profits from this book to the Schoodic Education Adventure residential program. Thank you for making a difference and for your support!

You can purchase fine art prints of any photograph in this book from the Colleen Miniuk-Sperry/CMS Photography website. For each sale of a photograph from Acadia National Park, I will donate 10% of the profits to the National Park Service. Images are also available for editorial and commercial licensing. Please visit my website at **www.cms-photo.com** for more information and to purchase.

Location Listing

Mount Desert Island...44

1. Thompson Island 48
2. Bar Island 50
3. Bar Harbor Shore Path 54
4. Compass Harbor Trail 56
5. Great Meadow 58
6. The Tarn 60
7. Sieur de Monts 62
8. Jesup Path 66
9. Beaver Dam Pond 68
10. Sand Beach 70
11. Great Head 72
12. Newport Cove Overlook 74
13. Thunder Hole 76
14. Monument Cove 78
15. Gorham Mountain Trail 84
16. Boulder Beach 86
17. Otter Cliff 88
18. Otter Point & Cove 94
19. Little Hunters Beach 96

20. Day Mountain 98
21. Hunters Beach 100
22. Little Long Pond 102
23. Asticou Azalea Garden 106
24. Waterfall Bridge 108
25. Eagle Lake 110
26. Duck Brook Bridge 112
27. Cadillac Mountain 114
28. Bubble Pond 124
29. Bubble Rock Trail 126
30. Jordan Pond Shore Path ... 128
31. Jordan Stream 130
32. Deer Brook Bridge & Waterfall .. 132
33. Pretty Marsh Picnic Area ..136
34. Bass Harbor Head Lighthouse . 138
35. Ship Harbor Trail 142
36. Wonderland Trail 144
37. Seawall Picnic Area 146

Isle au Haut..184

46. Eben's Head Trail 188
47. Duck Harbor 194
48. Western Head Trail 196
49. Cliff Trail 198
50. Long Pond 200

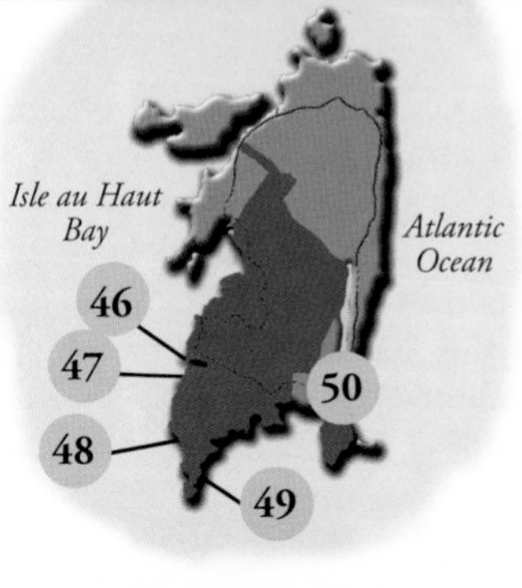

Maps not to scale. View and print the official Acadia National Park map at **www.nps.gov/acad**.

Isle au Haut Bay

Atlantic Ocean

46
47
48
49
50

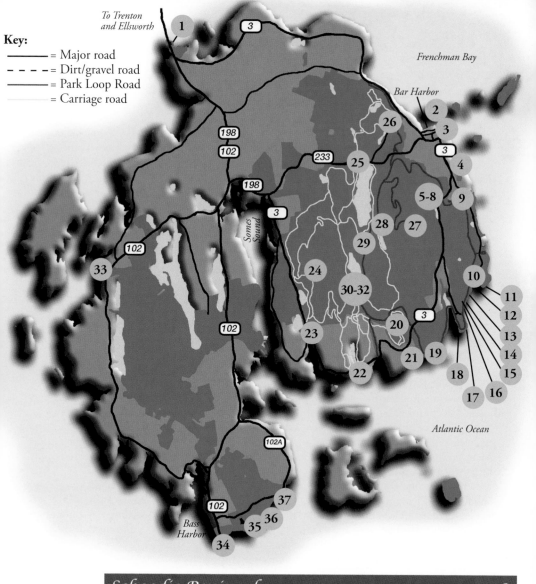

Key:
- ——— = Major road
- – – – = Dirt/gravel road
- —— = Park Loop Road
- —— = Carriage road

To Trenton and Ellsworth

1

3

Frenchman Bay

Bar Harbor

26

2

3

3

4

25

5-8

9

198

102

233

28

27

198

29

3

10

33

24

11

30-32

12

13

20

14

23

3

15

21

19

18

22

16

17

Somes Sound

Atlantic Ocean

102

102

102A

37

35

36

34

Bass Harbor

Schoodic Peninsula.................................148

38 Frazer Point Picnic Area ... 152

39 Schoodic Drive (West)...... 158

40 Ravens Nest 160

41 Schoodic Head 164

42 West Pond Cove 166

43 Schoodic Point 172

44 Little Moose Island 178

45 Schoodic Drive (East) 182

38

Winter Harbor

39

Schoodic Harbor

40

41

45

42

Atlantic Ocean

43

44

Introduction

*E*xperts dispute the origin of the park's name, "Acadia." Some believe the word derives from the Arcadia region in Greece, prized for its unspoiled wilderness. Over time, the "r" in the reference dropped—giving rise to the label "Acadia." Others attribute the label to the word "L'Acadie," which potentially stems from the French version of a Wabanaki Indian word meaning "the place." Rumors suggest that the first European settlers to Mount Desert Island may have also translated this term as "heaven on Earth."

When I first applied—sight unseen—to the Artist-in-Residence (AiR) program with Acadia National Park, I called the opportunity simply an escape. The new adventure promised a peaceful refuge to create my art in a place so far away and different from my home in Arizona. Although the name suggested a captivating place, I never intended to fall in love.

Starting in November 2009, I spent three glorious weeks in Acadia and discovered a treasure trove of natural, historical, and cultural resources that taught this desert dweller what the "A" stood for on the Jordan Pond Gatehouse shutters, where the glacial erratic rests on Schoodic Point, and how sedges differ from grasses—"sedges have edges!"—at Sieur de Monts.

The freedom to create a new photographic portfolio, the serenity of the scenery found in every corner of the park, and the kindness of the national park staff and local people made an unforgettable first impression. The AiR program gave me the unrivaled chance to grow, create, and appreciate immeasurably, allowing me to accomplish much more than I could have ever hoped. Except for one thing—giving back.

Unlike any other national park in America, Acadia was formed exclusively through many generous donations of land. Over the years, people have graciously contributed their time, talent, precious resources, and land to make the diverse park a unique national gem. Today, the distinctive giving tradition continues.

However, due to the unusual timing of my first residency, the opportunity to present school or public programs as outlined in the residency requirements did not exist. While this created incomparable and blissful independence, I left with an empty feeling. I had not given back to a park that had given me so much. With this in mind, I reapplied to the AiR program the following year in hopes I would have that chance.

In October 2010, during the height of autumn's spectacular display, I returned as an AiR with the sole purpose to work with the Schoodic Education Adventure (SEA) program. In the most rewarding experience of my career to date, I helped to establish the Photojournalism program and donated over 350 photographs of children participating in their studies for my project titled, "A Day in the SEA Life." In between these efforts, I relished and photographed the colorful change in season across the park. Much like my first residency confirmed, I knew I had found heaven on Earth on the Maine coast and yearned to see more.

Specifically, I wondered how winter would transform the places I had already enjoyed during the spring, summer, and fall. I applied a third time simply to learn more about "the place" in a new light. As Acadia's first winter AiR, I had paradise to myself for four weeks during January and February 2013.

After spending more than 100 magical days in four short years in the park (thanks to the AiR program, Arizona Highways Photography Workshops, and personal trips), I felt this burning urge to run up to the top of Cadillac Mountain and loudly yell so everyone in the world could hear, "COME TO ACADIA! COME TO ACADIA!"

Of course, to do so would violate the "Leave No Trace" principle of being considerate to others and maintaining quiet (and likely annoy a whole lot of people!) so I decided to write this

A glorious winter sunrise along the east side of the Schoodic Peninsula. Canon 5DMII, 16-35mm at 16mm, ISO 100, f/18 at 1/8th sec., three-stop graduated neutral density filter.

book instead. Consider this guide my invitation to you to experience, enjoy, and photograph Acadia through your own lens.

Whether you are planning your first or fifteenth visit, I hope the information shared here helps you make the most of your stay this enchanting national park. Mother Nature has left a world of wonder here while those who came before us have provided celebrated cultural and historical treasures. You need only to bring your camera and curiosity to record your own stories and experiences in this diverse place.

Roll up your pant legs and get your feet wet at Sand Beach. Listen carefully to the cobble clapping for you as the waves splash against Little Hunters Beach. Ponder what life must have been like for the rusticators as you stroll along the carriage roads. Photograph in horizontal rain atop Cadillac Mountain. Gaze in awe at the Milky Way above Jordan Pond. In doing so, I hope you find your place in "the place" and discover your own "heaven on Earth" at Acadia National Park.

But be forewarned! When talking about the magic of Acadia, locals and visitors alike often suggest there is something about this coastal park that grabs a hold of your heart and doesn't let go. Acadia has yet to let go of mine, and I hope it doesn't let go of yours either.

~Colleen J. Miniuk-Sperry

How to Use This Book

With such immense diversity within Acadia National Park, it is hard to know where to begin your photographic adventures!

Get started by acquainting yourself with the historical information about Acadia National Park starting on page 14. Then pack the necessary camera gear according to the guidance on page 22. Finally, polish your photography skills by reading the Photography Basics section beginning on page 26.

To help you plan your unforgettable journey, I have identified fifty top photographic locations and organized them by the three major regions of Acadia National Park in order of accessibility and popularity: Mount Desert Island, the Schoodic Peninsula, and Isle au Haut. In addition to the park maps on pages 8-9, each section begins with a local regional map identifying the specific locations covered in that section. Following the map is a brief overview of the region, where you will learn not only logistical information to make the most of your visit, but also the natural, cultural, and historical photographic highlights you will likely encounter.

For each recommended site, you will find pertinent location-specific details including:

- **Time of Year:** Each season in Acadia brings different light, moods, and weather, creating memorable photographic opportunities any time of year. That said, I have suggested the times of year associated with "can't miss" ephemeral events such as wildflower blooms, autumn leaf changes, ice formations, and wildlife migrations.

Unusual striations in the granite rocks along the Western Head Trail on Isle au Haut. Canon 5DMII, 16-35mm at 16mm, ISO 100, f/16 at 8 sec., three-stop graduated neutral density filter.

- **Time of Day:** Based on the area's geographical features and orientation towards the sun, I have recommended optimal times for photography in an effort to reduce your on-site scouting time and activities. That does not mean photographic opportunities do not exist outside of these time frames! No matter what time you visit—whether it is ideal or not—challenge yourself to find the best light for your subject matter.

- **Tides:** Water levels along the Acadia coast can vary by as much as 8 to 12 feet (2.4 to 3.7 m) between high and low tide, creating often dramatic changes to the associated landscape. If the level of water affects the location, I have noted the tide level I prefer. Before your outing, study tide charts provided by the National Oceanic and Atmospheric Administration

Close-up of hair-cap moss, which grows abundantly within Acadia's forests. Canon 5DMII, 100mm macro, ISO 100, f/4 at 1.3 sec.

(NOAA) Tide and Currents website at **tidesandcurrents.noaa.gov** or the Maine Tide Charts online at **me.usharbors.com** to determine what you will actually see upon your arrival. Remember, never turn your back on the ocean. Unpredictable rogue waves and strong currents can pull an unsuspecting person into the water, even while standing on dry land.

- **Hike:** If a location is "road kill" (meaning you can park the car, hop out, and start shooting with little to no effort), I rated the hike "Easy." If getting to the location requires a longer, arduous trek over steep terrain, I deemed the location "Strenuous." Everything in between is labeled "Moderate." Honestly consider your own capabilities and limitations prior to undertaking any physical activities. All of Acadia's maintained trails are clearly marked by either (or in some cases, both) stone-piles called cairns or blue blazes painted on the granite rocks and trees trunks.

You can reach all the featured locations in a two-wheel drive passenger car, making Acadia one of the most accessible national parks in the United States.

For quick reference, the Shoot Calendar on pages 204-207 outlines the above characteristics for all the locations. In addition, the Additional Resources section on page 203 lists a number of handy books and websites to help prepare you for your trip.

Although this guidebook provides details surrounding "when, where, and how" and "making the photo" stories to help you create memorable photographs, I hope it merely gives you a starting place for your own photographic expressions. Acadia possesses so much more than can ever fit in one single guidebook. I strongly encourage you to explore the park with your own vision, bringing your unique perspectives to light—pun intended!—in addition to learning from the examples offered here and by other photographers.

History of Acadia National Park

*L*ong before European settlers arrived on the Maine coast, the native Wabanaki people—whose name translates loosely as the "People of the Dawn"—lived off the abundant resources the land and sea provided along the northeastern shoreline. They referred to the mountainous island we know today as Mount Desert Island as "Pemetic" or "sloping land."

In 1604, King Henry IV of France granted French explorer Pierre Du Gua de Monts and his navigator, Samuel Champlain, permission to set sail to the New World. During their voyage, Champlain wrote in his journal of this 108-square-mile (173.8-square-km) isle, "It is very high, and notched in places, so that there is the appearance to one at sea, as of seven or eight mountains extending along near each other. The summit of most of them is destitute of trees, as there are only rocks on them. The woods consist of pines, firs, and birches only. I named it Isles des Monts Deserts."

Champlain's designation translates from French as "Island of the Desert Mountains," but over time the name evolved to simply "Mount Desert Island" (often abbreviated as MDI). Locals and visitors alike pronounce the word "Desert" in two different ways—as "desert" (DEH-zert) like the dry, dusty Sonoran Desert in Arizona or as "dessert" (Deh-ZERT) like the tasty treat you have after dinner.

Before 1844, few Americans outside of Maine knew of the area's wonders. In that year, painter Thomas Cole (founder of the Hudson River School art movement) visited the region, followed shortly thereafter by his student, Frederic Church. Their popular paintings of idyllic meadows, panoramic views of polished

The "A" carved into the wooden shutter on the Jordan Pond Gatehouse represents Grosvenor Atterbury's last name, the architect who designed the gatehouses during the construction of John D. Rockefeller Jr.'s carriage roads. Canon 5D, 24-105mm at 24mm, ISO 200, f/4 at 1/25th sec., polarizer.

mountains, and awe-inspiring craggy coastlines capped by unforgettable fiery skies attracted the attention of both other artists and the public at large.

By 1855, these stunning pictorial depictions served as a successful lure to wealthy businessmen living primarily in Philadelphia, Boston, and New York who were eager to escape the hustle and bustle of city life and see for themselves Mother Nature's grandeur in this isolated place. Referred to as "rusticators" or "summercators," they formed a veritable "Who's Who" list of prominent and wealthy families. Eventually, Rockefellers, Fords, Vanderbilts, Morgans, Asters, and Carnegies were "summering" in their luxurious mansions (quaintly called "cottages") and experiencing first-hand the very tableaus Cole and Church celebrated.

By the turn of the 20th century, many of these prominent residents began to worry that their treasured isle was in danger of becoming overdeveloped—a fear enhanced by the arrival of a portable sawmill. In 1901, Charles Eliot teamed up with George B. Dorr to establish the Hancock County Trustees of Public Reservations group with the intent of "...acquiring, owning and holding lands and other property in Hancock County [MDI's county] for free public use."

By 1916, Eliot and Dorr had collected almost 6,000 acres (2,428 hectares) across MDI, thanks to the integral land donations and financial contributions from John D. Rockefeller Jr. as well as numerous famous and not-so-famous people anxious to see the preservation of the island for widespread public enjoyment for generations to come. On July 8, 1916, President Woodrow Wilson officially declared the donated 6,000-plus acre (2,428-plus hectares) land package as the Sieur de Monts National Monument.

Three years later, Congress converted the monument into a national park and named it "Lafayette National Park" in honor of the famous French general who served under George Washington during the Revolutionary War. The new national park was the first to be created exclusively from donated lands as well as the first established east of the Mississippi River. Appropriately, the first superintendent to serve the park was none other than Dorr.

As additional donations continued to expand the park's reach on MDI, Dorr sought to acquire a 2,050-acre (830 hectares) tract of land across Frenchman Bay on the Schoodic Peninsula. John G. Moore, a Wall Street financier and Maine native, originally owned this scenic stretch of land. In the 1920s, the Moore heirs agreed to bestow the estate to the Hancock County Trustees of Public Reservations under two conditions: one, the land serve as a public park and promote scientific research, and two, the name "Lafayette National Park" change to something less French.

Dorr and the Moore heirs settled on the name "Acadia National Park," despite the word "Acadia" likely and ironically deriving from the French word, "L'Acadie." In 1929, after government legislation allowed the acquisition on the mainland, Dorr donated the Moore property to the newly renamed Acadia National Park.

While Dorr spent much of his time securing land gifts for the park, Rockefeller Jr. began carefully designing and personally overseeing the construction of an extensive network of pedestrian and horse-friendly carriage roads across these donated lands. Eventually, he and his meticulous crews completed 45 miles (72.4 km) of 16-foot-wide (13.7-m) carriage roads lined with white granite coping stones (also referred to as "Rockefeller's Teeth"), 17 uniquely designed stone bridges, and two French Romanesque-style stone gatehouses intertwined elegantly throughout the eastern side of MDI. Through Rockefeller Jr.'s sometimes controversial influence, the park restricted automobiles (which were becoming increasingly popular) from using the carriage roads.

After visiting Acadia in 1932, Frank Olmstead (the designer of Central Park in New York

History of Acadia National Park (continued)

City) foretold, "Driving in horse-drawn vehicles along narrow winding woodland roads amid beautiful and varied scenery, completely free from the annoyance, and even the dread of meeting motor cars, is so real and extraordinarily rare today that systematic provision for it may reasonably be expected to develop into one of the most unique attractions of the park and the island." Placed on the National Register of Historic Places in 1979, the carriage road system remains free of motorized vehicles and is popular with hikers, bikers, horseback riders, cross-country skiers—and photographers! Today, the non-profit Friends of Acadia (**friendsofacadia.org**) provides maintenance and upkeep of the carriage roads.

Realizing that he could not keep automobiles out of Acadia forever, Rockefeller Jr. also financed and designed the 27-mile (43.5-km) Park Motor Road (known today as the Park Loop Road) in an effort to control where cars could travel on this scenic island. However, preventing the completion of the picturesque drive was an United States naval radio station near Otter Cliff. Commissioned in 1917, the station was widely acclaimed as the Navy's best transatlantic radio receiver site due to its isolated location and clear path to Europe during World War I.

To secure the necessary lands, Rockefeller Jr. negotiated a land swap between the U.S. Navy and the National Park Service to relocate the military operations to the Schoodic Peninsula in early 1935. The Navy operated their radio station on a high perch near Schoodic Point until 2002, when the Winter Harbor Station shut down and the land transferred back to Acadia National Park. Today, after undergoing an extensive renovation in 2011, the former base now houses the Schoodic Institute on the Schoodic Education and Research Center (SERC) campus, which operates in line with the Moore heirs' original stipulations.

In 1943, the park was further enlarged with the donation of 2,728 acres (1,104 hectares)of land on the small Isle au Haut (French for "High Island") to the southwest of MDI. The park later acquired additional property on Little Cranberry Island (specifically the historic Isleford Historical Museum) in 1948, Baker Island in the 1950s, Bear Island in 1987, as well as parcels on a handful of tiny offshore islands in the Gulf of Maine and Frenchman Bay.

The patchwork quilt of donated park lands strewn across the Schoodic Peninsula to the northeast, on the rugged Isle au Haut to the southwest, and on the lobster-claw shaped MDI make Acadia National Park a magical, one of a kind place to explore and photograph. Within its boundaries lay an unprecedented diversity of not only historical remnants, but also natural gems, including 26 mountains, 26 freshwater lakes and ponds, pristine mixed forests, sand and cobble beaches, jagged granite headlands, and Somes Sound (a fjard—not a "fjord"). This grand landscape teems with an equally impressive assortment of mammals, fish, amphibians, invertebrates, and birds—both year-round residents and temporary migrants.

This variety attracts over two million visitors per year, making it one of the most visited parks in the National Park Service despite being one of the smallest at 49,000 acres (19,830 hectares).

Are you ready to make your own memories in Acadia National Park? Let's go!

OPPOSITE: Granite cliffs glow in early morning light along the Schoodic Peninsula. Canon 5DMII, 24-105mm at 28mm, ISO 125, f/14 at 1/8th sec., polarizer, three-stop graduated neutral density filter.

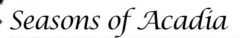

Seasons of Acadia

Winter (December through March):

Do not let the threat of blizzards and frigid temperatures scare you off! If photographing a winter wonderland in complete solitude sounds appealing to you, a visit to Acadia in winter will not disappoint.

According to the National Park Service, the park averages 61 inches (155 cm) of snow a year, most of which falls from December through March. Though the snow often melts relatively quickly after it falls, passing storms and nor'easters (the primary season occurring from September to April) generate magical fleeting moments of dancing light and moody clouds ideal for outdoor photography. Prolonged periods of below-freezing temperatures create ice formations beyond imagination along the coast and causes ethereal Atlantic sea smoke to rise out of the ocean as frigid air flows over warmer waters.

Essentially devoid of visitors and bugs, winter welcomes instead numerous bird species like common loons, common goldeneyes, common eiders, and even purple sandpipers migrating south to spend the cold season in warmer waters along the Acadia shoreline.

Seasonal closures prevent motorized travel on select paved and unpaved roads, including parts of the Park Loop Road. Snow and ice cover hiking trails and rock ledges across the park, making foot travel dangerous—if not impossible—without appropriate winter gear.

Though the days are short with just eight to nine hours of daylight, the sun traverses the sky lower on the horizon than in other seasons, making mid-day photography more productive with longer shadows and lower contrast throughout the day.

Advanced planning is essential for a winter stay, though, as many hotels, restaurants, and other services close for the season.

As the surface layer of the ocean begins to freeze, pancake ice forms in West Pond Cove on the Schoodic Peninsula. Canon 5DMII, 100-400mm at 150mm, ISO 100, f/20 at 0.3 sec., polarizer.

The deciduous forest along the Jesup Trail displays fresh spring greenery. Canon 5DMII, 16-35mm at 30mm, ISO 400, f/22 at 0.4 sec.

Spring (April through June):

As the snow melts and the air temperatures warm, the park ushers in more visitors than winter, but still far less than the masses to come in summer.

All winter road restrictions relax typically around late-April or early May, allowing shutterbugs full access to the park to see deciduous trees showing off fresh greenery. Under abundant sunshine, the snow and ice on the trails thaw, leading to somewhat muddy, but passable, conditions in early spring. As land temperatures start to increase, photogenic fog wraps around the bald mountain summits and sits along the coast, typically in the early mornings through the afternoon.

Hurricane season officially begins in May, though few ever reach these northern latitudes as full-blown hurricanes. Instead, these storms frequently turn into nor'easters which result in colder temperatures, high winds, pounding waves, and substantial precipitation. Depending on the amount of winter moisture and spring storms, black flies, mosquitoes, and "no-see-ums" commonly appear in May and June. By June, colorful wildflowers sprout along the coast, beneath dense forest canopies, and in serene meadows.

If the prospect of photographing peregrine falcons, warblers, and woodpeckers excites you, then time your trip for the end of May and early June to participate in the annual Acadia Birding Festival (**www.acadiabirdingfestival.com**). Though not in the national park, a stopover at the Maine Coastal Islands National Wildlife Refuge, which includes Petit Manan, is a worthy side trip for avian aficionados to photograph cute, clown-faced Atlantic puffins and agile, snow-white Arctic terns.

As the hours of sunlight lengthen from 14 to a peak of 17 hours around the summer solstice (June 20-22), pace yourself and set aside time for a refreshing nap if you plan to photograph sunrise, sunset, and the night sky in a long single day.

Summer (July through September):

In summer, visitors can expect pleasantly warm daytime temperatures offset by a steady, cool ocean breeze, which make some evenings feel downright chilly. Despite being the foggiest time of year (locals jokingly call August "Fogust" for good reason!), many of the estimated two-million-plus annual visitors that pass through Acadia's gates do so during these three months. This makes the summer Acadia's busiest season of the year.

Much like winter, advanced planning is essential, but not for the same reasons. Hotels book up well in advanced and a table for dinner can be hard to come by at restaurants, so make reservations for both prior to your arrival.

Because of the hoards of people arriving by automobiles and by cruise ships docking daily in Bar Harbor, plan to arrive at popular locations like Thunder Hole and Cadillac Mountain at first and last light. Even still, be prepared to share your space with flocks of people. Simply hiking a mere quarter-mile (0.4 km) or more off the main areas or visiting lesser-known Schoodic Peninsula and Isle au Haut will lead to greater solitude and quiet.

Throughout July and August, vibrant wildflowers continue to grace the emerald meadows, fragrant forests, and speckled granite. Blueberry season begins in late July and lasts until August, when the park permits picking for personal consumption. Mosquitoes are still prevalent around areas with standing water like Great Meadow, but steady coastal breezes generally keep pesky, biting insects from becoming a major problem along the shore.

Though the amount of daylight begins to decline following the summer solstice in late June, light chasers will still have 14-15 hours of sunlight with which to work. If astrophotography piques your interest, celebrate the stars above during the annual Acadia Night Sky Festival (**www.acadianightskyfestival.com**) each September.

TOP: A blanket of autumnal color graces the side of Cadillac Mountain. Canon 5DMII, 100-400mm at 370mm, ISO 100, f/8 at 0.4 sec., polarizer.
OPPOSITE: Morning fog hugs the coast along Ocean Drive. Canon 5DMII, 100-400mm at 160mm, ISO 50, f/11 at 0.4 sec., polarizer.

Fall (October and November):

During this time of transition, it may seem like the weather cannot make up its mind. Sunshine, clouds, rain, snow, and fog can occur at any time—and sometimes all on the same day!—so dress in layers to ensure you will be ready for the changes. The hurricane season officially ends in November, but nor'easters may arrive any time during the autumn season.

The Great Fire of 1947 scorched more than 17,000 acres (6880 hectares) of the east side of the island's spruce and fir forests, making way for healthy stands of deciduous trees to sprout out of the charred landscape. As a result, "color chasers" now flock to the park to catch a glimpse of birches, beeches, aspens, oaks, sumacs, and maples bursting into brilliant shades of reds, oranges, and yellows starting early October.

The timing can vary depending on precipitation, temperature, and sun, but the show typically peaks by mid-October. Color can linger in spots into early November if winter storms do not blow all the leaves off the trees first. Check **www.mainefoliage.com** for the current conditions.

As the days shorten to 9 to 12 hours of daylight, hawks, falcons, and sea ducks begin their winter migrations to the warmer waters along the Acadia coast. Catch the park's "Hawk Watch" program atop Cadillac Mountain before it wraps up in mid-October (see page 114 for more information).

Cruise ships still dock in Bar Harbor until late October, but at a much slower pace than summer. After Columbus Day, park visitation drops significantly, but so does access to services as many hotels, restaurants, and shops close their doors for winter. That said, local events like the Pajama Party and Bed Races in Bar Harbor in November make a visit during this time worthwhile.

Preparing for Your Outing

*E*ach location description suggests appropriate photography gear (in **bolded** font) to pack for your photographic outing to that location. However, the general gear checklist below lists the general equipment you should consider bringing with you to Acadia. Should you need to purchase any photographic equipment upon your arrival, stop by Hunt's Photo & Video (**www.huntsphotoandvideo.com**)in Portland before heading to the park.

As they say, "Less is more." Carefully consider the type of photography you will likely focus on during your outing and pack only the gear you need to accomplish those goals. That said, Murphy's Law suggests that the piece of equipment you leave behind will be the gear you will need the most during your shoot!

General Gear Checklist

- ❑ Camera
- ❑ Variety of lenses, ranging from wide-angle (shorter than 28 mm) to telephoto (longer than 100mm) and macro/micro lenses
- ❑ Tripod (I recommend Manfrotto, **www.manfrotto.us**)
- ❑ Cable release
- ❑ Polarizer
- ❑ Graduated neutral density filters
- ❑ Neutral density filters
- ❑ Reflector
- ❑ Diffuser
- ❑ Off-camera flash
- ❑ Gary Fong flash diffuser
- ❑ Multiple lens cloths
- ❑ Hoodman Hoodloupe™
- ❑ Headlamp or flashlight
- ❑ Photo vest
- ❑ Camera backpack
- ❑ Knee pads or gardening mat

For wildlife:
- ❑ Telephoto lens 200mm and longer
- ❑ Wimberley tripod head
- ❑ 1.4x or 2x teleconverter
- ❑ Visual Echoes "Better Beamer" Flash X-tender™

If windy:
- ❑ Wimberley Plamp™

If raining or snowing:
- ❑ Large golf umbrella
- ❑ Rain cover for camera
- ❑ Garbage bag, poncho, or rain cover for camera bag
- ❑ Rain jacket and pants
- ❑ Waterproof shoes
- ❑ Wool or neoprene socks
- ❑ Microfiber hand towels

If visiting in winter:
- ❑ Plastic garbage bag to reduce condensation on camera
- ❑ Hand warmers
- ❑ Gloves/mittens where individual fingers can be exposed (e.g., Simms®)
- ❑ Winter boots
- ❑ Wool socks
- ❑ YakTrax™ or snow cleats

Practicing "Leave No Trace"

*T*o avoid over-use and damage to the places we collectively love and want to protect the most, "Leave only footprints and take only pictures" when visiting Acadia National Park.

Adhering to the following "Leave No Trace" principles will help you enjoy these locations responsibly and ensure that future visitors and generations have the opportunity to see the same beauty you and I are fortunate to experience today:

- Stay on pre-existing trails when they are present, especially in extremely delicate and sensitive ecosystems like Cadillac Mountain and Little Moose Island. Step only on rock ledges and do not trample the vegetation.
- Leave all natural and manmade objects as you find them. Do not pick wildflowers, destroy live plants, or remove rocks from beaches. Do not remove fishing relics from the beach.
- Pack it in, pack it out. Take all your gear, food, and trash with you when you leave the park. In windy locations like the coast or the summit of mountains, store all belongings securely so they do not blow away.

Bobcat tracks in the snow at Thompson Island. Canon 5DMII, 16-35mm at 35mm, ISO 100, f/22 at 1/20th sec.

- Do not feed, approach, or otherwise interrupt the natural behavior patterns of wildlife you encounter.
- Carry a trail map. Prior to visiting, consult the Acadia National Park website at **www.nps.gov/acad** to download the park map and to determine if any special alerts for the park are in effect. Access rules and restrictions can change without notice.
- Be prepared for emergencies and changing or extreme conditions. Carry a map, basic first aid kit, flashlight or headlamp, matches, compass or GPS unit, whistle, pocketknife, extra food, and extra water when hiking.
- Inform others about where you will be going and when you expect to be back. Cell phone service is not always reliable within the park, so consider bringing a personal locator beacon like the SPOT™ Satellite GPS Messenger.
- Be respectful and courteous to other visitors, particularly other photographers you see in the field. Yield to others on trails and carriage roads. Talk in soft voices and avoid making loud noises.

For more information about Leave No Trace principles, visit **www.lnt.org**.

Cautions

Weather

Because of its location "downeast" along the coast (a historical reference from when boats sailed from Boston to Maine, or downwind but to the east), the year-round weather at Acadia National Park is generally more mild and moderate than found inland. However, conditions can—and often do —change in a heartbeat along the coast. Dress in wind-proof, water-resistant layers. Apply sunscreen and wear a hat year-round, but especially in spring and summer months.

Average annual rainfall tallies to 48 inches (122 cm) and precipitation is equally likely in all twelve months. Nor'easters (storms that can bring heavy rains, high winds, and larger-than-life surf) can occur at anytime, but most often happen between September and April. While exploring higher, exposed elevations and water-based locations, watch for lightning from approaching thunderstorms. While the moisture refreshes the landscape and makes for outstanding diffused photography, rain and snow also cause the granite rocks along the coast and on inland trails to become extremely slick. Boardwalks may also become slippery when wet. Ice makes many of the park's trails impassable during winter.

Hypothermia is most likely to occur on cold, winter days, but can affect visitors year-round whenever breezy, wet, and chilly conditions exist. Frostbite can occur after prolonged exposure to extremely cold temperatures. Should small white patches form on your skin, seek immediate medical attention, as this is an early symptom of frostbite. To prevent both hypothermia and frostbite, protect fingers, toes, nose, and ears with adequate clothing to stay warm and dry.

Prevent condensation from building up in your camera and lens' electronics by placing your gear in a tied garbage bag when you go indoors so that the interior temperatures gradually warm your equipment. Remember to remove your battery and memory card first!

To prepare yourself with the right clothes and equipment, keep a pulse on the NOAA National Weather Service (**www.weather.gov**) and the Weather Channel (**www.weather.com**) prior to and during your stay.

Coastal Rocks and Waves

Before any visit to the coast, particularly beaches and low-lying granite ledges, consult the NOAA Tide and Currents website at **tidesandcurrents.noaa.gov** or the Maine Tide Charts online at **me.usharbors.com** to determine whether the tide is high or low (as well as incoming or outgoing) to safely explore the shoreline.

Low tide reveals rockweed and algae-covered rocks of all shapes and sizes. Along the coast, wear hiking shoes with solid treads and watch your footing. Wet granite slabs, volcanic tuff boulders, and loose cobble are slicker than ice in a skating rink. Consider using your tripod or a hiking pole to help keep you steady if you plan to traverse these areas.

Though crashing waves can occur during storms and hurricanes, rogue sneaker waves can happen at any time. Especially during times with high seas, stay a safe distance away from cliff edges. To emphasize the point once again: never turn your back on the ocean.

Keep your lens free from salt spray by using a lens hood and a rain-cover (even when it is not raining) and frequently wiping the wet glass with a dry lens cloth. After your outing, wipe down your tripod and the external parts of your camera with a damp, clean, and absorbent cloth to avoid corrosion. If you expose your camera to the elements for an extended period of time, consider getting a professional cleaning after your visit.

Carriage Roads

Motorized vehicles are not permitted on any carriage roads, and bicycles are not permitted on paths residing on private property outside of the park boundary (e.g., near Little Long Pond).

No matter the carriage road, always walk or bike on the right. Bikers yield to hikers and everyone yields to horses. When biking, wear a protective helmet with a reflective surface to stay visible during low lighting situations. During winter, cross-country skiers will appreciate you not stepping in their clean ski tracks.

Wildlife

A broad variety of mammals, birds, reptiles, amphibians, and fish enjoy Acadia's natural hospitality, including whitetail deer, coyotes, porcupine, raccoons, foxes, muskrats, beavers, squirrels, chipmunks, bald eagles, peregrine falcons, seagulls, bullfrogs, and snapping turtles. Because much of the park resides on islands, rarely seen

Many of Acadia's trails (like Ocean Path shown here) are impassable due to ice in winter. Canon 5DMII, 24-105mm at 28mm, ISO 400, f/7.1 at 1/30th sec., polarizer.

are moose and black bear, which are more common on the mainland. Never approach or feed wildlife, even if some nosy creatures—like seagulls—attempt to approach you. Keep the "wild" in wildlife by putting trash in the garbage receptacles located throughout the park.

Though few intertidal creatures present a threat to humans, sensitive animals found in tide pools like sea urchins and starfish should not be touched or handled. Likewise, if you come upon a harbor seal pup seemingly "abandoned" along the shore (especially from late April to June), do not touch or approach the animal. Its mother is likely off-shore and will return to fetch her baby.

Insects

Following a wet winter and spring, mosquitoes and black flies breed in the standing water and can become a nuisance during June and July. Use bug spray and wear permethrin-treated clothing, tuck pant legs into your socks, and tighten long-sleeve shirt cuffs around your wrists (with rubber bands if needed). Though ticks are not common in the park, check yourself for the blood-sucking insect if you have tromped through the forest.

Poison Ivy

Though not common in the park, watch for the distinctive "leaves of three" as you visit the coast, wooded areas, and meadows. Should you inadvertently touch poison ivy or if you notice a red rash developing on your skin, immediately wash the area with ample cold water or with an over-the-counter remedy like Tecnu® to deactivate the plant's toxins.

Staying Hydrated

Drink at least one to two gallons of water per person per day, particularly if you plan to hike the Acadia trails. If you feel thirsty, you are already dehydrated. Drinking untreated water directly from Acadia's many streams and ponds is not advisable, as you risk contracting a giardia infection, which can cause diarrhea and dehydration.

Photography Basics

*T*hroughout this guidebook, I offer suggestions about what camera equipment to bring and possible techniques and approaches to get your creative juices flowing. I will also refer to a number of different photography terms, considerations, and camera settings that can enhance your photographic results and help produce images of which you can be proud. This section describes key photography concepts and points to consider when setting up your camera and making pictures in the breathtaking, photogenic coastal park.

RAW or JPEG File Format?

You can create a successful photograph in either format! A raw file (also referred to as RAW file) is a large file format that captures the entire range of data in an uncompressed format, providing the most options and flexibility in post-processing. The photographer must convert the RAW image into a usable, modifiable format before a computer can read it. Since post-

processing does not affect the data, this lossless format allows the photographer some leeway in exposure, color balance, and composition when creating the photograph. However, capturing the best photograph possible in the field will help increase the efficiency and the effectiveness of your post-processing activities.

JPEG (which stands for "Joint Photographic Experts Group") is a smaller file format that contains a compressed subset of the RAW data that is instantly readable by almost all computers. This format type does not require conversion before post-processing or viewing, but has less flexibility when making later adjustments to the image. Considered a lossy format, each time a photographer modifies and saves a JPEG photograph, the file progressively loses data and image quality degrades. This means there is slightly more pressure on the photographer to capture the best possible image in the field.

A slow ISO speed, slow shutter speed, and small aperture help render silky water while recording extensive depth of field along the Schoodic Peninsula's scenic Schoodic Drive. Canon 5DMII, 16-35mm at 16mm, ISO 100, f/18 at 3.2 sec., four-stop graduated neutral density filter.

If you are undecided as to which format to use, shoot in both RAW and JPEG. While it takes up more space on your memory card, you can record the best of both worlds while deciding which format to pursue.

Exposure Overview

The word "photography" comes from the Greek words meaning, "to paint with light." True to the definition, photographers need to record an adequate amount of light to render a photograph. The term "exposure" refers to the total amount of light collected by your camera when you create a picture.

There are three settings that control exposure: ISO/film speed, shutter speed, and aperture. Measured in "stops" of light, modifications to these exposure settings affect how much light the camera records. When you increase exposure by one stop of light through any of the exposure settings, the camera will record double the amount of light. Consequently, when you decrease the

A cluster of barnacles cling to the rocks at Sand Beach. Canon 5DMII, 100mm macro, two 12mm extension tubes stacked, ISO 100, f/2.8 at 1/125th sec., diffuser.

exposure by one stop of light, the camera will only record half as much light.

The statement, "open up" means you should add stops of light through one or a combination of these exposure settings. Conversely, "stop down" simply means you should reduce the light the camera records.

Different cameras manage these settings differently. Point-and-shoot and phone cameras automatically adjust these settings without the photographer getting involved. However, some of the fancier compact cameras allow for manual adjustments as well, much like their digital Single-Lens Reflex (dSLR) cousins which permit photographers to modify the three exposure settings through various camera modes such as program (P), aperture priority (Av), shutter speed priority (Tv—time value—or S), and manual (M). Since camera models vary, please consult your instruction manual to determine your camera's specific capabilities.

ISO/Film Speed

The International Standards Organization (ISO) has a widely-used numerical scale for measuring the light sensitivity, or speed, of camera film known as the ISO speed (often called 'ISO' for short). Most modern digital cameras allow you to specify an ISO speed and thus configure the digital sensor to perform similar to film of the same speed. Common ISO speed settings (from slowest to fastest) include ISO 100, 200, 400, 800, and 1600.

Changing the ISO setting affects how long it takes the camera to record an image. Lower numbers indicate the sensor is less sensitive to light and records an image more slowly. On the other hand, higher numbers suggest the sensor will record an image faster because the sensor is more sensitive to light.

To help freeze the motion of moving waves, wildflowers, or wildlife, select a faster ISO speed such as ISO 400 or higher. When photographing static subjects like landscape scenes or

when you wish to blur movement instead, use a lower ISO speed such as ISO 50 or 100. Use as low of a film speed as you possibly can to achieve your desired image to keep unnecessary noise or grain out of your photograph and preserve the best image quality possible.

ISO/film speed can be summarized as follows:

50	100	200	400	800	1600	3200	6400
Low ←			Sensor's sensitivity to light			→	High
Slow ←			Speed in recording image			→	Fast
Longer ←			Exposure times			→	Shorter
Lower ←			Noticeable grain/noise			→	Higher
Greater ←			Ability to enlarge without noise			→	Lesser

Shutter Speed and Depicting Motion

The shutter speed setting determines the amount of time the shutter stays open during the exposure. Measured in seconds, a fast shutter speed lets in a small amount of light and helps to freeze any action you see in your scene. However, a slow shutter speed allows the camera to record more light and helps to blur motion.

Many cameras permit shutter speeds as fast as 1/8000th of a second and as slow as 30 seconds. Some cameras also have a Bulb mode, which allows the shutter to remain open as long as the photographer depresses the shutter release, usually through a locking cable release (historically called the "bulb"). This mode enables photographers to capture images with shutter speeds longer than 30 seconds, so long as the cable release button is depressed.

The chart below shows examples of various shutter speeds and how each setting depicts motion in an image. Note that the numbers without the tick mark are fractions of a second (e.g., "1000" equals 1/1000th of a second) and those with the tick mark are in seconds (e.g., 4' equals 4 seconds):

1000	500	250	125	60	30	15	8	4	2	1'	2'	4'	8'	16'
Fast ←					Speed					→				Slow
Short ←				Amount of time shutter is open						→				Long
Frozen ←				Type of motion recorded						→				Blur

Aperture and Depth of Field

Aperture refers to the circular hole in the camera lens, called the diaphragm, which controls the amount of light allowed to pass on to the digital sensor (or film) during an exposure. The size of the opening is referred to as an "f-stop" (which is a complex calculated ratio of the lens's focal length to the diameter of the entrance pupil). Even though they refer to slightly different things, photographers often use the terms "aperture" and "f-stop" interchangeably.

A wide aperture such as f/4 or f/5.6 allows the camera sensor to collect a lot more light during the exposure. However, a small aperture such as f/16 or f/22 will let in a small amount of light.

Besides collecting light, the aperture setting is one way to control depth of field, which defines the extent to which objects at different distances from the camera will remain in sharp focus. The smaller the aperture number (e.g., f/4 or f/5.6), the smaller the depth of field will appear. With very large apertures, only objects near the focal point will stay in focus while objects that are closer or further away will be increasingly out of focus. Conversely, a bigger

This scene at Eagle Lake covered an extensive depth of field from the rocks and plants in the immediate foreground to the mountains in the far distance. To ensure everything remained in focus, I utilized a wide-angle lens, a small aperture and set my focus point on the large rock on the right, which was approximately at the hyperfocal distance of 6 feet (1.8 m). Canon 5DMII, 16-35mm at 35mm, ISO 125, f/22 at 1.3 sec., four-stop graduated neutral density filter.

aperture number (e.g., f/16 or f/22) will provide a deeper depth of field, meaning objects will stay in focus across a wider range of distances.

In addition to the aperture settings, the focal length of a lens and the camera-to-subject distance also affects depth of field. For a given aperture, the longer the focal length of the lens, the shorter the depth of field will seem. On the other hand, the shorter the focal length of the lens, the larger the depth of field will appear.

Regardless of the focal length of your lens, if the distance between your camera and subject is small, the resulting depth of field will be smaller. Alternatively, if the space between your camera and subject is large, the depth of field will be larger.

To capture extensive depth of field in your image, focus at the hyperfocal distance, which produces the maximum depth of field for a given aperture, lens, and subject-distance. The hyperfocal distance is the point where everything from half the hyperfocal distance to infinity is acceptably sharp. Because the set hyperfocal distance varies based on the aperture, focal length of the lens, and camera-to-subject distance, it is possible that you might need to focus behind or in front of your subject to get your desired depth of field. Internet resources such as the Depth of Field Master website (**dofmaster.com**) can help identify this distance for your equipment and composition.

To summarize aperture settings and their impact on an image:

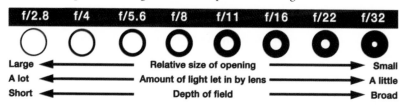

Photography Basics (continued)

Putting the Exposure Together

The ISO/film speed, shutter speed, and aperture work together to regulate the amount of light the sensor collects. Specifically, there is an inverse relationship between aperture and shutter speed. As the aperture gets smaller, the shutter generally needs to be open longer to record an adequate amount of light. As the aperture gets larger, the shutter speed does not need as much time.

Multiple combinations of aperture and shutter speeds exist to record the same amount of light. While this gives photographers a multitude of options to choose from, how do you know which setting to choose?

Start by adjusting your ISO speed to a single consistent setting such as ISO 100 to keep things simple. Then ask yourself whether you want to depict motion or record a specific depth of field.

If you wish to capture a frozen or blurred subject and you care little about depth of field, set your shutter speed first. On the other hand, if you wish to show either a short or a broad depth of field in your scene and are not as concerned with motion, change your aperture first. When both motion and depth of field are of equal importance, modify both shutter speed and aperture.

Sometimes conditions are not conducive to getting the exact settings you want. If you desire faster shutter speeds or smaller apertures (less light), choose a faster ISO speed. Conversely, if you wish for slower shutter speeds or wider apertures (more light), choose a slower ISO speed.

The Histogram

Viewed on your digital camera's LCD screen, a histogram is a graphical chart of how much light your camera captured during the exposure. This instant feedback helps photographers understand whether the camera recorded the appropriate amount of light and how to adjust the exposure if you do not like what you see.

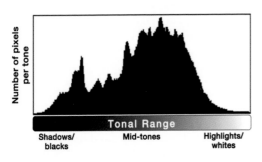

The left side of this graph represents the shadows captured in the image, while the right side shows the highlights. The middle displays the mid-tones.

Generally, a correctly exposed photo will show a balanced distribution of tones towards the center if you are shooting in JPEG format (see "RAW or JPEG?" section on page 26) or slightly to the right of the histogram without blowing out the highlights to maximize the amount of data your sensor records in RAW format.

Based on the resulting histogram, you can adjust the exposure to either add or subtract light to a follow-up image. If you see a spike on the left-most side of the graph, the image may have areas that are underexposed. To record sufficient detail in those dark spots, add light to the exposure in one of three ways:

1. In P, Av, or Tv modes, increase light through Exposure Value (EV) compensation ("+").

2. In Manual mode, open up the aperture but keep shutter speed the same. Or slow your shutter speed and keep the aperture the same.
3. Use a faster ISO speed, keeping aperture and shutter speed the same.

However, if you see a spike on the edge of the right side of the histogram, the camera has recorded too much light in certain areas. If your camera has the "Highlight Alert" function available and enabled, the overexposed spots will appear as blinking black and white areas when you review the photograph on your LCD screen (an indication the camera has not recorded data in those places). Post-processing software cannot currently recover or recreate this lost information. In this situation, you will want to subtract light in one of three ways:

1. In P, Av, or Tv modes, decrease light through EV compensation ("-").
2. In Manual, stop down the aperture but keep shutter speed the same. Alternatively, increase your shutter speed and keep the aperture the same.
3. Use a slower ISO speed, keeping aperture and shutter speed the same.

White Balance

Measured in degrees Kelvin (K), white balance describes how the camera sees the color of natural light and makes internal adjustments to render this color neutrally in the photograph. Some common measures of the color of light throughout the day include:

- Sunrise and sunset = 2000-3500 degrees K, which appears orange or "warm."
- A sunny clear day at high noon = 5000-5500 degrees K, making it a neutral color which is neither warm nor cold.
- An overcast day = 7000 to 9000 degrees K, which appears blue or "cold."

Auto White Balance (AWB) enables your camera to interpret the light and make modifications to deliver what it thinks is the "right" color in your photograph. Common preset settings such as Sunny, Overcast/Cloudy, Shade, Tungsten, and Fluorescent offer more control over how your camera sees the light's color. Simply set the white balance to match the conditions you see in the outdoors.

However, if you would like additional warmth in your photograph, consider changing the white balance to Overcast/Cloudy or Shade when it is sunny, as this tricks the camera into adding an orange tint to your photograph to balance the blues, similar to the effect of a warming filter.

Filters

Sometimes it takes more than a camera body and lens to create the photograph you desire. Filters can help extend your creative vision and assist in recording the scene more closely to the way your eye sees it. While post-processing software allows fine-tuning after recording the image, filters can help make similar adjustments in the camera as you create the photograph.

Though primarily used to protect a camera lens from scratching or breaking, an **ultraviolet (UV) filter** prevents ultraviolent rays from hitting the camera's sensor. Because it is transparent to visible light, this filter does not impact the exposure setting. While it reduces haze, particularly at high altitudes, you are unlikely to see any great effect at the sea level altitudes found in Acadia.

Photography Basics (continued)

A **polarizing filter**, often simply referred to as a "polarizer," attaches to the front of your lens and filters out reflected light our unaided eye sees as glare from non-metallic, polarizing surfaces such as water, rocks, and leaves. A polarizing filter reduces exposure settings about one to two stops of light, and as such, it can also double as a neutral density filter (read more about neutral density filters below).

A polarizer benefits your work in multiple ways. First, it helps reduce atmospheric haze and reflected glare that might appear in your natural scene. Second, this filter can intensify the color saturation in your photograph, most notably in a blue sky. Third, and finally, a polarizer can enhance or eliminate unwanted reflections in water like the ocean, ponds, and streams, an effect post-processing software cannot currently reproduce.

After placing it on your lens, rotate the front part of the filter, turning it slowly to see a visible effect on the amount of haze, color saturation, and/or reflection. Where you leave the polarizer during the rotation is a personal choice, but watch for over-polarization, where the sky becomes unnaturally dark blue.

If you do not see the effect of the polarizer in your viewfinder before you shoot, ensure you are rotating the filter around the lens slowly. Changes in polarization will be most obvious in the sky or in a water reflection.

In addition, a polarizer achieves maximum intensity when positioning your camera at a 90-degree angle from the sun. To determine the area of the sky that will be most affected, use a technique called, "Shoot the Sun." Extend your thumb and pointer-finger as if you were shooting a gun (so that your thumb and pointer-finger form a 90-degree angle). Then point your "gun" directly at the sun and rotate your arm so that your thumb rotates along an imaginary circle around the axis of your finger. The directions where your thumb points are the directions where your polarizer will have maximum effect on your photograph. When photographing in a different direction than where your thumb points, the polarizer will have little to no effect in your photograph.

As you turn the filter, look out for uneven polarization. This can occur when shooting at angles between 45 and 90 degrees, particularly with wide-angle lenses. One part of the sky will be darker than the other parts, which appears unnatural in the resulting photographs. To avoid uneven polarization, reduce the intensity of the effect by simply turning the filter slightly until the shades of the sky match better.

Because of our digital cameras white balance capabilities, perhaps the least-useful filter in digital photography is the **warming filter.** However, if you are still utilizing film to create images, this color-correcting filter is a "must-have" in your bag!

When placing this filter in front of your lens, it reduces the bluish hues in a scene by adding a subtle orange coloration. Much like the "Cloudy" or "Shade" settings on your digital camera's white balance, this filter is most useful for overcast days or open shade where the light appears very blue to the camera (even when not so apparent to our eyes!). Different strengths are available from a variety of manufacturers, such as the 81 series (81A, 81B, 81C, & 81D) and the KR series (KR3 or KR6). Warming polarizers are available for purchase if you wish to use these two filters simultaneously without having two separate filters in your bag.

A **neutral density filter**, which appears light grey in color, decreases the amount of light the camera's sensor sees without affecting the color of light. It is most helpful in slowing shutter speeds. A neutral density filter is available from manufacturers like Singh-Ray, Lee, and Hoya in varying strengths from 1-stop to 10-stops.

Occasionally, the scene we compose contains areas that are too bright for the camera to record while still properly exposing the rest of the scene. This frequently results in images where the landscape in the foreground looks perfectly exposed, but the overexposed sky appears white and washed out. Your camera may have a "Highlight Alert" feature that warns of this scenario (see the histogram section on page 30).

A **graduated neutral density filter**—also referred to as a "split neutral density filter" or "grad ND" for short—reduces the bright areas of the frame while exposing the rest of the photograph properly. Like the neutral density filter, this filter displays a grey tint, but only across part of the filter (hence the terms, "graduated" and "split").

To use a graduated neutral density filter, first switch the camera's shooting mode to Manual so you can more easily adjust the exposure settings as you decide which strength of filter to apply. Then, change your metering mode to spot metering to identify precisely the correct exposure for the foreground and background.

Next, determine how strong of a filter you need. Find the correct exposure for the dark area by aiming your camera at the darker spots in your foreground and noting the shutter speed and aperture that appear on your meter. Then, meter for the bright area (most commonly in the sky), and again, note the exposure readings.

Lastly, calculate the number of stops between the two exposures. The difference in exposure equals the strength of the graduated neutral density filter to use. For example, a three-stop difference in exposure indicates a three-stop filter would work best. Manufacturers like Singh-Ray and Lee sell gradual neutral density filters in one-, two-, three-, four-, and five-stop strengths. Stacking multiple filters sometimes helps manage extreme lighting conditions.

Once you have decided which filter to put in front of your lens, reset your exposure settings to the aperture and shutter speed you metered for the dark area.

Look for a natural horizon or diagonal line between the light and dark areas to match the horizon line. Soft-edged filters are more forgiving with an odd-shaped horizon than hard-edged ones. If the horizon line falls at an angle, tilt the filter to match the horizon line.

To get a better idea of where to place the filter, hold down your depth of field preview

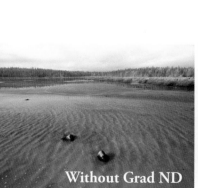

Though the rocks and ice in the foreground at Seawall Pond showed proper exposure, the sky appeared overexposed (left). A three-stop graduated neutral density filter positioned in front of the lens such that the dark section of the filter covered the sky helped to reduce the light in the clouds and match the exposure levels across the rest of the frame (right). Canon 5DMII, 16-35mm at 18mm, ISO 50, f/22 at 1/13th sec., three-stop graduated neutral density filter.

button (if available on your camera) while positioning the filter. Stopping down to a smaller aperture like f/16 or f/22 will make the placement of the graduated line more apparent.

Instead of using graduated neutral density filters, some photographers prefer capturing multiple frames at differing exposure levels to blend together later in post-processing software—or in some cases, in camera—to create High Dynamic Range (HDR) images. Specialized filters within post-processing software can also mimic the effect of a graduated neutral density filter for a single image.

Working with Natural Light

Our eyes do not see the world the same way our camera does. While humans naturally see three dimensions, our camera only sees two. Because our camera cannot "see" depth, photographers need to create the illusion of this third dimension in their pictures by recording shaping natural light. Whether you are photographing a small macro or a broad landscape scene, look for either side or backlight to help produce the feeling of depth within your frame.

Side light illuminates the subject from the side, where the shadow appears next to an object. This type of light allows the camera to capture the visual contrast between the highlights and shadows in order to produce a sense of shape and form.

Back light occurs when the sun lights the subject from behind, causing a visible, bright halo around an object. This glow separates the subject from the background, creating the appearance of depth in the scene. When shooting backlit scenes, remember to use a sunshade like a lens hood, your hand, or even a hat held between your camera and the sun to prevent lens flare from unintentionally occurring in your photograph.

Generally, the two types of light to avoid when photographing any scene are **top** and **front light**. Since the shadows are not visible to your camera in both situations, your subject may appear flat and shapeless when the sun illuminates the object from the front or from the top at mid-day.

To visualize the light direction and the height of the sun in the sky for your composition,

Side lighting occurs when the shadow falls to the side of an object within your frame. Canon 5DMII, 100mm macro, ISO 100, f/22 at 1/80th sec.

consult the Photographer's Ephemeris (**www.photoephemeris.com**) and utilize the Sunlight feature on Google™ Earth before heading out on your photo shoot. Once you arrive in the field, carefully observe and position yourself based on the direction of light falling on your subject.

In addition to positioning our cameras to "see" the contrast between light and shadow, we also need to consider the quality of light that exists and how it will affect our final photograph.

The night begins its transition from dark to light (in the morning) and from light to dark (in the evening) when "astronomical twilight" begins. During this time (which occurs approximately 90 minutes prior to sunrise and after sunset), a person cannot pick out any discernible detail in the landscape or identify a horizon line in the distant without the aid of artificial lights. The period between evening and morning astronomical twilight is the darkest part of the night and is the best time for photographing moving star trails using lengthy exposure times (e.g., one to six hours). Experiment with light painting by using a strong flashlight to illuminate a dark object in the frame.

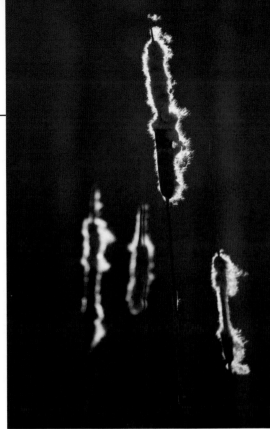

The glow around the edges of the cattails resulted from backlighting. Canon 5DMII, 100-400mm at 400mm, ISO 100, f/5.6 at 1/320th sec.

About 60 minutes before sunrise, "nautical twilight" begins when a person can distinguish land from sky on the horizon but still has difficulty seeing details within the landscape. Because the sun still sits below the horizon, the natural light appears soft and blue in color to the human eye. Hence, some photographers aptly refer this time frame as "The Blue Hour"— despite the best blue light only lasting about 20 to 30 minutes (around the transition to civil twilight). This is a popular time to capture landscape photographs under the unique light using long exposure times (i.e., up to and exceeding 30 seconds).

Approximately 30 minutes prior to the sun breaking the horizon, "civil twilight" offers enough light to read a book without using any additional light from a flashlight or headlamp. Depending on the clouds in the sky and the amount of dust particulates in the air, the sun's rays may color the clouds overhead in vibrant, eye-catching variations of colors like oranges, pinks, and purple. Because of Maine's latitude, this colorful show can appear up to 45 minutes prior to sunrise and after sunset (in comparison, at my home in Arizona, the timing is typically 15 minutes). Utilizing a graduated neutral density filter over the sky in this situation can help you record the spectacular show while maintaining detail in the land during your exposure.

Once the sun rises, the next 60 minutes of direct light offers what outdoor photographers often call "sweet light" and "The Golden Hour." The light from the sun is direct, but not as harsh as appears in the middle of the day, leading to long shadows, rich highlights, and warm, orange-colored light. In the winter months in Acadia, these ideal lighting conditions extend well beyond a single hour, since the sun traverses a lower path across the sky when compared to the sun's path in the summer months.

Afterwards and until about one hour before sunset, bright mid-day light occurs as the sun shines brightly overhead. Not only is this type of light more direct, but it also falls on our subjects from the top down, rendering few shadows for the camera to create the appearance of shape. Also, the harsh contrast of mid-day light makes it difficult to expose properly for both the highlights and the shadows, since the camera can pick up only a limited range of tones. However, graduated neutral density filters and High Dynamic Range (HDR) imaging techniques allow photographers to record a broad set of tones no matter the composition. In the evening, 60 minutes before the sun goes down, a second "Golden Hour" begins, followed immediately by the official sunset, civil twilight, nautical twilight, astronomical twilight, and then finally dark until the next morning.

Overcast skies create diffused light any time of day. Even a passing cloud in front of the sun or the shade from a larger object like a rock or tree can create this softer lighting condition. When a bright sun lingers overhead, though, a diffuser proves invaluable in providing diffused light over a smaller scene (see page 37 for more on diffusers).

Because of the low contrast between the shadows and highlights (and therefore, more even illumination), the camera records improved color saturation in your photograph, making it ideal light for photographing close-up scenes of wildflowers, fall foliage, and smaller tide pool creatures. That said, passing storms can yield moody wide-angle landscape photographs as well, especially if you utilize a two- or three-stop graduated neutral density filter over the sky to darken the clouds.

Like diffused light, reflected or bounced light (when the natural light bounces off a separate object then illuminates the subject) offers less intense contrast between highlights and shadows.

With so many options available, what is the best light to make a photograph? It depends entirely on your subject matter and the story you wish to tell with your photograph. As Alfred Stieglitz once suggested, "Wherever there is light, there is a photograph."

Photographed about 30 minutes before sunrise, Boulder Beach takes on a bluish shade thanks to the blue-colored pre-dawn light. Canon 5DMII, 16-35mm at 16mm, ISO 100, f/13 at 30 sec., three-stop graduated neutral density filter.

Managing Light With Reflectors and Diffusers

Sometimes the natural light in the middle of the day is too harsh, too direct, and too bright to make phenomenal photographs, especially of broad scenic landscapes. Human eyes have the ability to see a broad spectrum of light, but the current digital cameras record a much smaller dynamic range. Because of this, the camera will "see" a mid-day scene as "contrasty"—bright white highlights coupled with dark black shadows and not a lot of mid-tones in between.

Using a **reflector** can help reduce the stark contrast across a smaller scene and create more pleasing light on your subjects during the middle of the day. A reflector is any reflective surface used to redirect the natural light back into the scene. Commercially made reflectors have different colored surfaces, but gold and white are the most useful for photographing the outdoors.

As the name suggests, gold provides golden orange tones, as it modifies the reflected natural light so the scene feels warmer in color. A silver-colored reflector produces cooler, bluer tones. A white reflector reflects the existing color of the natural light into the scene, producing the most neutral-toned light.

No matter which color you choose, hold the reflector with the reflective surface towards the sun and guide the light into the shadowed areas falling on your subject. You might have to turn the reflector back and forth subtly until the reflected light hits your subject exactly as you desire.

A cloudless day in Acadia National Park can generate harsh lighting conditions that are difficult for your camera to record. Fortunately, you can create an "instant cloudy day" over a smaller scene with a **diffuser**. A diffuser is any semi-transparent material stretched across a frame. Collapsible versions (similar to a car window shade) are handy when photographing in remote areas. If a store-bought diffuser is not available, consider using a white bed sheet, piece of paper, or thin white t-shirt instead. Alternatively, purchase a light tent to place over your smaller scene.

No matter the material, hold the diffuser between the sun and your subject. As you position it, ensure you use a large enough diffuser to cover the entire scene, else you are likely to record a dark subject against a bright background. A Wimberley Plamp™, an extra tripod, a nearby tree, or a friend can help hold the diffuser in place as you are shooting.

Working With Artificial Light: Flash

Using a flash is useful in smaller scenes when the sun does not provide the quantity or quality of light you desire. Specifically, flash helps balance a large contrast between the highlights and the shadow areas much like a reflector does, only more so. Flash also adds dramatic light to diffused lighting set-ups.

A pop of light from an on-camera flash softens the shadows by adding light evenly to your scene. On-camera flash is most effective in backlit situations where the subject appears dark and the surrounding ambient light is lighter than the light falling on the subject. Otherwise, the front light created by this type of flash can render subjects as washed out, flat, and lacking dimension.

An off-camera flash acts the same as on-camera flash, except the flash is physically separated from the camera by a cord or wireless transmitter (infrared or radio). Not only does this provide the most flattering light in most applications, but it also provides seemingly endless creative options in creating and recording side or backlight in your scene.

A ring flash (a circular light that fits around the camera's lens) emits light that surrounds

the subject. This helps evenly illuminate the entire subject when natural light produces odd shadows or highlights. To create a similar shadow-less effect as a ring light, some manufacturers make twin lights, where two separate lights sit on either side of the camera's lens.

The biggest challenge in using artificial light is balancing the natural ambient light with the flash output to expose the entire scene properly. To do this, consider lighting your photograph in two different layers—first, an ambient or background layer and second, a flash or foreground layer, controlling the light and exposure level for both of these layers separately.

Starting with the ambient layer, adjust your shutter speed and aperture to get a desired exposure for the background. Then snap a test shot for ambient exposure, keeping the flash unit turned off. Check your histogram to ensure you have captured a balanced ambient exposure. Your subject in the foreground might be dark, and that's OK!

Next, turn on your flash unit and select either Through-the-Lens (TTL) or Manual mode. The various TTL modes available will automatically calculate and provide the necessary flash output for you. Selecting Manual mode is much like shooting in Manual camera mode: you decide the appropriate flash output setting given your distance from the subject, ISO speed, focal length of your lens, and aperture.

Make an exposure with the flash. Now what do you see on your histogram? Evaluate your foreground to determine how to adjust the flash output only—not the ambient light in the background.

If the subject in the foreground looks too dark, increase flash output by adding light through the Flash Exposure Compensation (FEC) button "+" on the flash or camera if you're using TTL mode. If you are in Manual flash mode, you have other options:

- Increase the flash output in Manual flash mode.
- Move the flash closer to subject.
- Select a more sensitive ISO speed setting.
- Open up the aperture, then increase the shutter speed.

If the foreground appears too bright, subtract light through the Flash Exposure Compensation (FEC) button "-" on the flash or camera if you are using TTL mode. If you are in Manual flash mode, additional adjustments include:

- Decrease the flash output in Manual flash mode.
- Move the flash away from subject.
- Select a less sensitive ISO speed setting.
- Close down the aperture, then decrease shutter speed.

The effect of artificial light on the subject should be gentle, not harsh like a nuclear blast. If you feel the flash is adding sufficient light, but creating too much contrast, soften the light even further with a flash diffuser like Gary Fong's Lightsphere (for digital SLR camera flashes) or Puffer Pop-Up Flash Diffuser (for on-camera pop-up flash).

Flash follows the inverse-square law, which states that the intensity of light decreases with the square of the distance between the light source and the subject (Intensity = 1/relative distance^2). The non-technical translation of this formula? The light from a flash (or any other source), rapidly loses intensity the further it travels from its source. A flash lights a scene most

Because of overcast skies, this perfectly-intact sea urchin skeleton showed few highlights or shadows, but plenty of midtones. By adding a touch of flash (held off-camera on the right), the subject showed improved contrast between highlight and shadow. As a result, the photograph displayed better shape and dimension.
LEFT: Canon 5D, 100mm macro, ISO 100, f/32 at 1/5th sec.
RIGHT: Canon 5D, 100mm macro, ISO 100, f/8 at 1/80th sec., flash at -1 TTL.

effectively when positioned from 2 to 50 feet (0.6 to 15.2 m) away from the subject matter. This makes artificial light an ideal choice to illuminate wildflowers, autumnal leaves, seashells, and other objects where the photographer can set up his or her camera in close proximity.

However, wildlife photographers frequently cannot get that close to their subjects and often shoot in the low-lighting conditions at sunrise and sunset, when many animals are most active. For these situations, fill light from an on-camera flash can help freeze the motion of a sea duck in flight or a deer grazing in an idyllic meadow. To help project the light at significantly greater distances, mount a lightweight Flash X-tender™ (also known as Better Beamer) to your flash. The Fresnel lens in this piece of specialized equipment concentrates a focused beam of artificial light on far-away subjects and helps to create an attractive catchlight—a specular highlight or sparkle—in the animal's eye.

Composition "Rules"

Composition refers to the way a photographer organizes and places the various elements within the frame. We should seek to develop a sense of harmony among the different elements within the photograph and to create the illusion of three-dimensional depth in this two-dimensional media.

When setting up your camera to photograph a scene, keep the following compositional tips in mind:

Keep it simple: Sometimes, less is more. A photograph should have a clear, definitive center of focus or interest to help viewers understand what you are trying to accomplish with your image.

Photography Basics (continued)

Start by verbally expressing what enticed you to make a picture in the first place. Ask yourself, "What specifically do I like about this scene?" and "What is catching my eye?" By having a clear definition of what "it" is you want to capture, you put yourself in an excellent position to actually capture "it" with your camera.

As you compose, fill your frame with your key subject. Eliminate anything and everything that does not contribute to your vision. Pay particular attention to any odd shapes, bright backgrounds, and out of focus elements that could distract your viewer's eye away from your subject. As a final check before you click the shutter, ask yourself if every element in the frame is adding value and context to your visual message.

Moving your feet, instead of simply zooming in with a zoom lens will help focus on your primary subject and eliminate extraneous elements within your photograph. As world-famous photojournalist, Robert Capa, once indicated, "If your photographs aren't good enough, you aren't close enough."

Abide by the Rule of Thirds: The Rule of Thirds simply suggests that you do not put the subject in the center of the frame. Instead, imagine a tic-tac-toe board on top of your frame consisting of two equally-spaced vertical lines and two equally-spaced horizontal lines. Ideally, the main center of interest for your photograph would fall at one of the four intersections between the

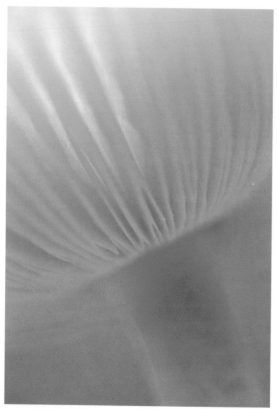

When I first saw this mushroom along the Witch Hole Pond Loop Carriage Road, I thought the gills looked like an upside-down ballerina's tutu. In order to convey this visual message, I did not need to include the entire mushroom (above), where the gills took up such a small part of the frame. Instead, I simplified the composition, filled my frame with only that subject, and tilted my camera in a Dutch tilt for a much more effective photograph (left). Canon 5DMII, 100mm macro, ISO 400, f/4 at 1/60th sec.

The granite cliffs near Monument Cove form an effective line from both corners, drawing the viewer into the frame and leading them through the photograph to the Otter Cliff in the background. Canon 5DMII, 16-35mm at 16mm, ISO 100, f/16 at 5 sec., three-stop graduated neutral density filter.

lines (i.e., the four corners of the center box in the tic-tac-toe board).

By doing this, you create asymmetrical balance which brings together a sense of unity among the various elements found within a photograph. The idea here is not that you hit the intersection points with precision, but rather to keep subjects out of the middle of the frame.

When you place the primary subject (or other key elements of the image) in the middle of the frame, you create static and symmetrical balance. Symmetry is often undesirable as it divides and creates competition among the various parts. For example, when the horizon line between the sky and land runs through the middle of the frame, this creates a dividing "half-and-half" composition. While you should generally aim for asymmetrical balance by placing the primary subject off-center, there are some scenes (like reflections in water) where you may wish to convey a sense of symmetry in nature. These situations often lend themselves well to breaking this rule.

Use leading lines: By introducing lines—whether subtle or blatant—into your composition, you offer a means for the viewer's eye to travel into and around the photographic frame. Lines also add a sense of depth and the illusion of space to your photograph when applied effectively.

Dynamic diagonal lines originating near—but not directly out of—the corners of your picture allow the viewer's eye to naturally and easily enter the scene. In addition to diagonal lines, look for converging lines, meandering S-curves, and Z-curves to establish a long path for your viewers and the illusion of depth within the image.

Keep in mind that a line should lead to some worthwhile payoff, like your primary subject, a prominent feature, or a well-illuminated shape. Take care to not lead your viewer out of the frame though, as we want to keep them looking at your image for as long as possible.

If no horizon is visible in your frame and you see an interesting, but rather static vertical or horizontal line, consider using the "Dutch tilt." In this cinematography technique, the photographer intentionally slants the camera a few degrees to the right or left while composing,

Photography Basics (continued)

which turns those static lines into visually pleasing diagonal lines.

As you experiment with this technique, tilt your camera in each direction, as a subject might look better when you slant your camera towards one way or the other depending on the arrangement of the flowers, rock patterns, and other smaller objects.

Create layers: To help create a sense of dimension, a photograph should contain multiple layers, including a foreground, mid-ground, and background, whether it contains a broad scenic view or an intimate macro detail.

Landscape photographers often create different visual spaces through the "near-far technique" where one positions the camera very close to an object in the foreground to make it appear larger in the frame and then utilizes a small aperture (like f/16 or f/22) to capture extensive depth of field from close up to the distant background. As you try this approach, look for complimentary framing elements like trees, grasses, and rocks on the bottom, sides, and top of the frame that add context to the rest of your image.

Macro photographers can also accomplish layering by setting a wide aperture (like f/4 or f/5.6) and selectively focusing on the mid-ground. The short depth of field blurs the objects closest to the frame as well as the background while keeping the primary subject in focus.

If the space between the foreground and the distant background is uninteresting, minimize the space it takes up in the frame by lowering your camera and tripod closer to the ground. On the other hand, if you wish to increase the mid-ground, then raise your gear.

Heed the Rule of Space: When photographing wildlife or people, position them such that they are peering into – not out of – the frame and allow enough space in front of their gaze to imply forward movement into – not out of – the photograph. Viewers connect with an animal's or person's eyes and then follow the direction of the subject's stare. If the subject looks out of the frame, your viewers will look there as well.

Follow the Rule of Odds: While arranging your subject, include an odd number of objects (e.g., one, three, five, seven) to create asymmetrical balance and dynamic tension within your frame. An even number of objects leads to symmetrical balance and a sense of calm, which can feel static to a viewer's eye.

Vary your perspective: Inevitably, the easiest and most comfortable way to photograph is at eye level. However, eye level may not necessarily yield the most effective composition for your scene. Look for opportunities to photograph your subject from the top down as if you had a birds-eye view of your subject. Do not be afraid to climb up on rocks or photograph from an airplane to get an aerial view of your subject (just do so very carefully!).

In addition, look for opportunities to photograph your subject from a bug's perspective – from bottom up. This naturally requires you to get low to the ground to observe your subject from this angle. Utilize the LiveView capabilities (if available on your camera) to help you compose when looking through the viewfinder is not an option.

Finally, consider whether to compose in a vertical portrait or horizontal landscape orientation. Vertical images feel more dynamic and possess more tension since less space exists for the various elements to work together. Despite having the same size real estate as vertical images, horizontal images conveys more peaceful and serene feelings since the elements have more apparent room to coexist. One orientation is not necessarily better than the other, so be

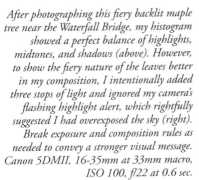

After photographing this fiery backlit maple tree near the Waterfall Bridge, my histogram showed a perfect balance of highlights, midtones, and shadows (above). However, to show the fiery nature of the leaves better in my composition, I intentionally added three stops of light and ignored my camera's flashing highlight alert, which rightfully suggested I had overexposed the sky (right). Break exposure and composition rules as needed to convey a stronger visual message. Canon 5DMII, 16-35mm at 33mm macro, ISO 100, f/22 at 0.6 sec.

sure to capture your image using both perspectives to see which one emphasizes your subject and best captures your vision.

Avoid mergers: A merger occurs when separate objects in the distance appear to intersect in our two-dimensional media. Typically, this overlap is distracting to the viewer's eye. A simple step to the left or the right to reposition your camera is usually enough to create a visual separation between the two elements.

Break the rules: View these compositional "rules" more like guidelines. Many situations exist where intentionally breaking the rules yields a very successful photograph. However, knowing the rules first can help you understand how to systematically, creatively, and effectively break them.

Work the Scene

Rarely does a photographer capture his or her exact vision with one snap of the shutter. More often, the best image results after a photographer diligently and persistently experiments with different angles, perspectives, lenses, exposure settings, depth of field, filters, lighting conditions, and creative ideas by clicking multiple photographs. During this process, check the camera's display in Playback mode to ensure you have recorded an image you envisioned and of which you are proud. Make as many frames as necessary until you are completely satisfied with your results. After all, with digital cameras, pixels are free, and the "Delete" button exists for good reason!

Countless egg-shaped boulders on Boulder Beach soak up the sun's morning rays. Canon 5DMII, 16-35mm at 16mm, ISO 100, f/16 at 0.4 sec., three-stop graduated neutral density filter.

Mount Desert Island

Mount Desert Island

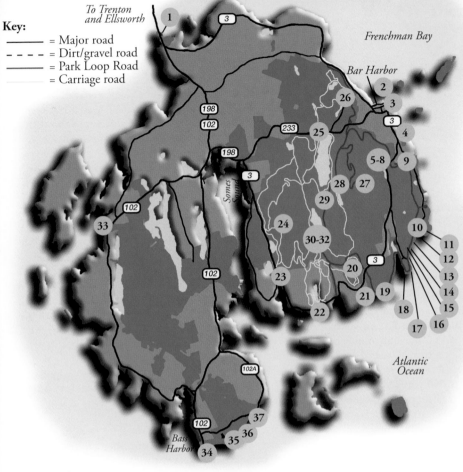

Key:
- ——— = Major road
- - - - - = Dirt/gravel road
- ——— = Park Loop Road
- ——— = Carriage road

To Trenton and Ellsworth

Frenchman Bay

Bar Harbor

Somes Sound

Atlantic Ocean

Bass Harbor

1	Thompson Island	48
2	Bar Island	50
3	Bar Harbor Shore Path	54
4	Compass Harbor Trail	56
5	Great Meadow	58
6	The Tarn	60
7	Sieur de Monts	62
8	Jesup Trail	66
9	Beaver Dam Pond	68
10	Sand Beach	70
11	Great Head	72
12	Newport Cove Overlook	74
13	Thunder Hole	76
14	Monument Cove	78
15	Gorham Mountain Trail	84
16	Boulder Beach	86
17	Otter Cliff	88
18	Otter Point & Cove	94
19	Little Hunters Beach	96
20	Day Mountain	98
21	Hunters Beach	100
22	Little Long Pond	102
23	Asticou Azalea Garden	106
24	Waterfall Bridge	108
25	Eagle Lake	110
26	Duck Brook Bridge	112
27	Cadillac Mountain	114
28	Bubble Pond	124
29	Bubble Rock Trail	126
30	Jordan Pond Shore Path	128
31	Jordan Stream	130
32	Deer Brook Bridge & Waterfall	132
33	Pretty Marsh Picnic Area	136
34	Bass Harbor Head Lighthouse	138
35	Ship Harbor Trail	142
36	Wonderland Trail	144
37	Seawall Picnic Area	146

Mount Desert Island Introduction

*A*long the coast in "Downeast Maine" sits Maine's largest island. Mount Desert Island (MDI) hosts the largest contiguous part of Acadia National Park (the park covers about 40% of the isle). The island serves as the heart of the national park and the lively town of Bar Harbor (located on the northeastern side of MDI) offers an ideal base during your visit.

Most out-of-state visitors choose to fly into either the Portland International Jetport (**www.portlandjetport.org**) or Bangor International Airport (**www.flybangor.com**). Located an easy three-hour drive away from Bar Harbor, Portland International Jetport provides year-round air transportation with major American and internationally-based commercial airlines.

The Bangor International Airport is a quick ninety-minute drive from Bar Harbor, but despite the "international" word in the name, Bangor does not currently have any scheduled international flights directly into or out of their airport. Several major domestic air carriers, however, provide connecting services across the United States.

During the summer months (typically June through September), several commercial airlines service the Hancock County/Bar Harbor Airport, which sits a mere 12 miles (19.3 km) from Bar Harbor. Private charters fly in year-round. Scenic Flights of Acadia (**www.scenicflightsofacadia.com**), who provide excellent airplane tours above Acadia and the surrounding area year-round, bases their operations out of this small, but friendly, airport. Look for their small red building along Route 3, though, not at the terminal.

Rental cars are available from all three airports. Although all park roads are accessible by a regular two-wheel drive vehicle, you might prefer to rent an all-wheel or four-wheel drive vehicle if visiting in the winter months when road conditions can vary from clear to icy and snowy.

The free, environmentally-sensitive Island Explorer park shuttle operates from late June until mid-October. Buses do not run at the early and late hours of the day when photographers typically head out to shoot, but they can help avoid mid-day parking challenges in the summer, especially on weekends and holidays. Before your outing, check schedules at **www.exploreacadia.com**.

No lodging exists within park boundaries, save for two campgrounds (Seawall and Blackwoods), but extensive options including hotels, resorts, bed & breakfasts, campgrounds,

Aerial view of Bar Harbor, Mount Desert Island, and Acadia National Park from a Scenic Flights of Acadia airplane. Canon 5DMII, 24-105mm at 32mm, ISO 1600, f/5.6 at 1/2000th sec., polarizer.

Cottage Street in downtown Bar Harbor bustles beneath a vibrant sunset. Canon 5DMII, 24-105mm at 60mm, ISO 100, f/8 at 8 sec., polarizer, three-stop graduated neutral density filter.

and hostels to fit any budget are located in Bar Harbor and other smaller towns on the island as well as in Trenton and Ellsworth on the mainland. Book early for a visit in between June through October to ensure you are able to reserve the dates you wish in the midst of high season. As many lodging options close for the off-season, contact your preferred hotel to ensure they are accommodating visitors in between mid-October and mid-June. Contact the Bar Harbor Chamber of Commerce (**www.barharborinfo.com**) for lodging information.

The only restaurant residing in the park is the historic Jordan Pond House (**www.thejordanpondhouse.com**) on the south side of Jordan Pond (see page 128). Ample dining options exist in Bar Harbor as well as Northeast Harbor, Southwest Harbor, Bass Harbor, and other small towns located on the island. Like the overnight accommodations though, dining reservations (if accepted) are a necessity during the summer's peak visitation times and many eateries shut down for the winter season. That said, the Hannaford's grocery store in Bar Harbor remains open year-round for provisions, as do stores and markets in nearby Trenton and Ellsworth on the mainland.

Once you arrive on MDI, stop by one of Acadia's visitor centers. From mid-May to mid-October, visit the main visitor center at Hulls Cove to pick up your park pass, read the *Beaver Log* park newspaper, study the large relief map of the park, and browse a healthy selection of books, calendars, and postcards to help you visualize the park. During the same time, Thompson Island also hosts a small welcome center with plenty of brochures and a helpful staff. From November to early April—except for Thanksgiving, Christmas Eve, Christmas Day, and New Year's Day—the Acadia National Park Headquarters on Highway 233 near Eagle Lake serves as the park's primary visitor center.

The park charges an entrance fee (for current rates, check the Acadia National Park website, **www.nps.gov/acad**). In both cases, your receipt is valid for entry for seven days. An Acadia National Park annual pass and other National Park passes (Annual, Golden Age Passport, and Golden Access Passport) are available at the visitor centers year-round or at the park entrance gate along Park Look Road/Ocean Drive from April to November.

With a park map in hand to navigate the somewhat confusing roads winding among public and private land, head to the 27-mile-long (43.5-km) Park Loop Road to explore natural icons like Cadillac Mountain, Thunder Hole, Boulder Beach, and Jordan Pond. However, make time to see lesser-known, but equally photogenic gems, like Little Hunters Beach, Gorham Mountain, and Day Mountain as well. Along the way, a lively landscape featuring bare mountain summits, serene meadows, cobble and sand beaches, jagged cliffs, and freshwater ponds offer homes and feeding grounds to a broad range of wildlife.

On par with the natural splendor, MDI is also home to remarkable historical landmarks, like the 45 miles (72.4 km) of carriage roads, 17 uniquely constructed stone bridges, 2 gatehouses, memorial plaques on multiple trails, and of course, the renowned Bass Harbor Head Lighthouse.

Thompson Island

A winter wonderland of fleeting ice formations and wintering birds

TIME OF YEAR	TIME OF DAY	TIDE	HIKE
December to March	*Sunrise and sunset*	*Low*	*Easy*

In winter, thin sheets of ice in Mount Desert Narrows collapse on top of boulders as the tide recedes. Canon 5DMII, 16-35mm at 16mm, ISO 50, f/22 at 1.6 sec., four-stop graduated neutral density filter.

Serving as the gateway to Acadia National Park for those traveling to MDI, the tiny Thompson Island provides visitors their brief first glimpse of the spectacular natural resources this national park protects. Sitting in the heart of the Mount Desert Narrows, the west side of the island features the classic evergreen-lined, rocky Maine coastal landscape. The east side showcases an open, grassy field where bird enthusiasts can spot red-breasted mergansers, buffleheads, common loons, common goldeneyes, and double-crested cormorants passing through the channel from October to May. In spring and fall, great egrets, snowy egrets, and great blue herons often hunt for food in the shallow wetlands to the south of the island.

Though photographers will want to stop here to start warming up their shutter finger in any season, winter offers the chance to create truly unique and difficult – if not impossible – to reproduce pictures. After long stretches of below freezing temperatures, a thin layer of ice forms on the sea, which moves with the ever-changing tide. At lower tides, as the water recedes, this ice shelf collapses around the boulders along the ocean's shore, creating intriguing volcano-like

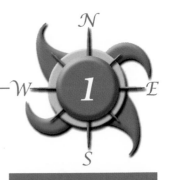

The high tide swallows the low tide's sheet of ice in the Mount Desert Narrows, resulting in ample, ever-changing compositions of winter. Canon 5DMII, 16-35mm at 35mm, ISO 200, f/13 at 1/80th sec.

Directions

From the intersection of Main Street and Route 3 in Ellsworth, travel 9 miles (14.5 km) southwest along Route 3. After crossing the Trenton Bridge, turn left into the signed picnic area. In winter, park instead at the Thompson Island Visitor Center (which closes for the season from mid-October to mid-May) directly across from this turnoff on the west side of street.

shapes protruding above the sheet of ice.

Since the scene changes with every rise and fall of the tide, if you see something you like here, photograph it immediately! The fleeting moment will only last until the next incoming tide or a warm front melts the breathtaking icy scene away.

Wide-angle, **normal**, and **telephoto lenses** coupled with a **polarizer**, **tripod**, and **cable release** can all help record a visual story of this short-lived effect. Create a sense of depth by setting your camera up low to the ground and utilizing the lines in the ice to lead your viewers from the foreground to the background. Take care to not lead your viewers out of the scene though, and find lines that payoff with something of significant interest.

A visit at sunrise will produce direct light on the east side of the island at the Thompson Island Picnic Area. At sunset, though, a wall of trees blocks the sun's rays and casts a distinct shadow across this spot on cloudless days. No matter the time of day, watch your histogram closely while you shoot. Camera meters aim to "see" average, middle grey tones within a scene, which causes your camera to underexpose a brightly lit landscape. Add light through your exposure settings to ensure the snow and ice appears a natural white color in your photograph—and to prevent both from looking dull grey.

To emphasize the feeling of cold, photograph in pre-sunrise or post-sunset light when the light tends to appear bluish. Also, setting your white balance to Sunny or even Tungsten will trick your camera into providing an increased bluish tint to your winter scene.

As you explore this area, watch your footing and do not venture onto the ice off the shoreline, as the tidal flow remains constantly active, though masked, under a fragile, thin layer of ice.

Pancake ice collects along the western shoreline of Thompson Island. Canon 5DMII, 24-105mm at 58mm, ISO 100, f/22 at 1/6th sec., polarizer, two-stop graduated neutral density filter.

Bar Island

Sweeping views of Bar Harbor from small isle accessible at low tide

TIME OF YEAR	TIME OF DAY	TIDE	HIKE
May to October	*Sunrise and sunset*	*Low*	*Moderate*

TOP: View of Bar Harbor and Champlain Mountain from the Bar Island summit. Canon 5DMII, 100-400mm at 135mm, ISO 1600, f/5.6 at 1/60th sec., polarizer, two-stop graduated neutral density filter. OPPOSITE: Visitors walk across the exposed gravel bar between the town of Bar Harbor and Bar Island. Canon 5DMII, 24-105mm at 105mm, ISO 800, f/9 at 1/200th sec., polarizer.

𝒜 stone's throw from Bar Harbor, this small spruce-covered remains inaccessible and simply something beautiful to admire from the downtown pier much of the time. However, for a mere hour and a half on either side of low tide, receding waters reveal a gravel sand spit connecting this tiny island with the shore, which gives the town its name. It allows adventurous shutterbugs to scuttle across and explore remote photographic treasure on Bar Island.

To safely enjoy your three-hour window on the island, consult the tide charts for Bar Harbor on the NOAA Tide and Currents website at **tidesandcurrents.noaa.gov** or the Maine Tide Charts online at **me.usharbors.com**, as well as The Photographer's Ephemeris (**www. photoephemeris.com**) to help plan your outing for when the low tide and the sunrise or sunset times coincide. During your jaunt, carefully monitor your time such that you return to MDI prior to the next incoming tide. If your travels occur during the dark, pack a **headlamp** or **flashlight** to illuminate your path.

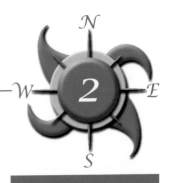

As Bridge Street disappears underneath a layer of packed sand, the exposed bar immediately offers intriguing patterns and shapes left behind by the retreating waves. Sunrise offers the better time to record footprint-less compositions than during mid-day or at sunset, but in any light, a **macro lens** will help isolate smaller arrangements on the temporary beach.

Just off-shore, flocks of herring gulls study passers-by from their rock perches while sea ducks nonchalantly paddle along Frenchman Bay. To photograph the colorful plumage of common eiders and common goldeneyes, bring a long **telephoto lens**, **teleconverter**, **on-camera flash unit**, and a **Flash X-tender™**. As you focus with fast shutter speeds—and as a result, wide open apertures—ensure the animal's eye closest to the camera is in sharp focus.

To survey the island, saunter 0.4 miles (0.6 km) across the sand bar towards the southwestern tip to join up with the Bar Island Trail, which casually meanders through serene forests and meadows. In June, purple, pink, and white lupines bloom prolifically in the clearings along the short 0.5-mile (0.8-km) hike en route to the 120-foot (37-m) summit.

After a short, uphill climb and a quick stroll just beyond the triangular, large pile of rocks marking the high point of the island, an unmatched view awaits of Bar Harbor's Main Street, the Victorian-style Bar Harbor Inn, and photogenic ships in the harbor with Huguenot Head and Champlain, Dorr, and Cadillac mountains serving as a backdrop. A telephoto lens ranging from 100 to 400mm will help isolate details of buildings and boats while a wide-angle or normal lens will enable you to frame your scene with the surrounding foliage. A polarizer and graduated neutral density filter will help darken the sky and balance the exposure. The lower light levels early in the morning and late in the evening will slow shutter speeds enough to necessitate a tripod and cable release to keep your images sharp.

To turn the glowing lights of Bar Harbor into sunburst-like stars against the rich pre-sunrise or post-sunset sky, remove all filters from your lens and set your camera to a small aperture such as f/16 or f/22.

Directions

From downtown Bar Harbor, travel north on Main Street until it dead-ends. Turn left onto West Street. Drive about 0.2 miles (0.3 km), and then turn right onto Bridge Street. Though a very small, informal gravel parking area exists at the north end of Bridge Street when the sand bar is exposed, it disappears at mid- and high tides. You might find it more convenient and safer to park along West Street instead. From the intersection of West and Bridge streets, walk 0.1 miles (0.2 km) to the start of the crossing.

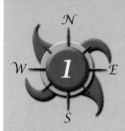

Psychedelic Skypools

"One should not only photograph things for what they are but for what else they are."

~Minor White

Maps possess a mysterious draw for me. If I pull one out, hours disappear, as I peer over the space between place names, intertwining road of all sizes, and special features along the way. A map does more than just help me get from point A to point B in my various journeys, though. Pointing my finger at familiar spots triggers fond memories of days past while unknown locations tease with the promise of new adventures. In addition, my endless fascination with these drawings not only makes getting to my next destination or photo shoot relatively straightforward, but it also subconsciously influences how I see and photograph the world around me.

While soaking in the ocean views from Ocean Drive's granite ledges one autumn morning, I marveled at the breathtaking tango of colors and psychedelic patterns of elliptical shapes dancing on the water's surface. As the undulating waves along the shore caught reflected light from the sky and the land, I was not only looking at the surf, but also lines and shapes reminiscent of topographical maps.

Formally called "skypools" and landpools," the colors of these rolling ovals depend on the time of day, weather conditions, and land surroundings. The patterns change constantly based on the water's speed, the wave height, and the reflected objects' form. Like a map, the ever-changing designs hint at what might lurk beneath the unseen ocean world.

In the book, *Color and Light in Nature* by David K. Lynch and William Livingston, the authors suggest viewing this lighting spectacle from a higher vantage point, approximately 15 degrees above the water. Though difficult to see with your own eyes, a fast shutter speed freezes the fleeting moments.

Anxious to record my own roadmaps, I made a few interesting snaps using a fast shutter speed and a wide aperture on continuous shooting drive mode (to make several instantaneous frames), I saw small, bright circles reflecting along patterns in my images. The sun had started to peek out from behind mostly cloudy skies.

Switching to a small aperture, I recorded the reflections of sun stars among the transforming designs. However, fully revealed, the sun's glare appeared too bright on the water's surface and distracted from the skypools. I waited until clouds partially obscured the light to render faint rays of light instead, which added a spark to my original idea of conveying the inconspicuous meeting of the land, sea, and sky. I also aimed to record the map-like patterns to invite my viewers to look at the ocean for more than what appears on the surface and to consider not only where you have been or where you are going but also the consistency of change.

Land, sea, and sky meet in a magical skypool of patterns, shapes, and sun stars off the Acadian shoreline. Canon 5DMII, 100-400mm at 400mm, ISO 400, f/25 at 1/1600th sec.

Bar Harbor Shore Path

Historic shoreline path reveals intriguing geology, glacial erratic

TIME OF YEAR	TIME OF DAY	TIDE	HIKE
Year-round	*Sunrise to late morning*	*Any*	*Easy*

Colorful Bar Harbor Formation rock leads into Bar Harbor. Canon 5DMII, 16-35mm at 16mm, ISO 400, f/16 at 1/10th sec., three-stop graduated neutral density filter.

*T*hough technically not in the national park, I would be remiss to *not* mention this historic path. Since the 1880s, people have ambled leisurely along the Bar Harbor Shore Path, a 1-mile (1.6-km) flat, well-maintained gravel path in front of grand Victorian-style inns and even grander private estates along the coast.

Despite its location in the middle of bustling Bar Harbor, the path offers a fine place to watch and record waves lapping against multi-colored, layered sandstone and siltstone of the Bar Harbor Formation (the second oldest rock formation on the island behind the Ellsworth Schist) with little effort.

Thanks to the Bar Harbor Chamber of Commerce, "Museum in the Streets" interpretive signs point out man-made and natural features along the way, including the well known glacial erratic referred to as "Balance Rock." To learn more, pick up a map and brochure at the Bar Harbor Chamber

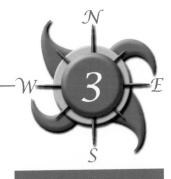

A solitary glacial erratic, called "Balance Rock," sits in the calm waters of Frenchman Bay. Canon 5DMII, 24-105mm at 65mm, ISO 125, f/9 at 30 sec., polarizer, two stop graduated neutral density filter.

of Commerce located at 2 Cottage Street in downtown Bar Harbor.

A **wide-angle lens** can help you bring home a memory of the 180-degree panoramic view of Frenchman Bay, the Porcupine Islands, and in the distance, Egg Rock and the Schoodic Peninsula. However, since the broad landscape scenes are more limited here than elsewhere in the park, if space is at a premium in your camera bag, pack instead a **macro** or **telephoto lens** to focus on the more plentiful intimate shoreline scenes or fishing boats heading out to sea.

Bring a **tripod** and **cable release**, as well as a **polarizer filter**, if you wish to capture the waves splashing over the rock with slower shutter speeds (around 1/4th of a second or slower). To turn static vertical and horizontal lines into more visually appealing diagonals, try isolating intriguing patterns and tilting your camera to one side or the other in a Dutch tilt, if needed.

Though direct light at sunrise and late morning is ideal for this east-facing trail, morning fog commonly occurs in June, July, and August. This makes for excellent conditions to record intimate scenes of vibrantly-colored rocks and otherworldly photographs of the landscape and boats in the harbor. Remember to check your histogram to ensure you are not blowing out the sky during these times and utilize a **graduated neutral density filter** to darken the sky in your frame for even moodier pictures.

Directions

From downtown Bar Harbor, travel north on Main Street until it dead-ends. Turn right onto West Street. Park here or in the lot on the north side of the street. Walk east towards the pier near the Bar Harbor Inn. The trail begins at the Shore Path sign. Very limited parking is also available along Hancock Street, where the trail ends.

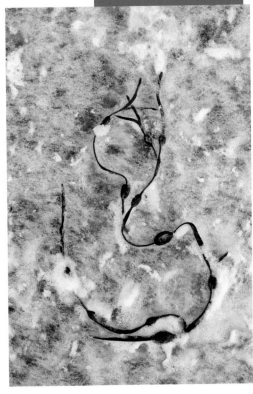

Washed onto shore by the high tide, rockweed in an abstract position sits along the Bar Harbor Shore Path. Canon 5DMII, 100mm macro, ISO 100, f/8 at 1/25th sec.

Compass Harbor Trail

Lesser-known coastal views featuring lupine and historical ruins

TIME OF YEAR	**TIME OF DAY**	**TIDE**	**HIKE**
Year-round	*Sunrise*	*Low to mid*	*Easy*

Lupine grow along the Compass Harbor in June. Canon 5DMII, 16-35mm at 27mm, ISO 200, f/20 at 1/20th sec., two stop graduated neutral density filter.

One of the more overlooked overlooks on the coastline along Ocean Drive, this little-known gem of a trail has two things the other coastal vistas don't have: a handful of perfectly positioned lupines along the cove come June and remnants of George B. Dorr's "Old Farm" family residence.

After a short, flat, easy meander through the serene forest, scenes of evergreen and maples give way to a panoramic ocean view of Frenchman Bay, Bald Porcupine Island, the Egg Rock Lighthouse, and the Schoodic Peninsula at the tree-lined, crescent-shaped Compass Harbor. A protected cobble beach exists on the north side while a cove with jagged volcanic boulders beneath the rugged Sols Cliffs offers additional photographic opportunities on the south end. In June, perky purple lupine grow on the eastern-most point separating these two different shorelines.

No doubt, the coastal scenery will

Sparkling ice encases a maple leaf along the Compass Harbor Trail in winter. Canon 5DMII, 24-105mm at 65mm, ISO 125, f/9 at 30 sec., polarizer.

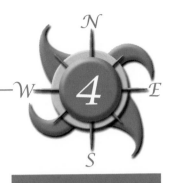

grab your attention, but compose tightly using a **normal** or short **telephoto lens** to eliminate the houses scattered around the cove. Getting low to the ground and tilting your camera towards the sky will exaggerate the height of the lively blooms against a cobalt blue sky. The vertical nature of the tall lupine lends itself to vertical compositions, but you can showcase the serenity of the broad scene through horizontal compositions as well. In either orientation, an aperture setting of f/16 or f/22 will maximize your depth of field and keep your entire scene in focus.

Consider bringing along a long telephoto lens as well to record a passing fishing boat or cruise ship headed into nearby Bar Harbor. Should you wish to include the sky in your frame, use a **polarizer** and **graduated neutral density filter** to aid in recording well-balanced exposures.

To get a taste of Acadian history, locate the faint path along the southwestern edge of the southern cove until you find stone steps leading deeper into the forest. Only these steps, a stone foundation and herringbone-style brick floors remain of what was once the glorious multi-storied mansion of "The Father of Acadia." Before passing away in 1944, George B. Dorr spent nearly his entire estimated $10 million fortune in his passionate and undying commitment to buy land and donate it to the park. A normal or telephoto lens will help record the remaining minute details of a more prosperous time.

Even though a distinct path will lead you to the coast, if you plan to shoot before the sun rises, scout the trail the day prior to your shoot (if you have the time) so you can easily find your way through the forest in the dark. Bring a **headlamp** or **flashlight** to illuminate the path on your morning stroll. Though there are many easy-going footpaths to follow, take care not to venture onto nearby private property.

Directions

From the intersection of Main Street and West Street in downtown Bar Harbor, travel south on Main Street/ Route 3 for 1.3 miles (2.1 km). Turn left into the unmarked, unsigned dirt parking lot. The only indication that you are in the right place is a small "Entering Acadia National Park" sign on the east side of the parking area.

The Schooner Head Path begins behind the "Fire Road. Do Not Block" sign. Walk the Schooner Head Path (the fire road) for about 0.2 miles (0.3 km) until the path splits. Veer left, and follow the Compass Harbor Trail less than 0.5 miles (0.8 km) to the coastline.

Great Meadow

Wildflowers and wildlife in a glacially-carved, idyllic meadow

TIME OF YEAR	TIME OF DAY	TIDE	HIKE
June and October	*Late morning to early afternoon*	*N/A*	*Easy*

TOP: Non-native lupine grow among aspen and birch in the Great Meadow. Canon 5DMII, 16-35mm at 16mm, ISO 250, f/16 at 1/60th sec.
OPPOSITE: Close-up of oxeye daisy. Canon 5DMII, 100mm macro, ISO 640, f/7.1 at 1/100th sec., diffuser, reflector.

There is no question Acadia National Park contains the most plain, but aptly descriptive, names for its grand features. Great Meadow is no exception to this naming scheme. It is indeed one great meadow, peacefully sitting in a U-shaped glacially-carved valley with Dorr and Cadillac mountains to the west and Huguenot Head and Champlain Mountain to the east.

Though brown and bare during the winter (and requiring a short hike from the Sieur de Monts parking area along the seasonally-closed, and often snow-covered, Park Loop Road), this expansive freshwater marsh showcases a brilliant wildflower show come springtime.

In late May and early June, extensive swaths of flashy, vibrant pink rhodora cover the ground. As if that was not enough of a show, in June, oversized pink, purple, and white lupines as well as delicate white-pedaled oxeye daisies interspersed with groves of birch and aspen trees make for an idyllic scene best photographed in late morning through early afternoon. The area does not get direct light at sunrise, thanks to the rounded mountains to the east. Similarly, the sun drops behind the horizon of Dorr Mountain well before sunset.

After a rainy spring, the

Directions

From the intersection of Main Street and West Street in downtown Bar Harbor, travel south on Main Street/ Route 3 for 0.8 miles (1.3 km). Turn left onto Cromwell Harbor Road. Proceed west for 0.2 miles (0.3 km). Turn left onto Great Meadow Drive (also referred to as Ledgelawn Drive). Drive another 0.8 miles (1.3 km) until you reach the T-intersection with the one-way Park Loop Road. No formal parking areas exist, so find a wide previously-used pullout on Great Meadow Drive or the Park Loop Road to park. This section of Park Loop Road closes to motorized vehicles in winter from December to mid-April.

lupine here grow almost to shoulder-height (and I'm nearly 6 feet [1.8 m] tall!) so in addition to bringing the more obvious lens choice for photographing wildflowers—a **macro lens**—use a normal or **wide-angle lens** even when trying to capture a close-up image of this invasive species within the park.

That said, a macro lens and **extension tubes** will still come in handy to record the multitude of details found here. Position your **tripod** low to the ground, set a wide aperture to blur the background, and maximize the effective depth of field range by keeping your lens parallel to the plane of the stem and flower head. If wind is present, utilize a **Wimberley Plamp**™, which gently clamps to the base of the flower. Remember to compose such that the handy contraption is not visible in your frame though!

The same deciduous trees providing a canopy over these beautiful blooms display their autumnal yellows, reds, and oranges during the first two weeks in October, offering a second chance to record ever-changing beauty and color. Across the meadow, at the base of Dorr Mountain, maples add fiery reds to the fall palette. Bring a wide range of lenses from wide-angle to **telephoto** as well as a **polarizer** to this ephemeral event.

Whether spring or fall, wildlife lovers will enjoy white-tailed deer grazing on foliage or owls silently flying overhead. Pack a telephoto lens with a **1.4x or 2.0x teleconverter** as well as a **Flash X-tender**™, which will throw artificial light farther than using an **on-camera flash** alone and will add a touch of attention-grabbing catch-light in the animal's eye.

The Tarn

Small pond teeming with reflections, wildflowers, and fall colors

TIME OF YEAR	TIME OF DAY	TIDE	HIKE
June to October	*Early morning*	*N/A*	*Easy*

Autumnal colors from deciduous trees on the side of Dorr Mountain reflect into the rush-filled tarn. Canon 5DMII, 100-400mm at 105mm, ISO 100, f/11 at 0.4 sec., polarizer.

*T*hough it is small in size, The Tarn is big on photographic opportunities! Like the Great Meadow to the north, The Tarn sits in the same glacially-carved valley surrounded by Dorr and Cadillac mountains to the west and Huguenot Head and Champlain Mountain on the east. Despite both being considered wetlands, unlike the Great Meadow, this stream-fed pond contains water. No deeper than 5 feet (1.5 m), this small 8-acre (3.2-hectare) fresh-water pond is home to a multitude of aquatic plant life, including the water-loving arrowhead, bayonet grass, pickerelweed, and water lilies.

Arriving at this location at first light is not necessary, as Champlain Mountain to the east obscures the sunrise. Instead, arrive no later than an hour after sun-up to catch illuminated and colorful deciduous trees clinging to the east-facing cliffs reflecting in the shadowed waters.

Although windless days produce striking mirror-like reflections, smooth the ripples in the water caused by a passing breeze by using slower shutter speeds around one second or slower. To reduce the speed of your shutter by one to two stops and to intensify the reflection, use a polarizing filter as well. To reduce the amount of light even further, place a neutral density

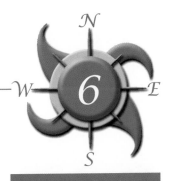

filter on your lens. As you do so, however, note that the lily pads and rushes waving in the wind and water will move during your longer exposure, which can create a visually appealing impressionistic view of the scene.

Keep your compositions simple and focused. If you have trouble identifying a subject, ask yourself what you like about the scene and consider creating a title for your frame before you snap it to provide extra focus. As you compose, include only the most essential elements within your photo. Scan the edges of your frame before snapping the shutter to ensure no distracting objects (such as out of focus branches or bright lighting) appear along the borders of your composition. A **telephoto lens** (100mm or longer) will help isolate details and eliminate extraneous elements.

In mid- to late June, colorful lupine blooms in the open spaces on the north shoreline and across the street from the pond at the entrance to the Beachcroft Trailhead. Though you might consider using a **macro lens**, the flowers are large enough such that even a **wide-angle** or a **normal lens** will also be useful here.

Because you will be photographing in the diffused shadow of Champlain Mountain, a **tripod** and **cable release** can help keep your camera still and your pictures sharp during slower shutter speeds. If you intend to include the illuminated western shoreline in your frame alongside the darker areas on The Tarn, utilize a **graduated neutral density filter** to maintain an acceptable exposure for both the highlights and shadows.

Directions

From the intersection of Main Street and West Street in downtown Bar Harbor, travel south on Main Street/ Route 3 for 2.4 miles (3.9 km). Immediately after the signed turnoff to Sieur de Monts, turn right into the small paved, unmarked parking area. The trail begins on the south side of the parking area or you may wish to walk carefully along the broad shoulder of Route 3.

Lupine grow in the open areas along the northern end of The Tarn each summer. Canon 5DMII, 16-35mm at 35mm, ISO 200, f/6.3 at 1/100th sec.

Sieur de Monts

Historically significant spring, plethora of wildflowers, and two museums

TIME OF YEAR	TIME OF DAY	TIDE	HIKE
Year-round	*Sunrise to early afternoon*	*N/A*	*Easy*

TOP: Sedges dance in the summer wind near The Wild Gardens of Acadia at Sieur de Monts. Canon 5DMII, 16-35mm at 35mm, ISO 100, f/22 at 30 sec., polarizer.
OPPOSITE: Sheep laurel blooms in the Coniferous Woods section of The Wild Gardens of Acadia. Canon 5DMII, 100mm macro, ISO 400, f/13 at 1/5th sec.

*I*n the early 1900s, commercial developers seeking to provide fresh water for the town of Bar Harbor defaulted on their loan while tapping into a hidden spring at the southern end of the Great Meadow. Upon learning this, George B. Dorr inquired about the purchase price—a steep $5,000 (equivalent to about $130,000 in today's money)—and requested that he receive the first right of refusal should someone else show interest in purchasing the property.

In 1909, a group of eager townspeople had raised enough money to buy the option on the spring. Dorr was given a meager one hour to decide to purchase this valuable 10-acre (4.1-hectare) tract—or else lose the land. According to Dorr's memoirs, his representative arrived at the Village Green with Dorr's decision with a mere two or three minutes to spare.

Immediately after taking ownership, he named the property, "The Wild Gardens of Acadia," and the spring "Sieur de Monts" to honor the 17th-century French explorer Pierre

Du Gua de Monts. Then, he encased the spring in a Florentine-style octagonal building and carved "Sweet Waters of Acadia" onto a nearby boulder, inspired by his travels and experiences with two springs in

A white, Florentine-style octagonal building houses the Sieur de Monts Spring. Canon 5DMII, 16-35mm at 30mm, ISO 400, f/22 at 0.3 sec., polarizer.

Turkey: The Sweet Waters of Asia and The Sweet Waters of Europe. Finally, Dorr established seven commemorative trails (including the Jesup Path on page 66) radiating into the woods from the tranquil spring.

Dorr eventually donated the 10-acre (4.1 hectare) parcel of land and spring to the Hancock County Trustees of Public Reservations, making it one of the first pieces of property bestowed in the spirit of forming what we know today as Acadia National Park. In 1916, President Woodrow Wilson proclaimed this land, along with 6,000 additional acres (2,428 hectares) across MDI, as the "Sieur de Monts National Monument."

Today, the enclosed spring still flows beneath the white arched dome behind the Nature Center. The nearby boulder with Dorr's historic etching serves as an excellent foreground to the Spring House in the background when using a **wide-angle lens**.

In addition, the now-cultivated grounds of The Wild Gardens of Acadia contain over 400 species of native flowers, trees, shrubs and other plants divided into 12 neatly-maintained habitats in less than an acre (0.4 hectare) of land. Open from dawn to dusk and free of charge, the gardens bloom consistently from May to October. A **macro** or **telephoto lens** will help you hone in on the yellow lady's slipper orchids in May and June in the Mixed Woods section, the regal blue flag iris along the Seaside area, the bizarre-looking carnivorous pitcher plant in the Bog section in July, and then the vibrant asters in the Meadow unit in August. As you explore, snap a photo not just of the beautiful blooms you spot, but also the accompanying signs that name the species so that you can identify the flowers later when you process your images at home.

Shutterbugs could easily start at sunrise and spend an entire day exploring all the photographic opportunities this area offers—especially if combined with the Jesup Path—but by late afternoon, aptly-named Dorr Mountain shadows much of the area, which can create excellent diffused light for close up details, but flat light for broad scenes. No matter your subject, look for side light, back light, or shade as you set up your compositions. If the sun

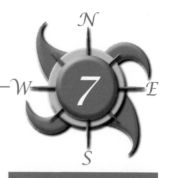

directly and harshly illuminates your subject, utilize a **reflector** to open the shadows or a **diffuser** to create more even lighting across the scene.

If bird photography is more your forte, pack a **telephoto lens**, **teleconverter**, **on-camera flash**, and a **Flash X-tender**™. Occasionally, peregrine falcons soar overheard, exploring territory away from their primary cliff-side breeding area near the Precipice Trail. The Sieur de Monts area is a prime, if not the best, place on the island to spot a warbler, flycatcher, or woodpecker. Set your ISO speed to a fast 400 or 800 setting to ensure faster shutter speeds at wide apertures, and then patiently look to the trees and sky.

Cultural and natural history lovers should spend time at the Nature Center and the Abbe Museum located on site. The small Nature Center is free of charge, while the Abbe Museum—listed on the National Register of Historic Places—charges a small admission fee to explore its thorough Wabanaki cultural and historical exhibits.

Both open their doors from late May to October, but the Abbe Museum's sister location with the same name in downtown Bar Harbor welcomes visitors year-round. Both sites also serve as a great place to take cover during a passing rainstorm.

Before you pack up for your next location, walk south from the Nature Center to see the small monument recognizing Dorr, now widely considered the "Father of Acadia," and to thank him for his swift purchasing decision in 1909.

Directions

From the intersection of Main Street and West Street in downtown Bar Harbor, travel south on Main Street/ Route 3 for 2.4 miles (3.9 km). Turn right at the signed turnoff to Sieur de Monts. Drive 0.1 miles (0.2 km) and then turn at the first left turn. Veer to the right when the road turns into a one-way street. After driving an additional 0.2 miles (0.3 km), ample parking exists in the paved parking lot.

A vibrantly-colored beech tree shakes its leaves during autumn. Canon 5DMII, 100-400mm at 400mm, ISO 50, f/40 at 8 sec., polarizer.

Jesup Path

Discover differing foliage from before and after the 1947 fire on easy stroll

TIME OF YEAR	TIME OF DAY	TIDE	HIKE
Year-round	*Sunrise to early afternoon*	*N/A*	*Easy*

Autumn leaves blanket the meadow along the Jesup Path. Canon 5DMII, 16-35mm at 30mm, ISO 400, f/16 at 1/5th sec., polarizer.

Though the Jesup Path resides on the stretch of land originally acquired and then donated to Acadia by George B. Dorr, the trail name celebrates the affection Morris and Maria DeWitt Jesup held for the island and developing park as summer residents.

In New York, Morris Jesup made his fortune in banking before dedicating his remaining life to philanthropy. Starting in 1884, he served as the founder and eventual president of the American Museum of Natural History in New York City—just one of many accolades he collected before passing away in 1908. In 1911, his wife, Maria, gifted the Jesup Memorial Library to Bar Harbor in memory of her late husband. Upon her death in 1914, she bequeathed $8.45 million (the equivalent of $20.6 billion today) to numerous public and charitable institutions. Today, a small plaque at the far southern end of the Jesup Path memorializes this generous couple as "Lovers of this Island."

Established almost 100 years ago as one of three garden paths to connect

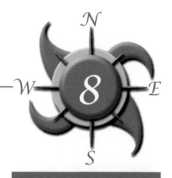

with Bar Harbor (the other two being the Cadillac Path and the Wild Gardens Path), the entire trail spans 1 mile (1.6 km) in length. Though the walkway officially starts at The Tarn and ends on the north side of the Great Meadow, parking at Sieur de Monts (see page 62) conveniently allows easy exploration in either direction.

After you locate the path to the west of the Nature Center, a relaxed stroll to the north along a wooden boardwalk transports you into one of the few areas where foliage from both the pre- and post-1947 fire obviously intermix. The old hemlocks survived the devastating blaze on the western side, while the paper birch, maple, and other deciduous trees have since replenished the charred section in the open meadow on the eastern side.

In July, a blue flag iris may catch your eye among the florescent-green understory filled with ferns, sedges, and grasses. In August and September, purple New England asters and showy goldenrod appear towards the northern end of the trail. In October, the mature birch and maples create a harmony of autumnal color. No matter the season, **wide-angle** to **telephoto zoom lenses** will help record the broad range of photographic opportunities here.

Though sunrise through early afternoon offers ideal side and backlighting conditions (especially if clouds exist overhead to create photogenic diffused illumination), by late afternoon, Dorr Mountain shadows much of the area. Regardless, a **polarizer** will reduce the reflected light on the petals or leaves respectively and increase the apparent color saturation in your frame. However, because a polarizer reduces the amount of light hitting your sensor, zoom in on your picture with your digital camera's LCD screen while in playback mode to ensure you set a fast enough shutter speed setting to freeze your chosen subject (especially if a breeze prevails).

If you utilize a **tripod**, show courtesy to other passers-by and do not hog the boardwalk. If your visit falls in between June and August, bring ample bug repellent and wear long pants to deter the biting insects.

Directions

From the intersection of Main Street and West Street in downtown Bar Harbor, travel south on Main Street/ Route 3 for 2.4 miles (3.9 km). Turn right at the signed turnoff to Sieur de Monts. Drive 0.1 miles (0.2 km) and then turn at the first left turn. Veer to the right when the road turns into a one-way street. After driving an additional 0.2 miles (0.3 km), ample parking exists in the paved parking lot. The Jesup Path runs along the west side of the Nature Center and The Wild Gardens of Acadia.

An acorn rests in the palm of a maple leaf in fall along the Jesup Path. Canon 5DMII, 100mm macro, 12mm extension tube, ISO 400, f/16 at 0.6 sec., diffuser.

Beaver Dam Pond

Mirror-like reflections and wildlife at small pond

TIME OF YEAR	TIME OF DAY	TIDE	HIKE
October	Early morning to late afternoon	N/A	Easy

An unusual mirror-like reflection frames a beaver lodge in the aptly named Beaver Dam Pond. Canon 5DMII, 100-400mm at 115mm, ISO 100, f/18 at 2.5 sec., polarizer.

Under the cover of intermingling hemlock and birch trees, Bear Brook plunges down the wooded ravine in between Huguenot Head and Champlain Mountain before pooling into the Beaver Dam Pond, which is located on a forested piece of land that George B. Dorr inherited from his father and then donated to the Hancock County Trustees of Public Reservations to help establish the Sieur de Monts National Monument in 1916.

Named for its multiple beaver dams and lodges, a patient wildlife viewer can catch a glimpse of these crafty and resourceful creatures, which are most active around dawn and dusk. In addition to a rare beaver sighting, occasionally great blue herons, bald eagles, or flycatchers visit the area, so keep your **telephoto lens** handy.

Because steady coastal winds originating from the east side of MDI frequently cause ripples on the water surface, mirror-like reflections are not common here. However, if you notice still waters, photograph the unusual conditions as long as the reflection remains and your time

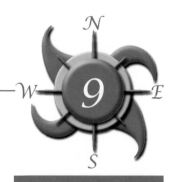

Winter brings a new palette of colorful reflections. Canon 5DMII, 100-400 mm at 350mm, ISO 100, f/11 at 0.6 sec., polarizer.

allows! If the breeze persists, though, slow your shutter speed down to smooth the small waves or speed it up to record the ever-changing skypool patterns created by the wind, water, and sky working magically together.

While a short to long telephoto lens (spanning 80 to 400mm) is the best option for isolating details in the water and surrounding forest, a **wide-angle lens** can help broaden your compositions to include the picturesque reeds along the shoreline as foreground. Do not be afraid to break the "Rule of Thirds" by placing the water's edge in the middle of your frame. Symmetrical compositions will emphasize and draw attention to the glassy mirror image reflecting in the water.

The northern end of the pond supplies an open view of the golden sun's side light illuminating the pond and surrounding foliage from early in the morning until late in the afternoon from March to October. The deciduous trees along the shore sport glowing spring and summer greens, which transform into a vibrant celebration of autumnal yellows, reds, and oranges in October. Using a **polarizer** will increase the color saturation in the neighboring trees, as well as intensify the water's reflection, no matter the season.

From November to February, the area is primarily backlit. To prevent unwanted lens flare from accidentally ruining your image, attach a sun shade or simply hold your hand between the sun and your lens.

Directions

From the intersection of Main Street and West Street in downtown Bar Harbor, travel south on Main Street/ Route 3 for 2.4 miles (3.9 km). Turn right at the signed turnoff to Sieur de Monts. Drive 0.2 miles (0.3 km) before turning right at the T-intersection with the one-way Park Loop Road (this section closes December through April). Continue another 0.5 miles (0.8 km) and then turn left into the signed Bear Brook Picnic Area. Park here and carefully walk to the northeast along Park Loop Road about 0.1 miles (0.2 km) to reach the pond.

Parking is also permitted in the right-hand lane along the Park Loop Road after the Beaver Dam Pond.

Sand Beach

Fleeting patterns of sand, water, and rock on unique sand beach

TIME OF YEAR	TIME OF DAY	TIDE	HIKE
Year-round	*Late morning to early afternoon*	*Any*	*Easy*

Smooth waters at Sand Beach. Canon 5DMII, 16-35mm at 33mm, ISO 100, f/8 at 87 sec., two-stop graduated neutral density filter, ten-stop neutral density filter.

*T*hough unusual given the cold waters surrounding MDI, the 300-yard (274-m) Sand Beach contains not only a blend of quartz and feldspar, but also calcium carbonate—the result of violent ocean waves shattering countless sea urchin and mussel shells into minuscule grain-sized particles along the protected Newport Cove. Besides being a geological gem, few other places along the Acadian shoreline enable such a close and personal experience with waves curling over a gently sloping beach.

Because of the beauty and easy access, the parking lot fills quickly by early morning in July and August, as the beach floods with relaxed sunbathers and daring swimmers eager to take a dip despite the seawater never warming beyond a bone-chilling 60 degrees Fahrenheit (15.6 degrees Celsius). Not surprisingly, Sand Beach is almost entirely devoid of visitors during winter.

After descending the stairs down to the south-facing beach, leave your shoes high on the beach and let the sandy grains seep through your toes during the spring, summer, and fall. In winter, though, water shoes and wool or neoprene socks will help you keep warm whether you wander on dry land or decide to dip your toes in the ocean while photographing.

Pack a **macro** or **short telephoto lens** (ranging from 80 to 200mm) as well as a **polarizer** and **neutral density filter** to study closely the waves, rocks, and sand intermingling in perpetually metamorphosing patterns—particularly on the far eastern edge of the beach. Here a small tidal creek originates from behind the fragile sand dunes and drains into the ocean near protruding small boulders covered in rockweed and barnacles. Observe the fleeting natural designs from a variety of perspectives (not just eye level) before snapping the shutter. The best perspectives might be from top-down, the side, or even lying on the ground!

In June and July especially, colorful wildflowers grace the dunes lining the northern side of the beach, but you will need to use a telephoto lens to photograph them, as this area is off-limits to travel and protected by a wooden fence. From December to March, the same lens coupled with a **flash** and **Flash X-tender**™ will help record wintering ducks like common loons, common eiders, and red-breasted mergansers paddling in the calmer waters.

Tucked in between the Great Head to the east and the Beehive to the west, diffused mid-day light offers the best lighting conditions for photography, as the Great Head prevents the sun's first light from illuminating Sand Beach. Similarly, as the setting sun dips behind the Beehive and Gorham Mountain, it casts a long shadow over the entire area starting in late afternoon.

In all seasons except winter, the park conveniently provides free fresh-water foot showers to rinse sand off both human and tripod legs after your photographic outing. Pack a beach or hand towel to dry off.

Waves swirl around barnacle-covered rocks along the eastern end of Sand Beach. Canon 5DMII, 16-35mm at 31mm, ISO 100, f/22 at 1/4th sec.

Directions

From the intersection of Main Street and West Street in Bar Harbor, travel south on Main Street/Route 3 for 2.4 miles (3.9 km). Turn right at the signed turnoff to Sieur de Monts. Drive 0.2 miles (0.3 km) before turning right at the T-intersection with the one-way Park Loop Road (this section is also referred to as Ocean Drive). Continue another 3.2 miles (5.2 km)—passing through the park's entrance station—before turning left into the signed parking area for Sand Beach.

From December to mid-April, access Sand Beach instead by driving south on Route 3 for 1.4 miles (2.3 km) from the intersection of Main Street and West Street in Bar Harbor. Turn left onto Schooner Head Drive and continue traveling south for 2.5 miles (4 km). Turn right onto the Schooner Head Overlook Road. Drive 0.1 miles (0.2 km). Turn left onto the one-way Park Loop Road/Ocean Drive and proceed through the entrance station. Travel 0.6 miles (1 km). Turn left into the signed parking area for Sand Beach.

Great Head

Panoramic coastal views atop rugged granite headland jutting into ocean

TIME OF YEAR	TIME OF DAY	TIDE	HIKE
April to September	Sunrise to early morning	Any	Moderate

Granite boulders along the eastern shoreline of the Great Head soak up the first rays of light at sunrise. Canon 5DMII, 16-35mm at 16mm, ISO 100, f/18 at 1.3 sec., three-stop graduated neutral density filter.

*I*n 1910, renowned financier and philanthropist J.P. Morgan purchased the wildly diverse landscapes of Great Head and Sand Beach for his daughter, Louisa Morgan Satterlee. She and her husband, Herbert, settled on the southwest end of Great Head, where they built a large home featuring a tower, tearoom, and observatory near its highest point.

Louisa died in 1946 and Herbert passed away the following year. Shortly thereafter, the Great Fire of 1947 burned the entire "Satterlee Field" homestead to its foundations—some of which are still visible today. Two years later, Satterlees' daughter, Eleanor, purchased the property from her father's estate. In May 1949, she donated both Great Head and Sand Beach to Acadia National Park—graciously granting the public the chance to revere panoramic coastal views from this rugged headland.

To catch the rising sun greeting the Great Head's easternmost shoreline cliffs with the ocean crashing below to the north, hike the trail counter-clockwise from the trailhead on the far eastern side of Sand Beach.

A slow shutter speed yields silky, cotton-like water, as seen here with the moving waves of the Atlantic Ocean viewed from Great Head. Canon 5DMII, 100-400mm at 400mm, ISO 400, f/5.6 at 0.5 sec., polarizer.

Directions

From the intersection of Main Street and West Street in Bar Harbor, travel south on Main Street/Route 3 for 2.4 miles (3.9 km). Turn right at the signed turnoff to Sieur de Monts. Drive 0.2 miles (0.3 km) before turning right at the T-intersection with the one-way Park Loop Road (this section is also referred to as Ocean Drive). Continue another 3.2 miles (5.2 km)—passing through the park's entrance station—before turning left into the signed parking area for Sand Beach.

From December to mid-April, access Sand Beach instead by driving south on Route 3 for 1.4 miles (2.3 km) from the intersection of Main Street and West Street in Bar Harbor. Turn left onto Schooner Head Drive and continue traveling south for 2.5 miles (4 km). Turn right onto the Schooner Head Overlook Road. Drive 0.1 miles (0.2 km). Turn left onto the one-way Park Loop Road/Ocean Drive and proceed through the entrance station. Travel 0.6 miles (1 km). Turn left into the signed parking area for Sand Beach.

Descend the stairs and walk to the eastern end of the beach. At high tide, you will need to cross a small tidal creek before reaching the granite steps leading to the Great Head trail. Wear water shoes to stay dry.

Use a **flashlight** or **headlamp** to help illuminate your way along the well-maintained trail in pre-dawn light.

After a 0.3-mile (0.5-km) stroll along the wooded trail to the south, a breathtaking scene appears to the west of the promontory, featuring serene Sand Beach, protected Newport Cove, and the weathered Beehive. However, the Great Head blocks the sun and casts a large unsightly shadow onto these locations until later in the morning. The best sunrise views lie another 0.2 miles (0.3 km) ahead on the east side near the 145-foot (44.2-m) summit. Pack a **wide-angle** or **normal lens**, **polarizer**, and **graduated neutral density filter** for the grand vista awaiting at the top!

As you approach the rounded peak of this rocky peninsula, the spruce and pitch-pine forest gives way to granite outcroppings with spectacular sweeping views of Frenchman Bay and Egg Rock Light as well as the Schoodic Peninsula off in the distance—an ideal setting for broad scale, landscape-style photographs. Watch your step on the rounded boulders along the cliff's edge, especially after rainstorms or dense fog.

Because these exposed viewpoints sometimes endure high winds, enable the image stabilization or vibration reduction feature on your camera if you intend to handhold your gear. However, if you use a **tripod** and **cable release** to keep your image sharp, remember to disable the image stabilization or vibration reduction function before shooting instead.

Whether you follow the entire 1.9-mile (3.1-km) loop around Great Head or retrace your steps to return to your car, stop to photograph the variety of wildflowers sprouting beneath the canopy of spruce, aspen, sumac, and birch trees from May to July with your **macro lens, reflector**, and **diffuser**.

Newport Cove Overlook

Breathtaking views of Acadian coastline from rugged cove to Otter Cliff

TIME OF YEAR	TIME OF DAY	TIDE	HIKE
October to March	*Sunrise*	*Mid to high, incoming*	*Moderate*

An October sun illuminates the granite cliffs at the Newport Cove Overlook. Canon 5DMII, 16-35mm at 18mm, ISO 100, f/13 at 1.3 sec., three-stop graduated neutral density filter.

$\mathcal{P}$erched high above the mouth of Newport Cove, this lesser-known, but highly photogenic location is easy to miss and the consequences of passing by the turnoff are inconvenient to say the least. If you unintentionally drive beyond the unmarked parking area, you will need either to walk with your pack from another distant parking lot along Ocean Drive or drive 8 miles (12.9 km) around the one-way Park Loop Road (assuming you take the shortcut via Highway 3), wasting precious time and ideal light for photographing. As with all locations along Ocean Drive, scout this location the day prior to your outing to ensure you have found the right spot!

Because the rugged granite cliffs extend south-southwest with views towards the prominent Otter Cliff, the optimal direct light from a rising sun occurs from October until March. In autumn and winter, arrive about 30 to 45 minutes before sunrise.

In contrast, from April to September, the Great Head to the east obstructs the sun's rays and creates a harsh, unattractive dark shadow line across the trees lining the rocky shore. If

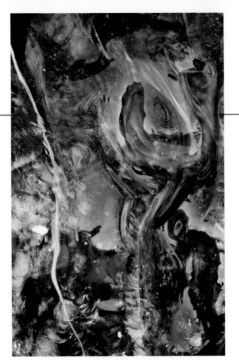

Intriguing ice formations appear along the cliffs and in puddles of water on top of the granite ledges. Canon 5DMII, 100mm macro, ISO 500, f/5.6 at 1/30th sec.

Directions

From the intersection of Main Street and West Street in downtown Bar Harbor, travel south on Main Street/Route 3 for 2.4 miles (3.9 km). Turn right at the signed turnoff to Sieur de Monts. Drive 0.2 miles (0.3 km) and turn right at the T-intersection of the one-way Park Loop Road (also referred to as Ocean Drive). Continue another 3.5 miles (5.6 km)—passing through the park's entrance station—before turning right into the marked and paved, but unnamed, parking area.

From December to mid-April, access Newport Cove Overlook instead by driving south on Route 3 for 1.4 miles (2.3 km) from the intersection of Main Street and West Street in Bar Harbor. Turn left onto Schooner Head Drive and continue traveling south for an additional 2.5 miles (4 km). Turn right onto Schooner Head Overlook Road. Drive 0.1 miles (0.2 km). Turn left onto the one-way Park Loop Road/Ocean Drive and proceed through the entrance station. Travel 0.9 miles (1.5 km) and then turn right into the parking area.

After parking, cross Park Loop Road/Ocean Drive to reach the gravel Ocean Path and turn left. Walk approximately 100 yards (91 m) and follow one of the steep informal social trails down to the granite rocks overlooking the cove.

spring and summer are your only chance to see this scene, arrive at least 45 minutes before sunrise to create images under pre-dawn's softer, more even lighting conditions.

With either a **wide-angle** or **normal lenses** (between 14 and 80 mm) in hand, create an effective visual line from the bottom right corner to the top left hand side of your frame leveraging the granite cliffs extending to the distant Otter Cliff.

Low to mid-tides below 8 feet (2.4 m) reveal prominent partially-submerged rocks to the left of the cliffs, and when included in your composition, provide an excellent way to create balance across a horizontally oriented photograph. A mid- to high tide of 8 feet (2.4 m) or higher, especially when an off-shore storm brews, sends much larger waves crashing into the land, which certainly adds drama to this scene. However, a tighter, vertical picture focusing on the wave action will ensure the left side of your composition does not appear so bare.

As the sun breaks the horizon, balance the contrast in light levels between the landscape and sky with a **polarizer** and **gradual neutral density filter**. Alternatively, use high dynamic range (HDR) imaging techniques to achieve a similar outcome.

No matter the season, small waterfalls appear on the sheer cliff walls after intense rainstorms. In winter, those same falls freeze, creating a vertical sheet of ice ideal for producing images of extraordinary patterns with a **telephoto lens**.

Those not wanting to make the short jaunt down to the cliff's edge (particularly when ice makes the trail and cliffs extremely slippery) should continue walking up the hill along the Ocean Path to get a spectacular view of the Ocean Drive coastline. During all seasons save for winter, use the ferns and other foliage in the foreground to create a sense of depth.

Thunder Hole

Narrow sea cave in granite creates explosive spray and thunderous sound

TIME OF YEAR	TIME OF DAY	TIDE	HIKE
Year-round	*Sunrise*	*Two hours before high*	*Easy*

Explosive ocean spray and a thunderous roar burst from a narrow slot in the granite shoreline and give Thunder Hole its name. Canon 5D, 24-105mm at 40mm, ISO 200, f/6.3 at 1/80th sec., polarizer.

When the stars align, Thunder Hole certainly lives up to its name. The best time to see and hear this unforgettable site occurs about two hours before high tide during high seas (minimally 3- to 4-foot [0.9- to 1.2-m] high waves) from an offshore storm with winds coming from the south. As the strong waves enter the narrow, fractured slot in the granite and pass into a small sheltered sea cove towards the back of the formation, the air trapped beneath the water suddenly releases, resulting in a thunderous "boom" and a violent plume of ocean spray exploding into the sky.

At all other times, you might see a few small waves splashing about and hear a little swooshing sound—certainly anti-climatic given its bold name. Even when Thunder Hole is not rumbling, though, the stunning views of the distant Otter Cliff to the south and Newport Cove to the north present numerous scenic opportunities to snap pixels.

Arrive about 30 to 45 minutes prior sunrise with a **wide-angle lens**, **polarizer**, and **graduated neutral density filters** in hand to take advantage of either Thunder Hole in action or the surrounding angular granite slabs pointing to rocky outcroppings in either direction. Or, isolate the constantly changing wave action against partially submerged rocks along the coastline with a telephoto lens. Set your camera to continuous drive mode, which will enable you to capture multiple frames per second, and hold your shutter down just before the wave hits the rocks. If you use a slow shutter speed (around 1/25th of a second or slower) to

13

Waters from the Atlantic Ocean move about partially submerged granite boulders off shore from Thunder Hole. Canon 5DMII, 24-105mm at 55mm, ISO 50, f/22 at 8 sec., polarizer.

render the movement of the exploding water, ensure you bring a **tripod** and **cable release**.

A set of rocky steps provides access to a fenced platform jutting onto the rocks overlooking the chasm. From here, photographers get a close-up view of Mother Nature at work. However, ocean spray makes the rock steps and surrounding granite slabs extremely slick, so firmly hold the handrail and wear shoes with good traction. Protect your camera with a **rain cover** and carry extra **lens cloths** to wipe your lens free of the copious amounts of salty sea spray.

The park rangers close this lower viewing area during strong storms or when other unsafe conditions prevail. In this case, heed all official directions, and stay a safe distance from the unpredictable waves and slick rocks so as not to repeat the tragic events of August 2009. As Hurricane Bill pounded the eastern seaboard during a spring tide (a point during the monthly tidal and lunar cycle when the high tide reaches its maximum height), a 12- to 15-foot-high (3.7- to 4.6-m) sneaker wave swept several unsuspecting onlookers at Thunder Hole into the Atlantic Ocean and unfortunately caused one seven-year-old girl to lose her life.

Since the parking area is steps away from your shooting location, also bring a **macro lens**, **diffuser**, and **reflector** to photograph the shrubby non-native pink rugosa rose and chokecherry blooming along the road and man-made pathways in June. If the morning sun illuminates these bursts of color from behind, utilize a touch of on-camera fill-flash set to underexpose one or two stops to showcase the detail in the shadows while rendering the rest of the landscape properly exposed.

Directions

From the intersection of Main Street and West Street in downtown Bar Harbor, travel south on Main Street/Route 3 for 2.4 miles (3.9 km). Turn right at the signed turnoff to Sieur de Monts. Drive 0.2 miles (0.3 km) and turn right at the T-intersection with the one-way Park Loop Road (also referred to as Ocean Drive). Continue another 3.9 miles (6.3 km)—passing through the park's entrance station—before turning right into the signed, paved parking area for Thunder Hole.

From December to mid-April, access Thunder Hole instead by driving south on Route 3 for 1.4 miles (2.3 km) from the intersection of Main Street and West Street in Bar Harbor. Turn left onto Schooner Head Drive and continue traveling south for an additional 2.5 miles (4 km). Turn right onto the Schooner Head Overlook Road. Drive 0.1 miles (0.2 km). Turn left onto the one-way Park Loop Road/ Ocean Drive and proceed through the entrance station. Travel 1.3 miles (2.1 km) and then turn right into the Thunder Hole parking lot.

Monument Cove

Soaring view of granite spire at the head of a cobble beach

TIME OF YEAR	TIME OF DAY	TIDE	HIKE
October to February	Sunrise	Mid to high	Easy

Morning light illuminates the prominent rock spire and surrounding cliffs in Monument Cove. Canon 5DMII, 16-35mm at 16mm, ISO 100, f/16 at 0.4 sec., three-stop graduated neutral density filter.

Though the entire coastline along Ocean Path suggests unforgettable landscape views, unmarked Monument Cove offers a unique bird's-eye view of a tall, weather-eroded stone spire tucked into the north end of this small, crescent-shaped cobble beach. Photographers familiar with southwestern United States rock formations might also refer to it as a "hoodoo."

Despite such a gorgeous scene, in the summer months, the rising sun's rays occur too far to the north to directly illuminate the rock formation, due to the cliffs lining the ocean to the east. However, from October to February, the morning sun stays low enough on the horizon such that it skims the pink granite shoreline and kisses the spire—bathing it in a luminous rich, golden glow.

To record the spectacular light show, arrive at least 30 minutes prior to sunrise to set up your **wide-angle** to **normal lens**, **polarizer**, **tripod**, and **cable release** and to scope out your

Blue flag iris blooms in the summer along the coastline near Monument Cove. Canon 5DMII, 16-35mm at 16mm, ISO 1600, f/10 at 1/6th sec., three-stop graduated neutral density filter.

composition along the thin social path. Should clouds grace the sky above, utilize a **graduated neutral density filter** to enhance the colors overhead. To display the moving waters below as a blur in your frame, add a neutral density filter to the front of your lens to aid in slowing your shutter speed, and wait for the waves to break before clicking the shutter. That said, starting the exposure immediately after the waves have crashed onto land and are beginning to recede back into the ocean can render intriguing silky white and blue patterns.

Just a few short minutes after the sun appears above the horizon, the scene becomes quite contrasty, such that recording multiple frames at varying exposures through High Dynamic Range (HDR) imaging techniques becomes the best option to maintain texture in both the shadow and highlight areas.

Once you have blasted away at Monument Cove proper, continue venturing south on the dirt trail to the pink granite cliffs for additional photogenic coastal opportunities. In June, showy, sun-loving blue flag iris, wild chokecherry, bunchberry dogwood, and rugosa rose bushes showcase their floral bouquets in the damp soil adjacent to the granite rocks. Then, in July, oxeye daisies and blue vetch grow in patches in the strip of forested land between the granite slabs and Ocean Drive.

From this viewpoint, point your **telephoto lens** paired with a **teleconverter**, **on-camera flash**, and **Flash X-tender™** out to sea to photograph common eider ducks casually floating along the shore any time of year. In winter, cormorants and mergansers also make an appearance in the seemingly endless sea below.

Directions

From the intersection of Main Street and West Street in Bar Harbor, travel south on Main Street/Route 3 for 2.4 miles (3.9 km). Turn right at the signed turnoff to Sieur de Monts. Drive 0.2 miles (0.3 km) and turn right at the T-intersection with the one-way Park Loop Road (also referred to as Ocean Drive). Continue another 4.2 miles (6.8 km)—passing through the park's entrance station—before turning right into the signed parking area for the Gorham Mountain Trail.

From December to mid-April, access Monument Cove instead by driving south on Main Street/Route 3 for 1.4 miles (2.3 km) from the intersection of Main Street and West Street in Bar Harbor. Turn left onto Schooner Head Drive and continue traveling south for an additional 2.5 miles (4 km). Turn right onto Schooner Head Overlook Road. Drive 0.1 miles (0.2 km). Turn left onto the one-way Park Loop Road/Ocean Drive and proceed through the entrance station. Travel 1.6 miles (2.6 km), and then turn right into the Gorham Mountain Trail parking area.

Cross Park Loop Road and walk north on the gravel Ocean Path. Turn left and continue walking about 150 yards (137.2 m) until you see the social dirt trail veering to the right on the north end of the cove.

The Ocean is Like the Desert

"Creativity is just connecting things."

~Steve Jobs

When I first applied to the Artist-in-Residence program in Acadia National Park, I sought only one thing: to create images in a place completely unlike my desert southwest surroundings in Arizona. I wished for a creative jolt to get out of my familiar habits and settings. Traveling almost 3,000 miles (4,828 km) across the country to explore a place I had never seen before seemed like the perfect remedy.

Because of the cool northeastern climate and Acadia's abundance of water—ocean, ponds, tarns, bogs, marshes, and streams—I quickly concluded that the coastal park appeared like nothing else at my home. With much delight, this new environment provided just the juice I needed to return to the Grand Canyon State re-energized about new photographic possibilities.

In October 2011, while leading an Arizona Highways Photography Workshop (AHPW) in Acadia National Park, our group stopped at a small coffee shop in Ellsworth en route to Portland. As I waited for my cup of Joe to brew, I struck up a conversation with the barista. When I mentioned the AHPW organization and I resided in Arizona, he exclaimed, "No kidding! My wife is from Arizona! She's from the Navajo Nation."

Curious about how they landed in Maine, I inquired about his story. After relaying his tale, I asked, "How does she like Maine? It is so different than Arizona!"

He responded, "She doesn't like driving down the highway much. She gets claustrophobic. There are too many trees lining the road. She has to visit the coast frequently to see the open sky, since the ocean is just like the desert."

I answered, "How fascinating!"

I froze as a myriad of thoughts raced through my head. No. No. No! The ocean is nothing like the desert. I come to Acadia to escape from Arizona. The ocean is not like the desert at all.

In the months following my conversation over coffee, I initially resisted the notion that Acadia and Arizona possessed much in common since I had specifically set out to this coastal park to experience something different than I would in the desert. Serendipitously, I read Austin Kleon's insightful book titled, *Steal Like an Artist*. In this short study on creativity, he shared what many experts believe: that nothing is original. Instead, everything new stems from the combination of two or more pre-existing ideas. What fresh ideas could come from embracing the concept that two seemingly unrelated places could be alike? I started to embrace and contemplate the notion.

As I returned to my place of refuge for my third residency, my new perception not only revealed an uncanny resemblance to the desert, but it also unlocked an abundance of new subjects I had missed during my previous visits. Weather-chiseled rock spires along the coastline transformed into hoodoos. The skeletons of frost-coated, leaf-less trees along Ocean Drive looked like jumping cholla. The soaring vistas from smoothed mountain summits opened to endless skies as big as I see from the top of prominent rock outcroppings in Sedona and Flagstaff. "My" ocean world turned into "my" desert.

In early February 2013, a nasty nor'easter (referred to as "Winter Storm Nemo" by The Weather Channel) blew through the region. Within two days, the storm dumped record snowfall across much of the Northeast. The Schoodic Peninsula, where I stayed, experienced blustery winds and heavy snowfall, though not to the same level inland Maine saw. Three hours

The morning after Winter Storm Nemo hit Maine, ice covers the coastal landscape along Ocean Drive, in between Monument Cove and Boulder Beach. Canon 5DMII, 16-35mm at 18mm, ISO 125, f/22 at 1.6 sec., three-stop graduated neutral density filter.

south by car, Portland, Maine received 31.9 inches (81 cm) of snow—setting a new city record.

The morning after the blizzard passed, I reluctantly dragged myself out of my warm, cozy bed at 4 a.m. to photograph sunrise on MDI. Battered and bruised from shooting at Schoodic Point the day before (see the "Making the Photo" story on page 174), I set out on the hour and a half drive with no particular destination in mind.

I first considered stopping at Thompson Island (see page 48) to record the spectacular ice formations common to this stretch of shoreline. When I crossed the bridge from Trenton, though, I noticed a clear cobalt blue sky overhead and a few clouds lingering in the distance over the horizon. In a split second decision, in hopes of catching a momentous sunrise, I chased the clouds until they brought me to Ocean Drive.

When I crested Park Loop Road above Newport Cove, I gazed with admiration at the horizon line transforming into a rainbow of colors. Chomping at the bit to start snapping pixels, I pulled off at the next parking area—Thunder Hole—to start recording this beauty.

Looking to the south along the coastline during a long exposure, I thought Boulder Beach a mere 0.5 miles (0.8 km) down the road might offer better broad landscape scenes given the rapidly developing morning show. Quickly, I returned to my car in hopes of making more eye-catching coastline compositions.

Immediately after passing by Monument Cove (and just before the parking lot for Boulder Beach), odd-shaped objects gleamed on the granite ledges to my left. Intrigued by these unusual subjects, I stopped for a closer look. A sheet of smoothed ice and countless sculpted ice hoodoos were scattered across a small stretch of coastline.

Overwhelmed with excitement, I grabbed my camera gear and ran towards the fleeting formations as the sky erupted into a memorable spectacle of pink, yellow, and orange. The sky's performance lasted 18 minutes, which was enough time for my brain (which had been conditioned extensively in photograph southwestern rock formations) to work on autopilot

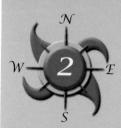

The Ocean is Like the Desert (continued)

mode using different lenses, settings, and compositions.

As the sun tucked behind a thick bank of clouds, a couple local women walking along the road stopped to admire the scene as well. During our brief exchange, they mentioned they had traveled this same route daily for 15 years and had not seen anything like the scene in front of them. Together, we contemplated how this normally granite-lined coast turned into an amazing winter wonderland.

The peak of Winter Storm Nemo occurred almost simultaneously with a higher than normal high tide on the afternoon of February 9, 2013, causing monster waves to pound a small section of the rocky shore. This fierce display by Mother Nature, combined with well-below freezing temperatures, created a wall of frozen sea spray, which plastered rocks and plant life alike with salty ice from the shoreline to Ocean Drive nearly 140 feet (42.7 m) away and nearly 50 feet (15.2 m) above sea level!

I returned to Ocean Drive the following morning to photograph sunrise and to check on this bizarre scene. Not surprisingly, the coastline ice hoodoos had melted in the warmer, sunnier weather after the clearing storm. Admiring the gift I had witnessed and photographed at the ephemeral scene the day before, I whispered, "Yes, of course, the ocean is just like the desert."

While soaking in the ocean sights, my thoughts turned to how the intriguing desert rock spires near my home in the desert southwest may seem robust and unyielding on the surface. However, wind and weather eventually prevails, taking solid sculpted stones and turning them into sand. Like the ice hoodoos along the coast, in due time, they too will disappear.

In that moment, my desert became my ocean.

OPPOSITE: Close-up of a sculpted ice after Winter Storm Nemo. Canon 5DMII, 100-400mm at 400mm, ISO 100, f/5.6 at 1/40th sec., polarizer.

Gorham Mountain Trail

Stunning aerial-like vista of coastline and prominent Acadia mountains

TIME OF YEAR	TIME OF DAY	TIDE	HIKE
April to November	*Sunrise*	*N/A*	*Strenuous*

View of the Beehive, Sand Beach, Great Head, and Frenchman Bay from the false summit. Canon 5DMII, 16-35mm at 16mm, ISO 100, f/16 at 0.5 sec., four-stop graduated neutral density filter.

*O*nce called "Peak of the Otters," potentially because of its proximity and view of the Otter Cliff, Gorham Mountain provides a different, yet equally impressive, look to the breathtaking Ocean Drive scenery. Though the entire trail travels 1.8 miles (2.9 km) round-trip, shutterbugs interested in seeing the most picturesque views of the mountain-lined coast below need only to make the steady ascent about 0.5 miles (0.8 km) from the parking area to the false summit about 300 feet above (91.4 m). The true summit, which offers a similar scenic overlook as the false summit, requires an additional heart-pounding 0.4-mile (0.6-km) trek uphill to reach the top of the 525-foot (160-m) peak.

The rising sun delivers a sheet of golden radiance across the landscape in any season, but the trail frequently ices over in the winter months, making the path treacherous or even impassible to hike (even with winter boot traction devices like Yaktrax™ or snow cleats).

However, during the spring, summer, and fall, set out on the well-maintained, but rocky, trail at least 60 minutes prior to sunrise to catch the first rays of light illuminating the Acadian coastline. Wear a **headlamp** or carry a **flashlight** to help you spot your way in the dark. For added safety, consider walking this route during daylight hours prior to your photographic outing here.

Goldenrod blooms among the granite ledges in late summer. Canon 5DMII, 100mm macro, ISO 200, f/22 at 8 sec.

N
W · 15 · E
S

As you emerge from the spruce forest, look for a small plaque embedded in a giant granite boulder commemorating Waldron Bates. Known as the "Pathmaker," Bates served as the head of the Roads and Paths Committee for the Bar Harbor Improvement Association from 1900 to 1909. As a result, he introduced the classic granite staircases, iron rung ladders, and stone cairns to many of Acadia's trails, including this one.

Immediately beyond this fitting tribute, the trail splits. Veer left to stay on the Gorham Mountain Trail and keep traveling until the path reaches an open granite ledge—the false summit—on the right. This elevated perch dotted with picturesque pitch pines offers 180-degree aerial-like views extending from Frenchman Bay and Sand Beach to the north to the open ocean beyond the Otter Cliff to the south.

In June, sheep laurel shrubs and mountain cranberry bushes interspersed among the granite slabs showcase pink flowers. From late July through August, as goldenrod and asters start to sprout, scrumptious wild blueberries along the trail offer a rewarding snack. Because the Great Fire of 1947 burned this area, deciduous trees and shrubs along the cliffs now dazzle with a spectacular color show in early October.

A **wide-angle lens** fitted with a **polarizer** and **graduated neutral density filter** will help record the true expansive nature of this scene. On the other hand, a **telephoto lens** with a polarizer will isolate the numerous intriguing details found in the mountains and shoreline. Either way, lug your **tripod** and **cable release** up the hill so you can keep your camera steady while photographing with slower shutter speeds at dawn and in possible windy conditions.

Adventurous geology buffs should make a quick side trip along the Cadillac Cliff Trail before returning to the parking area. When traveling downhill from either summit, veer left at the Bates plaque and trail marker. Then follow the challenging trail for 0.4 miles (0.6 km) to reach an ancient sea cave on the left. Now far above the current shoreline, the cave is a reminder of the higher sea levels here during the last glacial melt-off 12,000-plus years ago.

Directions

From the intersection of Main Street and West Street in Bar Harbor, travel south on Main Street/Route 3 for 2.4 miles (3.9 km). Turn right at the signed turnoff to Sieur de Monts. Drive 0.2 miles (0.3 km) and turn right at the T-intersection with the one-way Park Loop Road (also referred to as Ocean Drive). Continue another 4.2 miles (6.8 km)—passing through the park's entrance station—before turning right into the signed parking area for the Gorham Mountain Trailhead.

From December to mid-April, access the Gorham Mountain Trailhead instead by driving south on Main Street/Route 3 for 1.4 miles (2.3 km) from the intersection of Main Street and West Street in Bar Harbor. Turn left onto Schooner Head Drive and continue traveling south for an additional 2.5 miles (4 km). Turn right onto Schooner Head Overlook Road. Drive 0.1 miles (0.2 km). Turn left onto the one-way Park Loop Road/Ocean Drive and proceed through the entrance station. Travel 1.6 miles (2.6 km) and then turn right into the Gorham Mountain Trail parking area. The trailhead begins on the southwest side of the parking lot.

Boulder Beach

Beach full of egg-shaped boulders with close-range view of Otter Cliff

TIME OF YEAR	TIME OF DAY	TIDE	HIKE
Year-round	Sunrise	Low to mid, outgoing	Moderate

TOP: *Waves splash along the polished rocks at Boulder Beach at sunrise. Canon 5DMII, 16-35mm at 16mm, ISO 100, f/16 at 0.6 sec., three-stop graduated neutral density filter.*
OPPOSITE: *Snow resembling icing rests on top of the Otter Cliff after a winter snowstorm. Canon 5DMII, 100-400mm at 160mm, ISO 100, f/16 at 1/10th sec., polarizer.*

Given its simple name, one might expect the countless speckled egg-shaped boulders to serve as the salient feature of this crescent-shaped beach. However, its setting at the base of the picturesque Otter Cliff rising dramatically 110 feet (33.5 m) above the moody ocean is what makes this classic view truly remarkable.

Featuring larger and more smoothly polished rocks than other cobble beaches within Acadia's borders, Boulder Beach rightfully serves as one of the parks most iconic coastal landscapes. As a result, you can expect to share a morning photographic outing on this small stretch of shoreline with many other photographers anxious to bring home their own rendition during summer and autumn. Expect to have the place to yourself in winter, even on the weekends and holidays.

Despite its popularity, the unmarked trail down to the beach is difficult to locate, so try to

scout the location the day before if your schedule permits. Arrive about 30-45 minutes prior to sunrise dressed in waterproof or water resistant clothes like a rain jacket and pants (even on a clear day), water shoes, and wool or neoprene socks if you plan to get close to the splashing waves.

Before you leave the parking lot, pack your backpack with a **wide-angle** or **normal length lens**, a **polarizer**, **graduated neutral density filters**, a **neutral density filter**, **tripod**, and **cable release**. You might find it convenient to leave your photography bag high on the beach, while carrying critical gear in your pockets or a photo vest as you approach the ocean. Protect your camera gear from ocean spray and foggy mist with a **rain cover**—even when it is not raining.

The natural elegant curve of the shoreline serves as an obvious leading line for your compositions. Drop your camera low to the ground and utilize a side-lit boulder as a foreground anchor. Then time your exposure to occur simultaneously with the breaking waves to add visual drama. Use a fast shutter speed to freeze the action (e.g., 1/100th of a second and faster) or a slow shutter speed to blur the motion (e.g., 1/4th of a second or slower)—both approaches yield effective photographs.

An outgoing tide will reveal more rocks during your shoot—presenting new foreground material with every wave. An incoming tide leads to the water rapidly rising on you (and your tripod) up to 12 inches (30.5 cm) an hour! No matter the water level, keep yourself and your gear safe by heeding the old adage to never turn your back on the ocean.

The rocks here can get slick, especially when damp from the salty sea or after rain and snow. Keep one hand free to stabilize yourself and use your **tripod** or hiking poles to help keep a sturdy balance. Because the multi-sized boulders are rounded, it is sometimes challenging to find a level place for your tripod. A healthy dose of patience and creativity can go a long way in setting up the perfect frame here!

Additional, and equally as photogenic views, exist on the granite edges high above and to the north of the beach. Should you decide to position yourself here, do not fret if you have a few photographers in your frame. They will likely render small enough to edit them out in post-processing software.

Directions

From the intersection of Main Street and West Street in Bar Harbor, travel south on Main Street/Route 3 for 2.4 miles (3.9 km). Turn right at the signed turnoff to Sieur de Monts. Drive 0.2 miles (0.3 km) and turn right at the T-intersection with the one-way Park Loop Road (also referred to as Ocean Drive). Continue another 4.3 miles (6.9 km)—passing through the park's entrance station—before turning right into the marked, but unnamed, parking area.

From December to mid-April, access Boulder Beach instead by driving south 1.4 miles (2.3 km) on Main Street/Route 3 from the intersection of Main Street and West Street in Bar Harbor. Turn left onto Schooner Head Drive and continue traveling south for an additional 2.5 miles (4 km). Turn right onto Schooner Head Overlook Road. Drive 0.1 miles (0.2 km). Turn left onto the one-way Park Loop Road/Ocean Drive and proceed through the entrance station. Travel 1.7 miles (2.7 km) and then turn right into the parking lot.

From the parking area, cross Park Loop Road and walk roughly 100 yards (91.4 m) south on the gravel Ocean Path. Veer left when you see the steep social trail descending to the beach. If the cobble beach—which is Boulder Beach—comes into view while walking the Ocean Path, you have walked past the trail.

Otter Cliff

Striking overlook atop highest East Coast headland north of Brazil

TIME OF YEAR	TIME OF DAY	TIDE	HIKE
Year-round	*Sunrise*	*Any*	*Moderate*

TOP: *View of the Ocean Drive coastline from the top of the Otter Cliff at pre-dawn. Canon 5D, 24-105mm at 32mm, ISO 100, f/9 at 20 sec., polarizer, four-stop graduated neutral density filter.*
OPPOSITE: *The rocky south-facing headlands near Otter Cliff catch morning's first light. Canon 5DMII, 24-105mm at 67mm, ISO 100, f/20 at 0.5 sec., polarizer.*

*T*hough no sea otters live in the waters near Acadia (or along the entire East Coast for that matter), the dramatic Otter Cliff overlook may have received its name from the river otters found in Acadia's streams and ponds. While you will not see these mammals on your visit to this seaside bluff, the informal viewpoints along Ocean Path offer numerous magical places to watch and photograph resplendent sunshine gradually spotlighting each nook and cranny along the Acadia coast.

Plan to arrive about 30 minutes prior to sun-up to meander down the single flight of stone steps to the striking granite perch. Here, the volcanic rock of the Cranberry Island Formation juts out of the swirling sea to a height of 110 feet (33.5 m), qualifying this point as the highest headland along the Atlantic coast north of Rio de Janeiro, Brazil!

Record the first light splashing across the landscape with a **wide-angle** or **normal length lens**. Utilize the granite slabs as foreground to

help create a sense of depth and drop the horizon to the bottom third or fifth of the frame when colorful clouds grace the sky.

Add a **polarizer** to your lens to increase saturation across the scene as well as a **neutral density filter** to help slow the motion of the waves churning below. A **tripod** and **cable release** will keep your camera steady during slower shutter speeds or during the frequently breezy conditions on the exposed ledge.

During the summer months as the sun's azimuth peaks to the north, it is possible to include a sunburst in a horizontal frame using a **super wide-angle lens** at least 16mm or wider. To achieve this eye-catching effect, remove all filters from your lens and stop down to a smaller aperture (like f/16 or f/22) while pointing your camera into the sun.

The ringing bell buoy located offshore and to the south warns passing fishing boats of a partially-submerged hidden rock formation called the "Spindle." During high seas, waves crash violently over this hazard, offering impressive intimate and ever-changing scenes best photographed with a **telephoto lens**.

If you happen to spot a fishing boat heading out to sea or returning to Bar Harbor, you can utilize this same lens to isolate the ship against a rising sun. When photographing into the sun, however, remember to place a **lens shade** or use your hand to protect your photograph from unwanted lens flare.

Rock and ice climbers frequent the area, so you may see metal anchors attached to the top of the rocks where they attach their protective gear (e.g., ropes) during their climbs. As you explore the area, watch your footing, especially when the granite becomes wet or icy.

Directions

From the intersection of Main Street and West Street in Bar Harbor, travel south on Main Street/Route 3 for 2.4 miles (3.9 km). Turn right at the signed turnoff to Sieur de Monts. Drive 0.2 miles (0.3 km) and turn right at the T-intersection with the one-way Park Loop Road (also referred to as Ocean Drive). Continue another 4.7 miles (7.6 km)—passing through the park's entrance station—before turning right into a signed and paved, but unnamed, parking area immediately after the turnoff to Otter Cliff Road.

A more direct driving route exists if you do not plan to explore the Ocean Drive area prior to arriving at this location. From the intersection of Main Street and West Street in downtown Bar Harbor, travel south on Main Street/Route 3 for 2.5 miles (4 km) and then turn left onto Otter Cliff Road. Drive 1.9 miles (3.1 km) and turn right at Park Loop Road when the road ends. Turn right and then drive 0.3 miles (0.5 km) to the parking lot.

From the parking area, follow the crosswalk across Park Loop Road and proceed down the granite stairs on the right to the unofficial overlook.

A brilliant summer sunrise bathes the Acadia coastline along Ocean Drive in warm light. Canon 5DMII, 16-35mm at 16mm, ISO 100, f/20 at 1/4 sec., two- and four-stop graduated neutral density filter stacked.

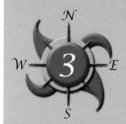

Expect the Unexpected

"If you do not expect the unexpected, you will not find it."

~Heraclitus

*B*y the middle of my second residency, I had visited Otter Cliff—one of my favorite vistas in the park—at sunrise no less than 14 times. Yet, the image I desired still eluded my camera. I was optimistic that on the fifteenth attempt, my luck would change and the perfect blend of light, weather, and tides would magically and finally come together.

I arrived pre-dawn to find the composition I had practiced and refined in previous attempts. I had hoped to witness an unforgettable sky graced with colorful clouds. Mother Nature had other plans, offering instead a common blue ceiling overhead. Unless I sought new creative ideas, the photograph I was about to make was not any different from so many I—and other photographers—had snapped before from this scenic locale. It would also leave me empty-handed on my fifteenth try.

I paused to consider a fresh vision when the humming sounds of lobster boats grabbed my attention. The noise from one early-riser continued to increase, as if the vessel was traveling in the cove below my rocky perch. I turned to confirm how close she had ventured to the ragged coastline on her way out to sea.

After locating his position and watching the direction of his travels, I saw a glint of light from the rising sun peeking over the horizon. Immediately I thought to myself, "What if the boat crossed in front of the sun?"

Without hesitation, I swapped my wide-angle lens for my 100-400mm telephoto lens. I quickly changed the ISO speed to ISO 200 and twirled my aperture dial (on Manual camera mode) to f/5.6. I fired a test shot to confirm my shutter speed, which needed to be fast enough to freeze the boat's forward progress. Within seconds, I had settled on the appropriate settings to achieve a balanced exposure while shooting directly into the sun. Now I needed the small craft to cross in front of the flaming ball of light to create my photograph.

As the boat approached the left edge of my composition, she cut his motor! Rolling my eyes as I pull back from my viewfinder, I wondered in frustration, "Really? Why would she do that?" Number 15 was becoming more of a tease.

Hoping the fishing boat would resume his initial path so my idea could come to fruition before the sun rose above the beautiful saturated light at the horizon, I noticed out of the corner of my right eye a substantially larger ship crossing from the other direction. With a few rapid, minor adjustments to my original composition, I recorded the sizeable dragger crossing in front of the sun. The bigger boat served as the perfect sized subject in my frame, creating a better visual balance than I could have achieved with the smaller fishing boat. (After the larger boat motored across the cove, the little boat cranked her engine back on and sped across the scene.)

On my fifteenth visit to Otter Cliff, I expected to bring home a landscape photograph worthy of this beautiful stretch of the coast. Instead of focusing so intently on an idea that was not coming together, I opened myself to other unexpected opportunities. By turning around and responding to my observations with my camera, I brought home an unpredicted, but a much stronger, storytelling image of life along the Maine coast.

OPPOSITE: Viewed from Otter Cliff, a dragger returns to Bar Harbor. Canon 5DMII, 100-400mm at 400mm, ISO 200, f/5.6 at 1/1000 sec.

Otter Point & Cove

Old naval radio station site offers easy access to shoreline, tide pools

TIME OF YEAR	TIME OF DAY	TIDE	HIKE
April to November	*Late afternoon to sunset*	*Minus low or high*	*Easy*

Remnants of Hurricane Ida formed a strong nor'easter in November 2009, causing strong winds and high waves, especially in exposed places along the coast like Otter Point. Canon 5D, 24-105mm at 24mm, ISO 200, f/18 at 1/200th sec.

*A*mid local controversy, John D. Rockefeller Jr. volunteered to personally finance and construct the Park Loop Road to regulate where motorized vehicles could travel on the island and within the park during the early 1920s. With the same meticulous, hands-on approach he used in building the carriage roads, Rockefeller Jr. wanted to design a roadway to showcase the diverse scenery on the eastern side of MDI from the Acadian coastline to the summit of Cadillac Mountain. The only problem? A highly-effective and widely-acclaimed United States naval radio station stood in the way on the northwestern side of Otter Point.

In 1933, Rockefeller Jr. suggested relocating the operations to the Schoodic Peninsula in exchange for the Otter Point land. The naval radio station moved 5 miles (8 km) across Frenchman Bay to an area near Schoodic Point in early 1935, allowing Rockefeller Jr. to remove the old buildings, donate the land to Acadia, and continue building his treasured thoroughfare. Though no remnants of the World War I outfit exist today, a plaque celebrating its commander, Lieutenant Alessandro Fabbri, marks the location of the old site across from the Fabbri Picnic

Bunchberry dogwood bloom in June in the forested areas lining Otter Point & Cove. Canon 5DMII, 100mm macro, ISO 400, f/18 at 0.5 sec.

Area along Rockefeller Jr.'s road.

Along the coastal stretch of Park Loop Road from Sand Beach to Otter Cove, the Civilian Conservation Corps built the meandering Ocean Path for hikers in 1938. Here at Otter Point, visitors now enjoy easy access to the granite shore (unlike the high precipice of neighboring Otter Cliff).

To explore the rich tide pools found along this section of the Ocean Path, plan to arrive one to two hours prior to a minus low tide (preferably coinciding with late afternoon or sunset light). Tide charts represent this measure in feet/meters, and when a minus low tide occurs (when water levels fall below the sea's average height), a minus sign ("-") appears in front of the listed number.

Barnacles cling to the rocks while green crabs, periwinkles, and limpets hide under rockweed. Closer to the receding water, starfish, and sea urchins take cover beneath kelp in the lowest intertidal zones. Carefully lift the rockweed or kelp to search for a photogenic specimen. For your safety (and the sea critters' too), do not touch or remove any creatures you find. Wear water shoes with a good tread and watch your footing—taking care not to slip on slick rocks or step on living creatures. Even at low tide, watch for rogue waves and never turn your back on the ocean.

Get close using your **macro lens**. If needed, employ a **diffuser** and **reflector** to tame overhead late afternoon light in your close-up composition. To selectively focus on the animal and blur the surrounding habitat, use a wide-open aperture (like f/2.8 or f/4) while focusing on your primary subject.

If grander landscape scenes appeal to you, venture north on the Ocean Path along the rocky, tree-lined western shoreline during high tide to position your camera (atop a tripod) with a **wide-angle** or **normal lens**, **polarizer**, and **graduated neutral density filter**. During the Golden Hour prior to sunset, the granite transforms from pink to orange as it soaks up the rays from a vanishing sun, making this spot one of the best year-round coastline locations in Acadia to catch sundown.

Directions

From the intersection of Main Street and West Street in Bar Harbor, travel south on Main Street for 2.4 miles (3.9 km). Turn right at the signed turnoff to Sieur de Monts. Drive 0.2 miles (0.3 km) and turn right at the T-intersection with the one-way Park Loop Road. Continue another 5 miles (8 km)—passing through the park's entrance station—before turning right into the signed parking area for Otter Point.

Alternatively, if you do not plan to visit the Ocean Drive area prior to arriving at this location, travel south on Main Street (which turns into Route 3) for 4 miles (6.4 km) from the intersection of Main Street and West Street in downtown Bar Harbor. Turn left onto Otter Cliff Road. Drive 1.9 miles (3.1 km) before turning right at Park Loop Road when the road ends. Turn right and continue 0.6 miles (1 km) to the parking lot. Follow the crosswalk across Park Loop Road to join the gravel Ocean Path.

Little Hunters Beach

Small, secluded, crescent-shaped beach filled with Shatter Zone cobble

TIME OF YEAR	TIME OF DAY	TIDE	HIKE
April to November	*Sunrise to late afternoon*	*Low to mid*	*Moderate*

TOP: Seaweed drapes over cobblestone from the Shatter Zone. Canon 5D, 100-400mm at 120mm, ISO 50, f/25 at 2.5 sec., polarizer. OPPOSITE: Sunrise at Little Hunters Beach. Canon 5DMII, 16-35mm at 16mm, ISO 100, f/22 at 0.8 sec., four- and five-stop graduated neutral density filters stacked.

Surrounded by granite cliffs to the east and dark volcanic outcroppings to the west, Little Hunters Beach delivers a peaceful, lesser-known setting for recording photographs of the ever-changing sea meeting the unyielding land. However, the coastline here has not always been so serene as it is today.

Approximately 420 million years ago, a large section of MDI sank into rising magma, causing substantial chunks of the land to either melt instantly or break into smaller pieces. Appropriately referred to as the "Shatter Zone," the broken rocks emerged in new forms as the molten lava cooled over time. As a result of this geological process, this small secluded crescent-shaped cove is now home to countless polished, patchy, and speckled granite cobblestones of all shapes, sizes, and colors.

Best photographed on overcast or foggy days, use a **telephoto lens** to compose smaller views of the persistent waves spilling over partially-submerged, fluorescent-green, moss-covered boulders revealed during low tide. With your camera set upon a **tripod** and equipped with a **cable release**, use a slow shutter speed (like 1/4th of a second)

to blur the water motion. Utilize a **neutral density filter** to reduce the amount of light hitting your sensor even further to create an ethereal scene. Alternatively, set a fast shutter speed (like 1/250th of a second) to freeze the airborne water droplets as the waves crash into the beach. Either way, wear water shoes in case you get wet!

Also, pack a **macro lens** to isolate the intriguing patterns in the small boulders. Add a **polarizer** to the front of your chosen lens to reduce the reflected sheen on the rocks and to enhance the color saturation.

Though the southeastern-facing cobble beach does not receive direct illumination at sunrise or sunset throughout the year, the evergreen trees lining the cove on the east side serve as the perfect obstruction to create a striking sunburst in your frame at first light. Point your **wide-angle** or **normal lens** into the sun, and then use a small aperture (like f/16 or f/22). Be careful not to look directly at the sun so as not to damage your eyes. Also, be wary of using your camera's Live View feature so as not to harm your camera's sensor.

Because of the extreme difference in exposure between the sky and land in this backlit situation, stack multiple **graduated neutral density filters** in front of your lens or snap multiple frames at varying exposure settings utilizing High Dynamic Range (HDR) imaging techniques to balance the bright sky with the backlit, shadowed beach.

Directions

From the intersection of Main Street and West Street in downtown Bar Harbor, travel south on Main Street/ Route 3 for 4 miles (6.4 km) and then turn left onto Otter Cliff Road. Drive 1.7 miles (2.7 km) and turn right at the road for Fabbri Picnic Area (if you miss this turn, don't worry! Proceed straight to Park Loop Road and turn right). Continue about 150 yards (137 m) to the intersection with the one-way Park Loop Road. Turn right and then drive 2 miles (3.2 km) to the paved, but unmarked, pullout on the right hand side of the street.

From the parking pullout, cross Park Loop Road and turn right. Walk down the wooden staircase to the beach.

Day Mountain

Panoramic coastal, autumnal view atop quiet mountain summit

TIME OF YEAR	**TIME OF DAY**	**TIDE**	**HIKE**
June to October	*Late afternoon to sunset*	*N/A*	*Strenuous (easy with carriage ride)*

Spectacular panoramic views await at the summit of Day Mountain. Canon 5DMII, 24-105mm at 40mm, ISO 100, f/16 at 8 sec., three-stop graduated neutral density filter.

*I*f spectacular Cadillac Mountain-style views without the hoards of visitors appeal to you, then Day Mountain is your spot! Though its elevation from the sea pales in comparison to the iconic mountain to the northeast—a mere 583 feet versus 1,529 feet (177.7 m vs. 466 m)—Day Mountain grants photographers a breathtaking 180-degree panoramic view of scenic Seal Harbor, the Cranberry Isles, and the Schoodic Peninsula. Despite its name, the best time to photograph here is sunset.

However, summiting Day Mountain takes a little more effort since a drivable road to the top does not exist like at Cadillac Mountain. Instead, the historic Day Mountain Loop Carriage Road, built by John D. Rockefeller Jr. in 1940, curls its way around the mountain along a 2.7-mile (4.4-km) path that is inaccessible to motor vehicles. No doubt a highlight of a trip to Acadia National Park is experiencing the carriage roads the way the rusticators did—by horse-drawn carriage.

Carriages of Acadia offers daily rides from late May to mid-October on a replica buckboard

to the summit—a trip worthy of your time. Make reservations for their two-hour sunset ride, especially if you are visiting during the peak of summer visitation or in October when the surrounding hillsides change into a rich, multi-colored tableau. For more information, visit **www.carriagesofacadia.com**.

The concessionaire permits small backpacks, so bring a **wide-angle** to **telephoto lenses, polarizing filter, graduated neutral density filter, tripod**, and **cable release** as well as a notepad and pen or a voice recorder to capture notes as the tour guides share interesting tidbits about the history of the carriage roads.

Photographers desiring unrestricted time limits to snap pictures from the summit at sunset and during the colorful post-dusk light may choose to make the less-traditional 0.5-mile (0.8-km) one-way hike on the Day Mountain Trail.

If you are concerned about hiking the short, but uphill, distance with a heavy pack, lighten your load by stowing a **normal** to telephoto lens, polarizing filter, graduated neutral density filter, tripod, cable release, **headlamp** or **flashlight**, and drinking water. Wear sturdy hiking shoes, as the route is rocky and steep in some areas. In winter, ice typically covers the trail, making it difficult to traverse even with snow cleats or other traction devices.

When photographing from the top in any season, as you point your camera to the southwest to compose, remember to shield your lens with a **lens shade**, hat, or your hand to prevent unwanted lens flare from the setting sun from ruining your final image.

Directions

From the Main Street and West Street intersection in Bar Harbor, travel south on Main Street/Route 3 for 4 miles (6.4 km) and then turn left onto Otter Cliff Road. Drive 1.7 miles (2.7 km) and turn right at the road for Fabbri Picnic Area (if you miss this turn, proceed straight to Park Loop Road and turn right). Continue about 150 yards (137 m) to the one-way Park Loop Road. Turn right and continue 4.1 miles (6.6 km) to a small gravel pullout on the right-hand side of the street just before the stone bridge.

Follow the "Path to Carriage Road" trail on the pullout's west side. Turn left at carriage road signpost 17 and cross the bridge. Then, cross the Day Mountain Loop carriage road, staying straight at signpost 37 to join the Day Mountain Summit Trail at the forest's edge.

To reach Carriages of Acadia, instead of parking in the pullout, continue driving underneath the bridge for an additional 0.3 miles (0.5 km). Turn right at their sign and then follow the "Carriage Road Tours" signs into their parking lot.

In addition to coastal views, an explosion of colors on nearby hillsides is visible in autumn from the summit. Canon 5DMII, 100-400mm at 400mm, ISO 100, f/11 at 1/10 sec., polarizer.

Hunters Beach

Bountiful compositions along tranquil brook and cobble-filled cove

TIME OF YEAR	TIME OF DAY	TIDE	HIKE
April to November	*Late morning to early afternoon*	*Low to mid*	*Moderate*

Hunters Brook cascades through a pristine forest along the trail to Hunters Beach. Canon 5DMII, 16-35mm at 16mm, ISO 100, f/16 at 1 sec.

Serving as another excellent example of Acadia's "Shatter Zone" from the dramatic Earth-changing geology events approximately 420 million years ago, Hunters Beach is comparable to Little Hunters Beach (see page 96) in many ways. As the similar names indicate, Hunters Beach offers a more extensive egg-shaped cobble beach than its smaller neighbor to the east. Though the opportunities for photographs are every bit as abundant, this spot offers something the Little Hunters Beach does not: the chance to photograph Hunters Brook along the 0.3-mile (0.5-km) one-way hike en route to the coast.

The easy-going dirt trail follows Hunters Brook as the babbling freshwater creek travels to Hunters Beach and the Atlantic Ocean to the south. Bring a **wide-angle** or **normal lens** to photograph the elegant stream lines meandering beneath a canopy of conifers and spotty deciduous trees (which sport their brilliant red, yellow, and orange

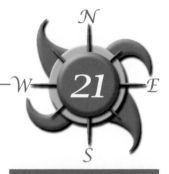

colors in October). A **telephoto lens** can isolate the remarkable details in the tumbling cascades. No matter your lens choice, utilize a **polarizer** to emphasize the vibrant reflections in the pools of water. Also, bring a **tripod** and **cable release** to keep your camera steady while using slow shutter speeds (e.g., 1/4th of a second or slower) to blur the brook's perpetual movement. If you do not have a cable release readily available, use your camera's self-timer feature instead to delay the shutter release as you remove your finger from pressing the shutter button.

Conscientiously compose your image such that the moving water travels towards your camera, appearing to flow from the top to the bottom of your frame. A composition featuring the water moving away from your lens often looks to defy gravity unnaturally as it flows from the bottom of your composition to the top.

After exhausting the ample creek-side photography opportunities, continue strolling south to Hunters Beach. Like Little Hunters Beach, the rising and setting sun does not illuminate the landscape directly due to its south-facing orientation as well as its position between Hunters Head to the east and Ingraham Point to the southwest.

Nevertheless, the picturesque assortment of speckled rocks, gnarled driftwood, wildflowers, and sea creatures hiding in tide pools at low tide suggest seemingly endless details to record with any lens in your camera bag, especially during overcast or foggy conditions. If bright conditions persist overhead, bring a **diffuser** along with a **macro lens** to mimic diffused light over smaller scenes.

Whether you decide to focus on the brook, beach, or both, wear water shoes, pack a few extra **lens cloths**, and leave a towel in your car in case you or your gear gets wet during your outing.

Directions

From the intersection of Main Street and West Street in downtown Bar Harbor, travel south on Main Street/Route 3 for 6.7 miles (10.8 km) and then turn left onto Cooksey Drive (also referred to as Sea Cliffs Drive on some maps). Drive 0.2 miles (0.3 km) and park in the small dirt parking area on the left. The marked trail begins on the southeast corner of the parking lot.

Ocean waves dance among the granite cobblestones on Hunters Beach. Canon 5DMII, 24-105mm at 90mm, ISO 100, f/18 at 1/4th sec., polarizer.

Little Long Pond

Idyllic setting for recording reflections, water lilies, and wildlife

TIME OF YEAR	TIME OF DAY	TIDE	HIKE
Year-round	*Sunrise to early morning*	*N/A*	*Easy*

The southern shoreline of Little Long Pond offers expansive tranquil views, especially in autumn. Canon 5DMII, 16-35mm at 16mm, ISO 100, f/13 at 2 sec., three-stop graduated neutral density filter.

*I*t is difficult to imagine a more idyllic place on MDI so close to a road. Bullfrogs croaking, lily pads lazily floating, and fog rising from the water's surface, combined with a picturesque boathouse and rounded Penobscot Mountain in the background make this 38-acre (15.4-hectares) lake a scene right out of a storybook.

Officially named "Long Pond," but referred to as "Little Long Pond" to reduce confusion with the larger lake to the west with the same name, this location does not reside in the park. Although the Rockefeller family owns the property, photo enthusiasts can saunter along the serene carriage road and the surrounding trails without seeking formal permission. Numerous dog walkers walk their dogs here, but sadly, not all clean up after their furry friends. Watch your step as you explore the area and keep your camera bag zipped to deter a curious canine from carrying off your gear. Note that bicycles are not permitted.

Broad landscape compositions from anywhere along the southern shoreline will not

Lily pads of all shapes and sizes grow in Little Long Pond. Canon 5DMII, 100-400mm at 190mm, ISO 800, f/20 at 0.4 sec., polarizer.

Directions

From the intersection of Main Street and West Street in Bar Harbor, travel south on Main Street/Route 3 for 8.4 miles (13.5 km). Veer right at the split in the road in Seal Harbor to follow Route 3. Drive an additional 0.8 miles (1.3 km) to the small gravel parking area on the north side of the road. Additional pullout space exists along the road just west of this parking lot. Please respect the posted "No Parking" signs along both sides of the street.

If these areas are full, continue driving an additional 0.3 miles (0.5 km) on Route 3 and turn right into the formal parking area marked "Little Long Pond Parking." The short dirt path back to the pond begins on the east side of the parking lot and leads visitors to the southwest side of the pond.

disappoint, especially at sunrise. Whether Mother Nature provides either direct light from the sun or diffused light from clouds or fog, pack a **wide-angle lens**, **polarizer**, **graduated neutral density filter**, **tripod**, and **cable release**. Unless lily pads cover the pond, drop your camera low to the ground to record ample foreground on the shoreline while minimizing the uninteresting middle ground.

When direct light exists, Little Long Pond is among the best places in Acadia to photograph reflections, especially during early to late morning light. When the trees along the west side reflect into the water, the copious amounts of lily pads and tall cattails can serve as visual anchors against lighter background. Remember to turn your polarizer such that it increases the reflection and saturation across the water.

Even with extensive wanderings around the pond, you will not be more than a 0.5-mile (0.8-km) walk from your vehicle, so also bring a **telephoto lens** if you wish to isolate the aquatic plants, including the bulbous yellow pond lilies blooming in July.

If photographing great blue herons, ospreys, and frogs are more your style, this same lens coupled with a **teleconverter** added in between your lens and camera will help fill your frame with the species of choice. Though a fast shutter speed will freeze the motion of flying birds, also try slowing your shutter speed down and panning the camera during the exposure as they soar overhead to freeze the bird against a blurred background.

This small body of water freezes in the winter and remains snow-covered much of the season, so the ice patterns common along the coastline are not prevalent here. However, since Little Long Pond is a popular place for the locals to ice skate, patterns in the ice and snow can make for interesting story-telling images.

Flying High!

"Life is either a daring adventure or nothing at all."

~Helen Keller

On my first visit to Acadia, I wanted to see and experience—not just photograph—the coastal park from as many different perspectives as I possibly could fit into my three-week stay in November. With autumn transitioning into winter, though, many businesses and services closed their doors in mid-October.

On my numerous 90-minute drives from the Schoodic Peninsula (where I was housed during all three residencies) to MDI, I saw one "Closed for the season" sign after another. Except for one. The Scenic Flights of Acadia in Trenton enthusiastically advertised "Open! Winter flights available!"

Although I had traveled in small planes before, I had never photographed from an airplane before. Eager to try a new experience and see the landscape from a different perspective, I immediately called to book an hour-long sunset flight around MDI.

At 3:30 p.m., I met my friendly pilot, Erik, on the Hancock County/Bar Harbor Airport tarmac. Before taking to the air, I cranked my ISO speed to ISO 400 on both of my cameras, to which I affixed a 24-105mm lens to one and a 100-400mm lens to the other so I could record both broad and compressed views from above respectively. I also changed my aperture to f/4, which would help ensure my corresponding shutter speeds would be fast enough to freeze the landscape while hand-holding my camera on a vibrating plane traveling 150-plus miles per hour (241.4 km/h).

From the moment the plane lifted off the ground, I started giggling, invigorated by the prospects of this new adventure. I had no idea what I was doing, but I knew I was going to have a blast doing it!

Over the drone of the propeller spinning, Erik graciously pointed out various features 1,000 feet (304.8 m) below us like Bar Harbor and Somes Sound as well as other, more remote, places I would have never seen unless I traveled by plane.

Once we were at a safe cruising altitude, Erik gave me the green light to pop open the window on my side of the plane. First, I removed my winter hat and gloves so they would not blow away. Then, I braced myself for the rush of chilled air as the window flung open and hugged the bottom of the wing.

Tapping into the "spray-and-pray" shooting methodology (where a photographer blindly shoots a large number of images in hopes a few turn out), I started photographing with a shutter speed of 1/100th. Although challenging to confirm while shuttering on a small plane, my first images looked a little blurry on the back of my camera's LCD screen. I quickly increased to ISO 500 (and eventually, as the sun set later in the flight, ISO 1600) so I could adjust my shutter speed to a faster setting.

Touring the outskirts of MDI, I physically extended my lens and head out the window, only to have the intense wind zoom my camera lenses to different focal lengths and force my head back into the cockpit. While photographing the Egg Rock Lighthouse, I placed my left hand on my 24-105mm lens to keep it from inadvertently moving during the exposure. One second I was photographing out the window; the next second, I had my lens in my left hand and my camera body in my right hand. In my attempt to gain more control over my equipment, I had accidentally pressed the lens release button. Without fast reflexes, my lens

Northeast Harbor at the mouth of Somes Sound catches luminous sunset light. Canon 5D, 24-105mm at 67mm, ISO 500, f/4 at 1/160th sec., polarizer.

could have easily dropped into the ocean below.

Stunned, I looked at Erik and quipped, "Oh boy! That's not a good thing!"

As he grinned, I added, "This could have been a VERY expensive flight, Erik!"

Reattaching the lens, I resumed laughing but decided to recoil slightly from the window in case I repeated my blunder (such that the unattached lens would only fall on my lap or on the plane's floor). The view six inches from the window was every bit as good as the one I was fighting to get by unnecessarily sticking my head out of the window. Besides, it was much more comfortable than getting battered by the wind!

Our exhilarating tour ended with a gorgeous tranquil sunset over island-dotted Blue Hill Bay on the west side of MDI. Awestruck by my aerial escapade, I laughed continuously for at least a half hour after we returned to Earth.

Four years later, during the unfortunate United States government shutdown which temporarily closed Acadia National Park, I knew how I could still see the park: from the air! I revisited Scenic Flights of Acadia, where I had the chance to reunite with Erik and enjoy another flight with my knowledgeable pilot, Alan. This trip, though, he showed me Frenchman Bay and the Schoodic Peninsula under mid-day, partly cloudy skies during the glorious height of autumn's colorful display.

Based on my learning's from the first flight, I did not need to "spray-and-pray," stick my head out the window, or hit the lens release button. I did, however, laugh and laugh as I admired the Acadian scenery from the sky. Like the first time, I was flying high.

Asticou Azalea Garden

Private garden brimming with azaleas, rhododendrons, and fall colors

TIME OF YEAR	TIME OF DAY	TIDE	HIKE
May to October	*Early morning to late afternoon*	*N/A*	*Easy*

Dainty bell-shaped blooms sprout in June on a Enkianthus tree near the Lily Pond. Canon 5DMII, 100mm macro, ISO 800, f/4 at 1/100th sec.

In 1956, a long-time MDI resident, Charles K. Savage, designed the breathtaking Asticou Azalea Garden, modeling it after a traditional Japanese stroll garden. Initially funded by John D. Rockefeller Jr., the 2.3-acre (0.9-hectare) garden's tranquil paths meander through a highly aesthetic, carefully manicured landscape—melting away visitors' daily life stresses and presenting shutterbugs ample photographic opportunities.

Located at the head of the charming Northeast Harbor, the property (which the non-profit Mount Desert Land and Garden Preserve organization now owns and oversees) does not reside within the Acadia National Park boundaries. Nonetheless, the 70-plus native and non-native species of azaleas, rhododendrons, and laurels blooming among the halcyon settings of the North Lawn, the Sand Garden, and Asticou Pond (followed by an autumnal display on par with anywhere in New England) make this a "can't miss" location while visiting the park.

Open to the public during daylight hours from

Abundant rhododendrons and azaleas show off their vibrant colors during the summer. Canon 5DMII, 100mm macro, ISO 200, f/6.3 at 1/160th sec.

Directions

From the intersection of Main Street and West Street in downtown Bar Harbor, travel south on Main Street for 0.3 miles (0.5 km). Turn right onto Mount Desert Street (which turns into Route 233/Eagle Lake Road). Drive 6.3 miles (10.1 km) and turn left onto Route 198 (also referred to as Sound Drive and Route 3) when you reach the T-intersection. Continue traveling about 4.2 miles (6.8 km) before turning left into the dirt Asticou Azalea Garden parking lot.

The park accepts and appreciates a donation in lieu of an entrance fee.

early May to late October, the color celebration begins in mid-May as the Japanese cherry trees flaunt delicate pink blossoms. Shortly thereafter, azaleas, rhododendrons, and laurels burst into every imaginable shade of pink and purple until the end of July. In August, blooming water lilies quietly line Asticou and Lily ponds. Not to be outdone by the spectacular spring and summer bloom, maple trees and other deciduous trees show off an artful collage of yellows, oranges, and reds towards the end of September and into mid-October.

Due to the narrow paths, leave your backpack behind and bring your **macro** or **telephoto lens** equipped with a **polarizer** to isolate blooms, leaves, and water reflections. Carry along a **reflector** and **diffuser** to manage the high contrast of mid-day light or stop by when overcast or foggy skies exist to photograph under naturally diffused light.

If you bring a **tripod** to keep your images sharp, please be courteous and respectful of other visitors along the path as you set up your shot. If you handhold your camera, enable your image stabilization or vibration reduction functionality and set your shutter speed to at least 1/focal length of your lens. For example, when handholding a lens set to a focal length of 200 mm, the shutter speed should be no slower than 1/200th of a second.

The Asticou Azalea Garden allows photographing for your personal enjoyment and usage. However, you must seek prior written permission from the Executive Director for any commercial usage. For more information, visit **www.gardenpreserve.org**.

Waterfall Bridge

Two historical carriage road bridges with waterfalls running beneath

TIME OF YEAR	TIME OF DAY	TIDE	HIKE
May to October	*Early to late afternoon*	*N/A*	*Moderate*

Hadlock Falls tumbles 40 feet (12.2 m) and meanders under the Waterfall Bridge. Canon 5DMII, 16-35mm at 16mm, ISO 100, f/18 at 1 sec.

The Waterfall Bridge area offers such a diversity of photographic subjects that you will not want to leave any of your photographic gear behind. However, that means photographers must lug a heavy pack on a short, but somewhat exhausting, jaunt up one of Acadia's steepest carriage roads. The worthy payoff, though, is not one, but two, dramatic stone bridges and the park's tallest waterfall.

After zigzagging up the gravel incline and then sauntering across a relatively flat section of the Hadlock Brook Loop Carriage Road with partially obstructed views of Upper Hadlock Pond and Northeast Harbor in the distance to the south, the first stone bridge—Hemlock Bridge—comes into view. Built in 1925 during John D. Rockefeller Jr.'s carriage road building extravaganza, this grand overpass spans majestically across the small cascades of Maple Spring Brook.

Compose with a **wide-angle lens** not only to exaggerate the bridge's length and height, but also to create a sense of depth in your image. A brief diversion along the Maple Spring Trail below the bridge reveals a closer view of the small cascades best photographed with a **normal** or **telephoto lens** outfitted with a **polarizing filter**.

Continue a mere 0.1-mile (0.2-km) to reach the equally impressive Waterfall Bridge. Constructed in the same year as its neighbor to the west, the stone structure provides an excellent platform on which to set your **tripod** and camera with a normal or telephoto lens fitted with a polarizer to record Hadlock

Lichen takes on an anthropomorphic shape on the rocks lining the carriage road. Canon 5DMII, 24-105mm at 65mm, ISO 100, f/22 at 4 sec., polarizer.

Directions

From the intersection of Main Street and West Street in downtown Bar Harbor, travel south on Main Street for 0.3 miles (0.5 km). Turn right onto Mount Desert Street (which turns into Route 233/Eagle Lake Road). Drive 6.3 miles (10.1 km) and turn left onto Route 198 (also referred to as Sound Drive and Route 3) when you reach the T-intersection. Continue traveling about 2.5 miles (4 km). At the signed turnoff for Parkman Mountain, turn left into the small paved parking area.

The carriage road begins on the northeast end of the parking area. Walk less than 100 yards (91 m) before turning right towards Upper Hadlock Pond. When you reach carriage road signpost 13, turn left. Walk 0.3 miles (0.5 km) and then stay straight/right when you reach signpost 12. Walk an additional 0.6 miles (1 km) to reach the Waterfall Bridge.

Falls tumbling 40 feet (12.2 m) and meandering beneath the bridge.

The Brook Trail—much like the Maple Spring Trail—allows photographers to snap closer compositions of the babbling brook emptying into small pools beneath the bridge. Using any lens ranging from wide-angle to telephoto, position yourself low to the ground and use a slow shutter speed (around a 1/4th of a second or slower) to show movement in the swirling pools. Should you decide to photograph near the falls, bring extra **lens cloths** to keep the front of your lens free of water droplets from the spray.

Both brooks flow heaviest in spring or after a heavy rainfall. They often slow to a trickle in late summer and autumn when showy maples, beech, and other deciduous trees fashion photogenic fall colors (particularly during October). A thick layer of ice hides Hadlock Falls in the winter, yielding interesting abstract studies when viewed through a telephoto lens.

An overcast or foggy day in the afternoon will provide the ideal shaping natural light as well as allow slow shutter speeds to blur the moving water beneath the bridges. If no clouds exist in the sky, arrive later in the afternoon to photograph in the shadow caused by Norumbega Mountain to the west obscuring the sunset in this area. Then, place a **neutral density filter** over your lens to help slow your shutter speed.

No doubt, the waterfalls and stone bridges here could fill your memory cards in a snap (or perhaps more appropriately, several hundred snaps!). As you explore this carriage road, though, pay attention to the photogenic, disc-shaped lichen anchored to the natural rock outcroppings and fabricated coping stones. Use a **macro lens** and a polarizer to isolate and enhance the different colors, shapes, and patterns you may find.

Eagle Lake

Large lake features stone bridge, wildlife, fall colors, and ice fishing

TIME OF YEAR	TIME OF DAY	TIDE	HIKE
Year-round	*Sunrise and sunset*	*N/A*	*Easy*

Eagle Lake's northern shoreline offers tranquil views of Cadillac (left) and Pemetic mountains (right). Canon 5DMII, 16-35mm at 16mm, ISO 200, f/11 at 30 sec., four-stop graduated neutral density filter.

Originally called Great Pond and Young's Pond, Acadia's second largest freshwater body (after Long Pond) was dubbed "Eagle Lake" by visiting artists in the mid-1800s who were inspired by the bald eagles soaring overhead.

In the early 1880s (prior to the Park Loop Road construction), eager tourists wishing to see the view from the summit of Green Mountain (known today as Cadillac Mountain) traveled from Bar Harbor to Eagle Lake to hop aboard a small steamship called the "Wauwinnet." After crossing the 436-acre (176.4-hectare) lake to the base of the mountain, visitors then boarded the Green Mountain Railway for a thirty-minute ride to the top of MDI's tallest mountain. After the cog railway declared bankruptcy in 1890, officials scuttled the steamer in Eagle Lake in 1893.

Although little remains from this storied past, a magnificent piece of history is still visible here: the Eagle Lake Bridge on the far northwest corner of the lake. Built in 1928 as one of Rockefeller Jr.'s seventeen carriage road bridges, the

Gothic-arch stone overpass is the only historic bridge one can drive an automobile across today, thanks to a widening project in 1974 to accommodate increasing island traffic.

After photographing the bridge with a **wide-angle** or **normal lens**, head to the water's edge along the northern shoreline. Multiple vantage points immediately reveal spectacular scenes of not only Eagle Lake, but also the surrounding Cadillac, Pemetic, and Sargent mountains, as well as the Bubbles to the south. Although the lake receives first morning light from April to September, Cadillac Mountain delays the sun's direct illumination from October to March for about 20-40 minutes after sunrise.

With the broad perspectives provided by a wide-angle or normal lens, the mid-ground here can feel overly expansive and visually empty due to the lake's long length. Position your camera low to the ground to minimize this bare, unnecessary space. No matter the lens, a **graduated neutral density filter** over the sky will ensure a balanced exposure, especially at sunrise and sundown if the clouds change into a colorful spectacle.

During the summer, a **telephoto lens** coupled with a teleconverter will isolate soaring bald eagles overhead as well as visiting ospreys, great blue herons, and common loons enjoying the undisturbed, protected waters.

Come October, the trees surrounding the lake, as well as the west-facing flanks of Cadillac Mountain, explode into a kaleidoscope of colors, thanks to the re-growth following the devastating Great Fire of 1947. Emphasize the ribbons of reds, oranges, and yellows from maple, beech, birch, and other deciduous trees using a normal or telephoto lens. Also, leverage a **polarizing filter** to intensify the hues in the water and the sky, as well as to remove the reflected sheen from the autumn leaves. By adding a polarizer, however, your shutter speeds will slow by one to two stops of light, so bring a **tripod** and **cable release** to keep your camera steady.

Though the tree-lined lake serves as a public water supply (and as such, swimming and wading are not permitted), in winter, cozy ice fishing huts spouting steam dot the frozen lake. Use a telephoto lens to photograph individual shelters or groupings scattered across the lake.

Directions

From the intersection of Main Street and West Street in Bar Harbor, travel south on Main Street for 0.3 miles (0.5 km). Turn right onto Mount Desert Street (which turns into Route 233/Eagle Lake Road). Drive 2.8 miles (4.5 km) until you see the large metal brown sign indicating "Carriage Road Entrance." Turn right into the dirt parking lot. The carriage road begins on the west side of the parking lot. Walk straight for about 50 yards (46 m) and then turn left to follow the carriage road under the Eagle Lake Bridge to reach the Eagle Lake shore.

A freshly-fallen maple leaf rests in a shallow pool of water. Canon 5DMII, 100mm macro, ISO 50, f/22 at 0.5 sec., reflector, diffuser.

Duck Brook Bridge

Small brook flowing beneath a grand historic carriage road bridge

TIME OF YEAR	TIME OF DAY	TIDE	HIKE
Year-round	Late morning to early afternoon	N/A	Moderate

Duck Brook parades through a canopy of fall color. Canon 5DMII, 16-35mm at 27mm, ISO 50, f/22 at 4 sec., polarizer.

John D. Rockefeller Jr. ensured each stone carriage road constructed in Acadia National Park retained its own character and charm. As such, no two bridges look alike. Arguably, Duck Brook Bridge is one of the grandest in park.

Built in 1929 as a triple-arched bridge spanning a deep ravine which is home to the jubilantly-flowing Duck Brook. The 200-foot (61-m) gravel deck features four regal semi-circle viewing balconies to allow visitors to soak in the surrounding beauty. Stairs on the east side, as well as a dirt path on the west side, of the bridge enable photographers to not only record a broad perspective of the historic overpass, but also get a closer view of the tumbling creek flowing through the forested canopy.

The south-facing bridge facade is photogenic in all seasons, especially in late morning or early evening when the sun provides shaping

sidelight to highlight the stone details. Bring a **wide-angle lens** to include the entire span within your horizontal frame. A **graduated neutral density filter** will hold back light from an overly bright sky above.

A cloudy day supplies the ideal diffused light to photograph Duck Brook with any lens from wide-angle to **telephoto**. If you position your camera looking south and upstream—and consequently into the sun to achieve backlighting—remember to protect your lens from lens flare with your **lens shade**, hand, or hat if the sun pokes out from behind a cloud.

To render silk-like moving water, use a slower shutter speed (e.g., 1/4th second or slower), using a **polarizer** and/ or a **neutral density filter** to lengthen your shutter speeds as needed to produce your desired effect. Do not forget a **tripod** and **cable release** to keep your camera steady during longer exposure time.

Though shutterbugs will no doubt busy themselves with photographing the bridge and brook, fleeting seasonal moments make this scenic spot even more attractive. In spring and summer, oxeye daisies, yellow oldfield cinquefoil, and pink sheep laurel line the stream. In autumn, splashes of color from maples, birch, and oaks dot the evergreen foliage. In winter, fleeting lacy ice formations come and go with each splash.

If you have any time left in the day after exploring the plethora of subjects at the bridge and brook, those seeking additional images of close-up forest details of ferns, lichen, mushrooms, and moss should consider a short stroll in either direction along the Witch Hole Pond Loop Carriage Road with a **macro** or telephoto lens, polarizer, **reflector**, and **diffuser** in hand.

Directions

From the intersection of Main Street and West Street in Bar Harbor, travel south on Main Street for 0.3 miles (0.5 km). Turn right onto Mount Desert Street (which turns into Route 233/Eagle Lake Road). Drive 2.5 miles (4 km). Turn right onto the unmarked Duck Brook Road. Travel an additional 1.1 miles (1.8 km) and then park along the side of the paved road at the carriage road entrance.

Ice graces a cascade along Duck Brook. Canon 5DMII, 100-400mm at 340mm, ISO 200, f/22 at 0.6 sec., polarizer.

Cadillac Mountain

Epic panoramic views at the summit of Acadia's tallest mountain

TIME OF YEAR	TIME OF DAY	TIDE	HIKE
Mid-April to November	*Sunrise and sunset*	*N/A*	*Easy to moderate*

Expansive vistas of Frenchman Bay, Porcupine Islands, and Bar Harbor from the Cadillac Mountain North Ridge Trail. Canon 5DMII, 16-35mm at 16mm, ISO 100, f/20 at 1.6 sec., three-stop graduated neutral density filter.

Were I challenged to name the crown jewel of Acadia National Park, Cadillac Mountain would likely rise to the honor. Standing 1,530 feet (466.3 m) above sea level, it is not only the tallest mountain in Acadia National Park, but also the highest rise of any landform along the Atlantic seaboard north of Sugarloaf Mountain in Rio de Janeiro, Brazil!

Because of its prominent position, from two weeks after September's autumn equinox until the two weeks prior to March's spring equinox, you can be among the first people in the United States to see—and photograph!—the rising sun over the Atlantic Ocean. Unfortunately, the drivable 7-mile (11.3-km) paved road to the top closes from late November until mid-April. This gives you a mere two months—October and November—to claim your title, unless you plan to hike, snowshoe, or cross-country ski the arduous uphill trek on the unplowed, snow-covered road or one of the frozen hiking trails in the winter.

Sun worshippers and shutterbugs alike flock to the paved 0.5-mile (0.8-km) Cadillac Summit Loop Trail to experience this momentous occasion. Arrive early—minimally 45 to 60

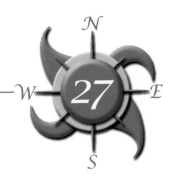

minutes before sun up—to set-up along this extremely popular path. Though it is tempting to wander off the trail to get away from the crowds, keep to the designated walkways or rock hop across the pink, speckled Cadillac Granite slabs so as to not trample the delicate vegetation growing in this extremely harsh environment. If solitude is what you seek, leave the crowds behind by hiking down the moderately strenuous Cadillac-Dorr Trail a mere 0.25 miles (0.4 km) or more instead for equally stunning scenes.

To record the sun's rising rays breaking the horizon across island-dotted Frenchman Bay, use a **wide-angle** or **normal lens** with all filters removed and a small aperture (such as f/16 or f/22) to create a radiating sunburst.

To create a panoramic photograph of the epic unprecedented view, start by picking two points that will define the opposite ends of your scene. Turn your camera to a vertical orientation (to render a taller, higher quality final panoramic image) and snap a series of multiple frames covering the area between your two defined points. Keep your camera level on your tripod and ensure each frame overlaps the previous frame by 30-40% to enable your post-processing software to stitch and blend the images seamlessly together. Check your histogram throughout the process to guarantee proper exposure, making exposure value adjustments as needed to compensate for too little or too much light across your scene. Because of the varying light levels between the land and the sky, also use a graduated neutral density filter over the bright sky as needed.

Once the sun rises, turn your lens to the south, where starting in early October, a carpet of color resulting from changing beech, birch, aspen, and maple leaves provides endless tighter compositions with a **telephoto lens**. Apply a **polarizer** to your lens to remove the reflected light from the leaves and to enrich the overall saturation of your scene.

Though sunrise views from the top are best facing south and east, sunset light is ideal

Summer fog burns off Frenchman Bay at sunset. Canon 5D, 100-400mm at 130mm, ISO 200, f/8 at 1/20th sec., polarizer.

Viewed from the summit looking south towards Otter Cove, low sweet blueberry and other deciduous plants show off a palette of color each October. Canon 5DMII, 16-35mm at 16mm, ISO 400, f/8 at 1/8th sec., three-stop graduated neutral density filter.

Cadillac Mountain (continued)

looking north and west. Once again, the Cadillac Summit Loop Trail offers plenty of photographic opportunities looking northwest towards Bar Harbor, the Porcupine Islands (named because of the way the pointy spruce trees appear on the rounded islands), and Frenchman Bay. Like sunrise, though, you will not be alone in enjoying the view.

The maintained Cadillac Mountain North Ridge Trail, which starts on the north side of the parking loop, offers a quieter experience. After a moderate 10-15 minute walk through low sweet blueberry bush (which turns a flashy lipstick red in mid- to late October) and stunted evergreens, eventually the subalpine terrain gives way to a wide, exposed clearing and breathtaking vistas to the northeast towards Bar Harbor and the Porcupine Islands.

Fog envelops the tundra-like summit landscape frequently throughout the year. Canon 5DMII, 24-105mm at 28mm, ISO 100, f/16 at 15 sec., polarizer, two-stop graduated neutral density filter.

Located a short walk to the west from the parking area, the Blue Hill Overlook offers unobstructed sunset views of Eagle Lake, the northwestern side of MDI, and Blue Hill Bay. Create a colorful silhouette as the sun drops below the horizon by aiming your camera in the sun's direction. While spot metering on an area of the sky, find a balance between your aperture and/or shutter speed settings so your camera's exposure meter lines up at the "0" mark. As you snap these backlit scenes, check your histogram, which should show no highlights and a heavy set of pixels on the left side to represents the blackened landscape.

Wildlife photographers interested in photographing migrating sharp-shinned hawks, peregrine falcons, bald eagles, and American kestrels should time their visit for late August through mid-October during the park's special "Hawk Watch" program. Weather permitting, park interpreters join visitors at a designated observation site along the Cadillac Mountain North Ridge Trail to help identify and count the thousands of raptors passing through the park overhead. Bring a telephoto lens, a **teleconverter**, and lots of patience to photograph this seasonal migration. To learn more about this

program and past years' results, read the Riding the Winds updates on **www.nps.gov/acad/naturescience/hawkwatch-update.htm**.

No matter the timing of your visit, high winds often pummel the summit. Bring a tripod and **cable release** to keep your camera still and your images sharp, but remember to turn off image stabilization/vibration reduction so the camera does not intentionally introduce camera shake. For smaller macro scenes, like sheep laurel blooming in June, use a **Wimberley Plamp**™ to hold your flower steady and build a wind block with your backpack or body to slow the movement of your specimen.

Fog can occur over the ocean at any time, but it is especially common in August. Sometimes, the low clouds encapsulate the entire mountain, making for moody backdrops among the granite slabs. Keep an extra **lens cloth** handy to keep your lens free from moisture and use a **rain cover** as needed to protect your camera (even when it is not raining). At other times, the haze spares the top of Cadillac Mountain, so visitors look down on a magical sea of clouds below.

Those seeking equally impressive viewpoints, while making less cliché and more unique images, should consider stopping at any of the numerous paved pullouts along the Cadillac Mountain Road at either sunrise or sunset.

On your way back into town after your photography outing, if you happened to catch sunrise, be sure to visit the Bar Harbor Chamber of Commerce and request your very own official "Cadillac Mountain Sunrise Club" membership card.

Directions

From the intersection of Main Street and West Street in Bar Harbor, travel south on Main Street for 0.3 miles (0.5 km). Turn right onto Mount Desert Street (which turns into Route 233/Eagle Lake Road). Drive 1.6 miles (2.6 km) and turn right at the signed entrance to Acadia National Park. Drive about 150 yards (137 m) and then turn left. Travel no more than 55 yards (50 m) and then turn left onto Park Loop Road. Drive 1 mile (1.6 km). Turn left at the signed Cadillac Summit Road. Drive an additional 3.3 miles (5.5 km) to reach the large paved parking area at the top of the mountain.

Distant view of Western Bay from the western side of Cadillac Mountain. Canon 5D, 100-400mm at 400mm, ISO 125, f/5.6 at 3.2 sec.

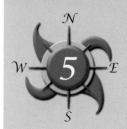

Chasing the Stars

"Reach high, for stars lie hidden in your soul."

~Pamela Vaull Starr

Conveniently, the annual Leonid meteor shower was set to occur in the middle of my first residency in November 2009. Due to the combination of the new moon and the expected height of astronomical activity, experts agreed the viewing conditions would be optimal in between 3:30 and 5:30 a.m. in the east-northeast section of the sky.

Despite requiring a substantial amount of daylight before I consider myself a fully functioning human (and even then, it still might be a stretch), I set my alarm for 2 a.m. so that I could travel from the Schoodic Peninsula to the summit of Cadillac Mountain to catch the show through my camera lens.

To keep myself awake during the 90-minute drive, I reviewed my game plan for the early morning's shoot. I planned to set up the camera on Cadillac Mountain facing east-northeast towards the night's show with a 24mm lens. Although I would run some test shots at higher ISO to confirm my exposure settings, I knew I wanted to record at least a 75-minute exposure on Bulb starting at 3:45 a.m. This approach would allow the stars to spin and the meteors to streak across my frame before the brighter twilight began to appear on the horizon ahead of the 6:30 a.m. sunrise.

While driving westward on Highway 1, a sudden, fiery blaze of light whizzing across the night's black sky interrupted my visualizations, which scared me enough to slam on the brakes and shout, "Whoa!" I nervously chuckled when I realized the unexpected shooting meteor was exactly what I had hoped to see on my middle-of-the-night journey.

When I eventually pulled into the parking lot at the top of Cadillac Mountain, three other cars were parked in the lot. Were they sleeping? Watching meteors? Early for sunrise? It was too dark to tell.

Under the guidance of my headlamp, I wandered along the trail to locate the spot I had photographed a week prior, which was a mere 0.25 miles (0.4 km) from the parking lot. Although I desired a simple composition with little to no foreground so I could fill my frame with stars and meteors, I was more excited to find a spot protected by large boulders so I could keep warm and my camera stabilized in the freezing winds howling across the face of the peak.

With just two 70-second test shots on ISO 3200, I determined a viable composition and appropriate exposure settings to prevent overexposing Bar Harbor's bright lights below. Racing against time, I triggered the third exposure on ISO 125 at f/4 on Bulb mode with the intent of leaving the shutter open for 75 minutes.

While my camera quietly worked, I curled into a ball and enjoyed the view. The heavens above spit out 20 to 30 meteors, though none as bright or as big as the one I saw earlier in the night on my drive. As the high winds ushered in a thin layer of clouds over Frenchman Bay and a glimpse of twilight appeared on the horizon, I decided to end my exposure early—after only 48 minutes.

By 5:30 a.m., I was enjoying sips of hot tea in the warmth of my car and analyzing the results on the back of my camera's LCD. I liked the star movement, but the lights of Bar Harbor and across Frenchman Bay on the mainland appeared too bright and distracting for my personal taste. I also did not record a significant amount of meteor activity, which I expected given the faint streaks I saw with my eyes. Ironically, even though I stopped the exposure

My final vision came together at the Ravens Nest beneath the Milky Way on October 11, 2010. Canon 5DMII, 16-35mm at 35mm, two exposures combined (the first at ISO 400, f/16 at 25 sec. for the cliffs; the second at ISO 3200, f/2.8 at 20 sec. about 40 minutes after the first exposure to freeze the stars).

Chasing the Stars (continued)

shorter than planned, the amount of light my camera collected looked correct based on the distribution of tones appearing in my histogram.

As with many ideas I have, some work out, but a fair number do not. In this case, I visualized an idea, executed it well, and yet, it still did not result in "the" image for which I had hoped. It was time to go back to the drawing board.

Four days later, excited by the prospects of the dark, moonless sky and determined to resolve the issues I identified in my initial night image from Cadillac Mountain, I ventured to Otter Cliff for a second try from a new vantage point away from the artificial lights of Bar Harbor. After a series of test shots, I determined similar exposure settings: ISO 100, f/4 at 45 minutes.

I happily reviewed the results of the single shot when the image flashed on the back of the camera's display. The stars swirled above Newport Cove and Ocean Drive as I had hoped. While I was certainly making progress on achieving my vision, the shadowed landscape rendered too dark to provide adequate detail in the cliffs. I thought, "What if I photographed the same idea under a rising crescent moon to illuminate the landscape?"

When I returned to my home base, I consulted The Photographer's Ephemeris (**www.photoephemeris.com**) to determine the exact date I needed to set up based on a rising crescent moon during astronomical twilight (which would provide enough light to illuminate the landscape, but not so much to overpower the star trails). Unfortunately, the stars—or in this case, more appropriately, the moon—were not going to align during the remainder of my time in the park.

After learning about my second residency, returning to Otter Cliff to try star trails again fell high on my wish list during my preparations. I revisited The Photographer's Ephemeris, scanning through each date of my three-week stay in October 2010. I noted that on October 5, a waning crescent moon would rise over the Atlantic Ocean at 3:49 a.m.

On October 5, I arrived at Otter Cliff at 3:30 a.m. anxious to make a new image. As Murphy's Law would have it, thick clouds covered the sky's dome. The layer turned an eerie reddish glow above the lights of Bar Harbor, but prevented me from recording star trails. I contemplated strike three. I would not get a second chance to shoot a rising crescent moon during my second stay. If I wanted to record the night sky over Acadia on this trip, I needed to shake up my vision once again. I thought, "What if I photographed during a *setting* crescent moon along a *western* shoreline?"

Checking The Photographer's Ephemeris revealed I had a two-day window on October 10 and 11 when a waxing crescent moon set during, or just after, astronomical twilight. On October 11, clear skies paved the way for my next attempt at star trails in the park. I headed to one of my favorite spots to photograph along the Schoodic Peninsula's western coastline—the remote and rugged Ravens Nest.

As day transformed into twilight, I recorded a series of images focused on the setting moon illuminating the rocky coastline. As twilight turned into night, I snapped additional frames of the slowly emerging Milky Way overhead. To combine the best light on the landscape and the night sky, I intended to combine multiple images in post-processing.

After chasing the stars across Acadia and evolving my vision with each attempt, I finally had recorded a visual message that matched what I wanted to share with my viewers.

Close, but not quite: attempt #2 at Otter Cliff beneath star trails on November 21, 2009. Canon 5D, 24-105mm at 24mm, ISO 100, f/4 at 45 min.

Bubble Pond

Reflections and historic stone bridge near enchanting pond

TIME OF YEAR	TIME OF DAY	TIDE	HIKE
May to October	*Late morning to early afternoon*	*N/A*	*Easy*

Boulders line the northern shoreline at Bubble Pond. Canon 5D, 24-105mm at 24mm, ISO 125, f/14 at 0.5 sec., polarizer, three-stop graduated neutral density filter.

*O*nce called "Turtle Lake," then "Twinhill Pond," and subsequently "Bubble Pond," this charming water basin acquired its modern name from the nearby Bubbles, even though the well-known formations are not visible from the pond. However, two other rounded peaks—Pemetic and Cadillac—frame the tranquil 32-acre (13-hectare) pool.

Due to its location within a U-shaped glacial valley, this spot does not receive direct light at sunrise or sunset. By the time the sun eventually rises above Cadillac Mountain or begins to disappear behind Pemetic Mountain, the light casts an unsightly shadow line across the landscape and results in high contrast in photographs. Calm, overcast, and foggy mornings offer the ideal weather conditions to photograph mirror-like reflections and the still foliage surrounding the little lake. By late afternoon, though, brisk winds often whip through the basin.

Though the Jordan-Bubble Ponds Loop Carriage Road skirting the western side of the water's edge provides glimpses of lake views through a screen of old-growth trees, you only need to walk less than 200 feet (61 m) from the parking area to a convenient clearing along the shoreline to make memorable images. Since you will carry your gear only a short distance, bring

a broad selection of **lenses—wide-angle**, **normal**, **telephoto**, and **macro**—to explore the multitude of diverse compositions within a small area.

When you arrive at the water's edge, look for a pleasing combination of rocks and rushes in the foreground while balancing the converging mountains flanks in the background. Position your camera low to the ground to keep the empty mid-ground water to a minimum (though tempting to dip your toes in the water to get closer to the foreground objects, the park does not permit wading at Bubble Pond since it serves as a public water supply).

To ensure you render the entire scene in sharp focus, set a small aperture (such as f/16 or f/22) and focus one-third of the way into your frame from the bottom—a quick way to approximate the hyperfocal distance. Consult the Depth of Field Master charts at **www.dofmaster.com** to learn the precise hyperfocal distance for your camera brand, lens, and aperture setting.

No matter your composition, use a **polarizer** to enhance the reflections in the water and darken the cobalt blue sky. The same filter will also remove the reflected sheen off the leaves of the trees surrounding the lake, especially when they show off a glorious riot of color during early October.

After exploring the pond, head to the historic Bubble Pond Bridge with your wide-angle or normal lens in hand. Located due east from the northern shore, the rustic carriage road overpass appears to span a defunct path to nowhere. When John D. Rockefeller Jr. constructed the 200-foot-long (61-m) stone bridge in 1928, the Park Loop Road traveled beneath the single arch. Later, the National Park Service re-routed the road to its current position about 200 feet (61 m) to the north.

Directions

From the intersection of Main Street and West Street in Bar Harbor, travel south on Main Street for 0.3 miles (0.5 km). Turn right onto Mount Desert Street (which turns into Route 233/Eagle Lake Road). Drive 1.6 miles (2.6 km) and turn right at the signed entrance to Acadia National Park. Drive about 150 yards (137 m) and then turn left. Travel no more than 55 yards (50 m) and then turn left onto Park Loop Road. Drive 2.4 miles (3.9 km). Turn left into the signed parking area for Bubble Pond.

Maple trees flaunt their vibrant autumn shades each October along the Bubble Pond shore. Canon 5D, 100-400mm at 130mm, ISO 100, f/18 at 1.6 sec., polarizer.

Bubble Rock Trail

Fourteen-ton glacial erratic resting on edge of granite cliffs

TIME OF YEAR	TIME OF DAY	TIDE	HIKE
May to October	*Late morning*	*N/A*	*Strenuous*

Also known as Balanced Rock, Bubble Rock is an enormous glacial erratic transported by ice 15,000 years ago from the Lucerne Lake area, which is about 20 miles (32.2 km) northwest of MDI. The glacial ice eventually melted, and the 14-ton boulder now rests precariously perched on a granite ledge on the South Bubble—a rounded mountain of 768 feet (234.1 m) in elevation.

Photogenic views of this famous rock reward shutterbugs willing to make the more strenuous trek up the mountain with a 400-foot (121.9-m) elevation change in a short 0.5 mile (0.8 km). In addition, a stunning aerial-like overlook of Eagle Lake looking north and Jordan Pond looking south lies ahead after your efforts.

The forest at the start of the trail offers an abundance of close-up scenes best recorded with a **macro lens**. Use a **diffuser** and/or **reflector** when sunny, dappled light filters through the golden leaves of autumn.

When headed to the

TOP: Bubble Rock floats in a sea of fog. Canon 5D, 24-105mm at 24mm, ISO 125, f/14 at 0.5 sec., polarizer, three-stop graduated neutral density filter.
OPPOSITE: Backlit aspen leaves cling to the final days of autumn. Canon 5DMII, 100-400mm at 220mm, ISO 400, f/14 at 1/60th sec.

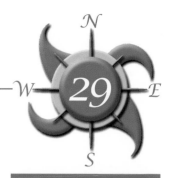

summit, also pack a **wide-angle** to **normal focal length lens**, **polarizing filter**, **graduated neutral density filters**, **tripod**, and **cable release** with you. At the top, position your camera such that Bubble Rock falls off center in your composition with either Eagle Lake or Jordan Pond serving as a scenic backdrop. Add another layer of depth by lowering your camera to the ground to include the lines from the granite joints extending from the foreground and into the frame.

Though located on a mountainous peak, Bubble Rock does not see the first nor last rays of sunlight, thanks to Pemetic Mountain to the east and Penobscot Mountain to the west. Plan instead to arrive about an hour or two after sunrise and wait for partly cloudy skies to obscure the sun, which helps to reduce the harsher contrast of mid-day light. In thick fog, the boulder can appear as if it is magically floating in clouds as the surrounding landscape disappears from view.

After you shoot, be sure to set your camera on a **tripod** and self-timer to record your very own photograph starring you as the mythological Sisyphus pushing the rock uphill (except in our case, let's hope—unlike the myth—he rock does not roll back down the hill!).

Especially when rain drenches the rocks or high winds howl through the valley, stay a safe distance from the edge as no handrails or fences exist along the cliffs. Due to ice covering the steep path, this trail is often inaccessible in winter, except to those wearing snow cleats and with previous experience in winter hiking. Those with a fear of heights might skip the visit to Bubble Rock.

Directions

From the intersection of Main Street and West Street in Bar Harbor, travel south on Main Street for 0.3 miles (0.5 km). Turn right onto Mount Desert Street (which turns into Route 233/Eagle Lake Road). Drive 1.6 miles (2.6 km) and turn right at the signed entrance to Acadia National Park. Drive about 150 yards (137 m) and then turn left. Travel no more than 55 yards (50 m) and then turn left onto Park Loop Road. Drive 3.4 miles (5.5 km). Turn right into the signed parking area for Bubble Rock. The dirt trail begins on the west side of the parking area.

Follow the Bubble Trail for 0.2 miles (0.3 km)—passing the Jordan Pond Carry Trail. When the trail splits for North and South Bubble, veer left following the signs to Bubble Rock and South Bubble. Follow the trail up the stair-like boulders for about 0.1 miles (0.2 km). At the second split, veer left again towards South Bubble and continue walking 0.2 miles (0.3 km) to reach the summit. Continue following the trail eastward, with the blue blazes on the rocks and trees as your guide, until you reach Bubble Rock on the far eastern side of the summit.

Jordan Pond Shore Path

Valley views and star trails along shore of Acadia's deepest lake

TIME OF YEAR	TIME OF DAY	TIDE	HIKE
Year-round	*Early afternoon to sunset; night*	*N/A*	*Moderate*

Sunset serenity along the southern shoreline of Jordan Pond. Canon 5DMII, 16-35mm at 33mm, ISO 100, f/20 at 1/8th sec., three-stop graduated neutral density filter.

*O*f the 26 lakes and ponds in Acadia, Jordan Pond is the deepest freshwater lake at 150 feet (45.7 m). The 3.3-mile (5.3 km) Jordan Pond Shore Path around the glacial remnant provides breathtaking views of the glacially carved North and South Bubbles, the staggering cliffs of Penobscot Mountain, and rounded Pemetic Mountain. However, arguably the most photogenic scenes fall along the entire southern end of the trail no more than a quarter-mile (0.4-km) stroll from the boat ramp. Though the western-most cove is most popular, continue walking east along the path for equally impressive set-ups and fewer onlookers.

Because the distant mountains loses direct light about 30-45 minutes before sunset depending on the time of year, arrive at least 60 minutes prior to last light with a **wide-angle** or **normal lens**, **tripod**, **cable release**, and **polarizer** in your camera bag. If Mother Nature showcases fiery clouds during civil twilight, use a **graduated neutral density filter** over your lens to accentuate the color.

As you wait for the final show of the day, use a **telephoto lens, flash**, and **Flash X-tender**™ to photograph common loons or common mergansers casually padding around the water's edge. Since this is a public water supply, you cannot join them in the water for a closer look.

Besides the western shoreline of the Schoodic Peninsula (see page 158), the southern end of Jordan Pond is one of the best places to photograph the night sky under a crescent or new moon. As day turns to night, Polaris—also known as the North Star—emerges above the Bubbles and acts as an anchor for spinning star trails.

Before the sun goes down, determine your composition and focus point for your chosen scene, as it will be difficult to do both in the dark. Set an **ultra-wide-angle lens** to a wide aperture (like f/2.8 or f/4.0) focused at infinity to not only allow you to record the rocks in the foreground but also the stars reflecting in the pond.

When the sky turns to night, make a few test shots to confirm your exposure settings. First, use a high ISO speed setting (like ISO 3200) as soon as astronomical twilight falls. Once you determine the correct shutter speed and aperture settings with the fast ISO (check your histogram), reset your ISO speed to ISO 100 or 200. Then, calculate the shutter speed required for your given aperture and desired ISO speed. For example, a two-second exposure with an f/2.8 aperture at ISO 3200 is equivalent to a 104-second exposure at f/2.8 and ISO 100 since the difference between ISO 3200 and 100 is five stops of light.

The amount of movement in the star trails is a matter of preference, but use Bulb mode and a locking **cable release** to open the shutter for at least 40-60 minutes (and up to several hours) to create a circular pattern in the sky. Should you wish to freeze the stars instead, use a faster ISO speed setting (e.g., ISO 1600) and subsequently a faster shutter speed, keeping your exposures less than 30 seconds to prevent star trails.

From mid-May to late October, taste a bite of history at the Jordan Pond House, the only restaurant within park boundaries. Sitting on the lawn, replenishing your energy with tea and popovers as the rusticators did in days past, makes for an unforgettable traditional Acadia experience. Jordan Pond House (**www.jordanpond.com**) accepts and suggests reservations for both lunch and dinner.

Directions

From the intersection of Main Street and West Street in Bar Harbor, travel south on Main Street for 0.3 miles (0.5 km). Turn right onto Mount Desert Street (which turns into Route 233/Eagle Lake Road). Drive 1.6 miles (2.6 km) and turn right at the signed entrance to Acadia National Park. Drive about 150 yards (137 m) and then turn left. Travel no more than 55 yards (50 m) and then turn left onto Park Loop Road. Drive 4.9 miles (7.9 km). Turn right at the signed turnoff for the Jordan Pond North Lot and then travel 0.1 miles (0.2 km) to the parking lot. The dirt trail to the pond begins on the northwest side of the parking area (to the right of the boat-launch ramp).

Vibrant autumn tones emerge in maple leaves along the trail each October. Canon 5DMII, 100mm macro, ISO 640, f/3.2 at 1/125 sec.

Jordan Stream

Cascades meandering beneath unique, historic carriage road bridge

TIME OF YEAR	TIME OF DAY	TIDE	HIKE
Year-round	*Early morning to early afternoon*	*N/A*	*Moderate*

Beech leaves showing autumnal color along the carriage roads. Canon 5D, 100mm macro, ISO 200, f/3.2 at 1/80 sec.

At first glance, Jordan Stream may look similar to the many cascading creeks gracefully weaving through Acadia's pristine forests. Unlike the others, though, this babbling brook originates at the south end of Jordan Pond, tumbles down a gentle hill, and crosses beneath the first carriage road bridge (Cobblestone Bridge) constructed in the park by John D. Rockefeller Jr. and his dedicated team.

As the perennial stream flows along the rocky, tree-covered banks, each season delivers its own fleeting beauty. In spring and summer, the surrounding woods boast vivacious greens. In autumn, the foliage flaunts a rainbow of reds, yellows, and oranges. In winter, after a snowfall, the trees quietly exhibit elegant lines of alternating white and grey.

No matter the month, even the shortest stroll along the Jordan Stream Loop Carriage Road brings to light ample photographic opportunities! Carry a **telephoto** or **macro lens** to help isolate smaller scenes of splendor. Utilize a wide aperture (like f/4 or f/5.6) to selectively focus and to keep the busy background blurred while photographing patterns on a lichen-covered rock, colorful leaf, or ice formation.

Walk no more than 0.25 miles (0.4 km) down the trail to find larger waterfalls more

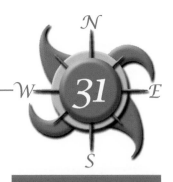

Jordan Stream cascades along the trail. Canon 5DMII, 24-105mm at 67mm, ISO 200, f/9 at 10 sec., polarizer.

suitable for **wide-angle** and **normal lens** compositions. A **polarizer** coupled with a **neutral density filter** will not only help increase saturation, but will also slow your shutter speed to render silk-like water. Place your camera on a **tripod** and use a **cable release** with slow exposures. Wear water shoes with good traction and stuff a **lens cloth** or two in your pocket in case the falls spray your lens. Utilize a **rain cover** or shower cap for complete protection, even when it is not raining. In fact, for creative effect, try photographing your scene through a clear shower cap to create a surrealistic, ethereal feeling in your frame.

Continue down the trail a little more than 0.25 miles (0.4 km) to photograph the historic Cobblestone Bridge (staying right at signpost 23 and again at signpost 24 before reaching the one-of-a-kind overpass). Rather than using rustic granite blocks (as they did with all future bridges), Rockefeller Jr.'s team utilized the area's cobblestones to create a more natural-appearing face when they constructed this bridge in 1917.

The semi-circle viewing turrets provide a glimpse of this unique design, but a dirt footpath and small wooden bridge allows access to the stream below. Depending on how far you wander down the streambed, a wide-angle or normal lens positioned low to the ground will help record compositions inclusive of both the rushing water and the bridge. So that the line of the bridge does not appear horizontal across your frame—and therefore visually static—move to one side or the other of the bridge to create a more dynamic angle and leading line from one of the corners of your frame.

An overcast day provides the best time to photograph the historic bridge, the babbling brook, and the surrounding foliage, as the dappled, direct light filtering through the trees may cause too much contrast for your camera to handle in one frame. If you arrive under clear, sunny skies, use High Dynamic Range (HDR) imaging techniques and look for smaller compositions in even, shaded lighting. Or, utilize a large diffuser to help create even illumination across your scene. Alternatively, arrive before the sun rises above the canopy trees to photograph in the morning's open shadows.

From the intersection of Main Street and West Street in Bar Harbor, travel south on Main Street for 0.3 miles (0.5 km). Turn right onto Mount Desert Street (which turns into Route 233/Eagle Lake Road). Drive 1.6 miles (2.6 km) and turn right at the signed entrance to Acadia National Park. Drive about 150 yards (137 m) and then turn left. Travel no more than 55 yards (50 m) and then turn left onto Park Loop Road. Drive 4.9 miles (7.9 km). Turn right at the signed turnoff for the Jordan Pond North Lot and then make an immediate left into the parking lot on the south side of the road. Park and then follow the marked dirt path on the southeast end of the parking lot for less than 0.1 miles (0.2 km) to reach the Jordan Pond House area.

The trail begins to the west of the gift shop at the sign declaring, "To Asticou and Jordan Pond Path." Walk down the stone steps and continue straight when you reach carriage road signpost 15 to join the Jordan Stream Carriage Road.

Deer Brook Bridge & Waterfall

Two stone bridges and a waterfall along scenic carriage road

TIME OF YEAR	TIME OF DAY	TIDE	HIKE
May to October	*Early to late morning*	*N/A*	*Moderate*

Deer Brook cascades beneath the historic Deer Brook Bridge. Canon 5D, 24-105mm at 24mm, ISO 100, f/9 at 8 sec., polarizer.

Though the historic Deer Brook Bridge (and tumbling cascades beneath it) provides ample photographic opportunities to portray the work of humankind and nature peacefully co-existing, the path en route to the bridge holds an even wider diversity of photogenic temptations. Hit the trail early in the morning to explore all this area has to offer!

Immediately after beginning your hike to the Deer Brook Bridge, saunter over the quaint Jordan Stream Bridge. After completing the Cobblestone and Little Harbor Brook bridges in 1917 and 1919 respectively, John D. Rockefeller Jr. and his crew built this smaller stone overpass in 1920 across the bridge's namesake, Jordan Stream. Its serene location at the convergence of Jordan Pond and the brook makes it pixel-worthy with a **wide-angle** or **normal length lens**.

Continue following the Jordan-Bubble Ponds Loop Carriage Road as it snakes through the dense old-growth forest—an area not affected by the Great Fire of 1947. As the season changes from summer to autumn, gleaming green birch, aspen, and maple leaves transform into a multi-hued range of reds, oranges, and yellows along the carriage road. Draw on your **macro** or **telephoto lens** (in conjunction with a **polarizer**,

Birch leaves and reflections along the Jordan-Bubble Ponds Loop Carriage Road. Canon 5DMII, 100mm macro, ISO 400, f/22 at 0.8 sec.

reflector, and **diffuser**) to burn through more memory cards here.

As the trail hugs the talus-covered eastern flanks of Penobscot Mountain, the trees eventually clear for spectacular aerial-like views of Jordan Pond below and Pemetic Mountain across the pond. Shortly thereafter, visitors reach the celebrated bridge. By dropping down the dirt path on the eastern side of the stone overpass, you will not only get a better view for photographs, but you will also catch a glimpse of the carved circular medallion indicating the year Rockefeller Jr. constructed this stone masterpiece—1925. Evergreens frame the bridge predominantly, creating a strong contrast with its grey-washed stone any time of year. A couple of young maple trees nearby provide a small splash of color in early and mid-October.

In addition to the healthy forest cover overhead, the nearby Bubbles and distant Cadillac and Pemetic mountains prevent the falls from receiving direct illumination until about 30-45 minutes after the sunrise depending on the time of year. Similarly, Penobscot Mountain casts a deep shadow on the area by mid-afternoon, making it possible to record even, but somewhat flat, lighting later in the day.

Utilize a wide-angle lens to include both the cascades and the bridge within your frame—experimenting with both vertical and horizontal orientations. Normal and **telephoto lenses** will help isolate smaller falls. No matter the lens, add a polarizer to eliminate reflected sheen from leaves and improve the overall saturation of your recorded scene. In addition, utilize a neutral density filter to slow shutter speeds to at least 1/4th second or slower to render streaking, cotton-like water. The long exposures make carrying a **tripod** and **cable release** up the hill a necessity.

Bring a clear shower cap or **rain gear** for your camera—even when it is not raining—to protect from spray, especially during spring and after rain storms when the creek flows at its highest. A **lens cloth** or two will also help keep your lens free of water droplets.

Directions

From the intersection of Main Street and West Street in Bar Harbor, travel south on Main Street for 0.3 miles (0.5 km). Turn right onto Mount Desert Street (which turns into Route 233/Eagle Lake Road). Drive 1.6 miles (2.6 km) and turn right at the signed entrance to Acadia National Park. Drive about 150 yards (137 m) and then turn left. Travel no more than 55 yards (50 m) and then turn left onto Park Loop Road. Drive 4.9 miles (7.9 km). Turn right at the signed parking area for the Jordan Pond North Lot and then travel 0.1 miles (0.2 km) to the parking lot.

Walk to the boat ramp on the northwest corner of the parking area and then follow the southern-most shoreline path until it connects with the carriage road. Turn right at the carriage road and then stay straight when approaching signpost #14. Continue 1.3 miles (2.1 km) to reach the bridge.

Ride With Me

"Never, never, never give up."
~Winston Churchill

While learning as much as I could prior to my first visit, I read an insightful book by Ann Rockefeller Roberts titled, *Mr. Rockefeller's Roads: The Untold Stories of Acadia's Carriage Roads.* Concerned the increasing number of automobiles traversing MDI would threaten the natural beauty and affect the peacefulness the isle provided to him, his family, and fellow community members, John Rockefeller Jr. envisioned setting aside land to establish a network of carriage roads limited to only horse-drawn carriages and pedestrians. By 1940, a carefully designed and developed system of integrated carriage roads existed for recreational purposes. Inspired by this story, I started to visualize the types of photographs I wanted to make when I experienced the historical paths firsthand.

After making the cross-country trek to the park in November 2009, I set out to travel almost every length of the dirt carriage roads by foot or bicycle. Occasionally, I stopped to make a photograph (or two or ten or fifty). Along the way, I felt I was capturing technically acceptable photographs. However, I never felt within my heart and soul that I had portrayed this unique feature in a creative manner nor successfully conveyed through my visual expression just how much excitement awaited those who visited these paths.

Reviewing my images at home confirmed the lackluster results. The photo below represented the best image of the carriage roads I had made during my initial visit. Would this photograph inspire you to go to Acadia and experience the carriage roads for yourself? (I am hoping you said a resounding, "NO!") Although I followed the composition and exposure rules, from a creative aspect, it was positively dreadful. Displeased with my results, I analyzed what went wrong and designed a new vision that would hopefully yield an improved image during my fortunate second chance in October 2010.

During the 10 months between visits to the park, I imagined what I wanted my final image to look like and how I would accomplish it. I quickly concluded that walking or running while photographing would not yield fast or smooth enough motion. I wanted to show an inviting perspective implying I was riding a bike along the carriage road instead.

As I cycled along the carriage roads, I would use a slower shutter speed to record my movement. Initially, I considered holding the camera up to my eye with one hand while

keeping the other on the handlebar, but that approach would likely result in both the bike and me inadvertently wrapped around a tree within seconds. To not only keep me safe, but also convey my message, I needed to determine how to keep both hands on the handlebars while moving and making photographs. But how?

I mulled the crux of the problem over with my husband, Craig, who promptly suggested I research what skydivers do to trigger the shutter hands-free when they toss themselves out of airplanes. With this recommendation in mind, I found a company online, Conceptus, Inc. (**www.conceptusinc.com**),

TOP: Ride with me on the Jordan-Bubble Ponds Loop Carriage Road! Canon 5DMII, 16-35mm at 16mm, ISO 50, f/20 @ 1/5th sec., polarizer, triggered by Conceptus tongue switch.
OPPOSITE: The Hemlock Bridge along the Hadlock Brook Loop Carriage Road. Canon 5D, 24-105mm at 28mm, ISO 100, f/20 @ 4 sec., polarizer.

who made camera switches for just this purpose. I traveled to one of their distributors in Eloy, Arizona to purchase a tongue switch (a cable-release that plugs into the camera and allows your tongue to trigger the shutter instead of your hands). After testing my new toy at the store, I knew this tool would help me capture my vision on my next trip!

Beaming with fresh enthusiasm for my idea, I returned to Acadia that autumn and biked the color-kissed, tree-lined carriage roads with my camera strapped to my mid-section with a basic cloth strap. After snapping test shots to gain the correct exposure settings, I then manually focused my 16mm wide-angle lens at infinity. With my tongue switch in my mouth, I pedaled as fast as I could downhill, experimenting with various shutter speeds to render just enough motion but not so much that the surrounding forest appeared like the streaked stars when the Millennium Falcon kicked into hyperspace mode in the movie *Star Wars*.

Six-hundred shots later—only four of which turned out to my liking—I can confidentially say the photograph above, titled "Ride With Me," is exactly how I felt about enjoying the carriage roads. More importantly, this image conveys precisely what I wanted to share with my viewers about that exhilarating feeling.

Whether you are photographing from a bike, an airplane, or with your two feet solidly planted on the ground, keep visualizing and shooting until you are pleased with the image on the back of your LCD before you move on to a new idea. If you do not, you are cheating yourself and your audience out of something very important you have to say about the scene in front of you. Work the scene by moving your position, changing lens, using light differently, modifying your exposure settings, applying filters, or whatever else you need to do to ensure you capture that vision. Once you have a spark of enthusiasm over an idea, do not walk away or give up until you have recorded it, even if it takes 10 months, 600 snaps, and a tongue switch to achieve it!

Pretty Marsh Picnic Area

West-facing cobble beach with unique sunset coastline views

TIME OF YEAR	TIME OF DAY	TIDE	HIKE
May to October	*Sunset*	*Any*	*Moderate*

Low tide reveals rockweed- and barnacle-covered boulders on the beach at Pretty Marsh. Canon 5DMII, 16-35mm at 16mm, ISO 100, f/16 at 4 sec., two- and four-stop graduated neutral density filter stacked.

With Acadia National Park's flair for obvious names, one might expect a gorgeous swampy area at the Pretty Marsh Picnic Area. Though there is no argument this location is pretty, it does not offer scenes of a marsh as the simple name implies. Instead, this quiet, lesser-known spot overlooks Pretty Marsh Harbor, a protected tree-lined cove along the Bartlett Narrows. Situated on the far western part of the park, the area presents one of the few locations along the MDI coastline to photograph sidelight at sunset.

Before descending the wooden steps down to the flat cobblestone shoreline, scan the towering spruce and other evergreen trees near the parking area for woodpeckers and nuthatches with a **long telephoto lens** (e.g., 400 mm or longer). A pop of **flash** coupled with a **Flash X-tender**™ will add a touch of dramatic catch-light to the bird's eye and enable faster shutter speeds under the dark forest canopy.

When you decide to head to the beach, grab a **wide-angle** to **normal focal length lens**,

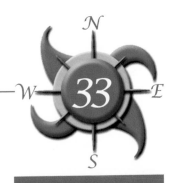

Mushrooms sprout in the moss lining the forest floor in the picnic area.
Canon 5DMII, 24-105mm at 85mm, ISO 100, f/11 at 0.5 sec.

polarizer, **tripod**, and **cable release**. Position your camera facing south towards the open waters or north towards Pretty Marsh Harbor to record the sun's radiant final rays illuminating the rounded stones from the side.

Although a landscape-style composition may feel most comfortable here, do not forget to try a vertical portrait orientation as well to display a more visually dramatic arrangement—especially if colorful clouds appear during civil twilight. One or more **graduated neutral density filters** held over your lens will help darken the multi-colored sky above while keeping the land perfectly exposed.

Because Pretty Marsh resides in a sheltered bay, waves here rarely do more than gently slosh against the shoreline. Should you wish to slow your shutter speed down to record a cotton-like effect of the dawdling water, utilize the slowest ISO speed setting your camera allows (e.g., ISO 50 or 100) and add a neutral density filter over your lens to lengthen your exposure as much as possible.

Directions

From the intersection of Main Street and West Street in Bar Harbor, travel south on Main Street for 0.3 miles (0.5 km). Turn right onto Mount Desert Street (which turns into Route 233/Eagle Lake Road). Drive 6.3 miles (10.1 km) and turn right onto Route 198 (also referred to as Sound Drive and Route 3) when you reach the T-intersection. Continue traveling about 1.4 miles (2.3 km). Turn left onto Route 102/Main Street and proceed another 0.9 miles (1.5 km). Veer right onto the signed Pretty Marsh Road and drive an additional 4 miles (6.4 km). Turn right into the signed Pretty Marsh Picnic Area. Follow the road into the parking area.

The Pretty Marsh Picnic Area closes to motorized vehicles from December to mid-April.

A lone seagull swims among skypools in Pretty Marsh Harbor. Canon 5DMII, 100-400mm at 400mm, ISO 400, f/11 at 1/1000th sec.

Bass Harbor Head Lighthouse

Active historic lighthouse along rocky shoreline at mouth of Bass Harbor

TIME OF YEAR	TIME OF DAY	TIDE	HIKE
October to March	Sunset	Mid to high, incoming	Moderate

With an incoming high tide swirling among the rocks, the Bass Harbor Head Lighthouse catches the day's final rays. Canon 5DMII, 24-105mm at 24mm, ISO 50, f/20 at 6 sec., polarizer, four-stop graduated neutral density filter.

*T*owering above the swirling Atlantic Ocean at the mouth of Bass Harbor, the stately Bass Harbor Head Lighthouse is widely considered one of the most iconic scenes within Acadia National Park. Dramatically located on the edge of precipitous, rugged cliffs, the white brick 26-foot (7.9 m) tower began guiding sailors through the surrounding shallow waters in 1858. Now listed on the National Register of Historic Places, the lighthouse remains active, but with an automated light since 1974.

Not surprisingly, since it is the only lighthouse on MDI and easily accessible, hoards of photographers and onlookers alike visit to catch a glimpse of this impressive site. As a result, expect to share your space with others on the rocks beneath the guiding light at sunset, particularly in summer and autumn (despite the sun's rays falling behind the lighthouse and a shielding stand of evergreen trees which casts a shadow across the entire scene). Crowds diminish significantly, except for weekends and major holidays, from November to February when the lighthouse, granite cliffs, and volcanic boulders catch stunning direct sidelight from the day's glorious last rays.

Arrive at least 60 minutes prior to sundown to find your favorite position among the rocks with a **wide-angle to normal lens**, **polarizer**, **tripod**, and **cable release**. Watch for convergence, though, when using a wide-angle lens. With this lens, the lighthouse and surrounding trees can appear to slant unnaturally. Compose broadly to correct the perspective later in post-processing software or keep the lighthouse straight in the field by making a subtle tilt movement with a **tilt-shift lens**. Then, time your exposure with the lighthouse's red

Off-shore jagged rocks surrounded by the ethereal sea. Canon 5DMII, 24-105mm at 92mm, ISO 200, f/8 at 243 sec., ten-stop neutral density filter.

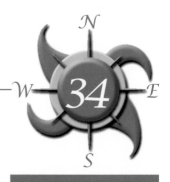

occulting light as it flashes brightly for three seconds (and then disappears for one second).

In addition, cover your lens with a **lens shade** or your hand to protect your photograph from inadvertently recording lens flare unless you decide intentionally to photograph a sunburst as the sun dances between clouds or kisses the horizon.

If clouds exist overhead, the superlative show begins once the sun drops below the horizon and up to 45 minutes thereafter. As the clouds erupt into a colorful fury, use a **three-stop or stronger graduated neutral density filter** or employ High Dynamic Range (HDR) imaging techniques to balance the bright hues in the sky with the shadowed landscape.

An incoming mid- to high tide (between 8 and 10 feet [2.4 and 3.1 m]) offers the ideal conditions in all seasons for photographing dramatic crashing waves over the dark rocks in the foreground. To smooth the wave action in your photograph, place a **neutral density filter** in front of your lens to slow your shutter speed. A **lens cloth** will help prevent ocean spray from building up on your lens during your outing.

At the highest tides, shutterbugs might find it challenging to achieve a pleasant angle from the rocks. After the high tides recede, though, small pockets of water remain on top of the volcanic rock, serving as reflection pools for the lighthouse. Get close and low to the water, while taking care not to merge any part of the reflected lighthouse with the surrounding rocks in the foreground. As you find your perfect composition, watch your step on the wet, slick rocks and do not turn your back on the ocean.

At the lowest tides, visitors can cross the boulder field to the west side of the light. In doing so, though, not only will you likely be in front of other photographers' cameras on the east side (and therefore, somewhat unpopular), you will also be working with unflattering, flat front light on the lighthouse.

Because a United States Coast Guard family lives here year-round, the park prohibits visitation at the lighthouse from 10 p.m. to half an hour before sunrise. The gatekeeper house is off-limits to the public.

Directions

From the intersection of Main Street and West Street in Bar Harbor, travel south on Main Street for 0.3 miles (0.5 km). Turn right onto Mount Desert Street (which turns into Route 233/Eagle Lake Road). Drive 6.3 miles (10.1 km) and turn right onto Route 198 (also referred to as Sound Drive and Route 3) when you reach the T-intersection. Continue traveling about 1.4 miles (2.3 km). Turn left onto Route 102/Main Street and proceed another 8.6 miles (13.8 km). Turn left onto Route 102A and then travel 2.2 miles (3.5 km), following the signs to the Bass Harbor Head Lighthouse parking area.

The trail down to the coastline begins on the southeast side of the parking area (south of the bathrooms). Stay on the trail as it descends the wooden stairs and proceeds onto the granite boulders.

Turning the Tide

"Learning is the only thing the mind never exhausts, never fears, and never regrets."

~Leonardo da Vinci

*P*rior to my first residency, I knew very little about Acadia. I knew much of it fell along the Maine coast (and hoped it looked similar to one of my other beloved locations, the Oregon Coast). I heard it displayed a spectacular fall color show in October. And I understood you could be among the first in the United States to see the sunrise atop Cadillac Mountain. It was all of the unknowns, though, that made visiting the park that much more attractive to me.

To make the most of my three weeks on location, though, I did not want to arrive completely blind so I spent an enormous amount of time learning about the various sites I might see. In web searches about the park, a few photogenic park icons flooded the results list, including the Bass Harbor Head Lighthouse. I scribbled the spot into the "must-see" category on my shot list, a spreadsheet I created to catalog my thoughts about different locations and ideas for a given park, area, or trip.

After learning where on MDI the lighthouse resided and how frequently the light flashed, I picked out a few images online I enjoyed and then studied them closely to understand how they approached the scene. I performed a critique of each image, defining what I liked and did not like about the image. I also outlined how I would change the image. I considered many "what if" scenarios. What if I arrived at sunrise instead of sunset (which seemed to be the time most photographers frequented the spot)? What if I stayed higher on the cliffs? What if I used a telephoto lens? I closed my eyes and imagined myself standing on the rocks working through all these different situations in changing weather conditions.

This analytical process not only helped increase my excitement for photographing the lighthouse, but also started defining a creative vision before jumping on a plane to Maine. Based on my varying ideas, I used The Photographer's Ephemeris (**www.photographersephemeris. com**) to identify the best timing to record direct light on the lighthouse given the sun's angle in November. I tapped into Google™ Earth (**www.google.com/earth**) to confirm my compositions. Based on my findings, I determined that sunset would likely yield the best chance for direct light on the lighthouse and most photogenic views were from the east along the rocky shoreline.

While enjoying Acadia, I monitored the weather with my ideas for the lighthouse still brewing. During a convenient break in a passing storm, I headed to the lighthouse to see if my visualizations matched reality and to hopefully create a worthy image of a park icon.

The lighthouse appeared the same, but the swirling waves and dark volcanic rocks beneath the beacon of light did not. I climbed on top of the sharp boulders, but water surprisingly inched up with every snap of my shutter, causing me to move higher and higher on the rocks to stay safe. The influx of water changed my composition every few frames as I moved inland. Despite my naiveté over the waves' encroachment, I enjoyed the memorable lighting and weather conditions Mother Nature provided at sunset.

After the shoot concluded, I realized I had been working against a rising tide. Throughout all my research and planning, I had forgotten to consider the tides! While I was familiar with the notion of tides, changes in the ocean's water levels are not something we concern ourselves much with in the desert. However, along this stretch of coast, the sea rises almost 12 inches (30.5 cm) an hour!

During a winter sunset, the last rays of the day illuminate the Bass Harbor Head Lighthouse and the granite cliffs it rests upon. Canon 5DMII, 24-105mm at 24mm, ISO 50, f/20 at 6 sec., polarizer, four-stop graduated neutral density filter.

That evening, I checked the tide tables for Bass Harbor (which was, not surprisingly, the closest harbor to the iconic lighthouse). This stretch of coast experienced a 10.8-foot (3.3-m) high tide at 5:32 a.m. and an 11-foot (3.4-m) high tide at 5:58 p.m. The single low tide for the day occurred at 11:47 a.m. at a 0.7-foot (0.2-m) level. Since the sun dropped below the horizon at 4:10 p.m., I had experienced an incoming mid- to high tide around 8.5 feet (2.6 m).

A year later, I visited the lighthouse at low tide, hoping to position myself far south onto the rocks. While I had timed my arrival perfectly to coincide with the day's lowest water level, I felt I lost the imperative connection between the lighthouse and the waters it protected. I determined that I had luckily experienced what I considered ideal conditions on my first visit.

From this experience, I learned that simply knowing that tides existed was not enough. I developed precise opinions on high or low tide, incoming and outgoing, and the specific water level for a given spot to create the type of photograph I desired. From then on, I added a necessary and important layer of complexity to my visualizations for not just Acadia, but any coastal location I visited in the future.

Ship Harbor Trail

Wildflowers and waves along small, craggy, granite-lined peninsula

TIME OF YEAR	TIME OF DAY	TIDE	HIKE
Year-round	Late afternoon to sunset	Minus low or high	Moderate

Granite cliffs along the western side of the trail glow in sunset light at low tide. Canon 5DMII, 16-35mm at 16mm, ISO 100, f/14 at 2 sec., four-stop graduated neutral density filter.

Legend holds that an American ship escaping a British gunboat became entrenched in the mud of Ship Harbor during the Revolutionary War. However, no one has ever located the shipwreck remains (the cove all but dries out during a minus low tide if you wish to confirm for yourself!). What photographers will find instead are abundant wildflowers and crashing waves along this craggy peninsula.

Set out in the late afternoon to begin hiking the 1.3-mile (2.1-km) figure-eight loop counterclockwise. Allow ample time to make the moderately strenuous saunter through the lovely spruce forest, which bursts with beautiful blooms from bunchberry dogwood and rhodora in June. However, time your stroll such that you find yourself on the southwestern-most tip of the peninsula at sunset to explore the tide pools and granite coastline soaking up the warm last rays of daylight.

Pack a **macro** and/or a **telephoto lens** to record the smaller treasures you find in the woods along the way. To help control the light over your composition, also bring a **reflector**, **diffuser**, and **flash**. This same equipment will also come in handy when you finally emerge from the forest to photograph the delicate sea urchins, starfish, snails, and other tide pool animals revealed at minus low tide levels.

A break in a winter storm highlights a wave crashing into the granite cliffs along the trail. Canon 5DMII, 24-105mm at 60mm, ISO 50, f/22 at 0.3 sec., polarizer.

Directions

From the intersection of Main Street and West Street in Bar Harbor, travel south on Main Street for 0.3 miles (0.5 km). Turn right onto Mount Desert Street (which turns into Route 233/Eagle Lake Road). Drive 6.3 miles (10.1 km) and turn right onto Route 198 (also known as Sound Drive) when you reach the T-intersection. Continue traveling about 1.4 miles (2.3 km). Turn left onto Route 102/Main Street and proceed another 8.6 miles (13.8 km). Turn left onto Route 102A and then travel 1.6 miles (2.6 km) before turning left to follow Route 102A. Drive 0.8 miles (1.3 km) to the signed Ship Harbor Trailhead parking lot. The trail begins on the south end of the paved parking area.

The pink granite ledges on the southwestern edge of the trail make it a clear choice for watching storm waves thunder into the coast—especially at high tide and as the sun drops below the horizon. The cracks and joints along the rocky coastline make for effective leading lines and foregrounds, but a keen eye will catch blossoming beach pea growing in June, sea lavender from July to September, and New England aster from August to September to include in your frame as well. A **wide-angle** to **normal lens** coupled with a **polarizer** and **graduated neutral density filter** will enable you to not only include ample foreground, but also ensure the best color saturation and exposure levels during a brilliant sunset.

To freeze an exploding wave, use a faster shutter speed (e.g., 1/100th of a second). Keep an eye on slowing shutter speeds as the light levels fall with the setting sun, and if necessary, increase your ISO speed to enable you to freeze the motion. To blur the action instead, set your shutter speed to 1/4th second or slower. Either way, time your snap of the shutter for precisely the moment the wave makes contact with the land and continue to shoot through the receding waves to record silky waterfalls flowing back into the ocean.

As you photograph along the rocky coastline, stay a safe distance away from the cliff edge and watch for sneaker waves. If it is windy, as it often is on this exposed peninsula, bring an extra **lens cloth** to keep your lens free from sea spray during your outing.

Dew collects on New England asters along the shoreline. Canon 5DMII, 100mm macro, ISO 400, f/6.3 at 1/125th sec.

Wonderland Trail

Utopia of cobble, tidal creatures, wildflowers, and wildlife

TIME OF YEAR	**TIME OF DAY**	**TIDE**	**HIKE**
Year-round	*Late morning to early afternoon*	*Minus low*	*Moderate*

At low tide, sea snails rest upon rockweed along the shoreline on the Wonderland Trail. Canon 5DMII, 100mm macro, ISO 100, f/32 at 4 sec.

As the name implies, the Wonderland Trail reveals bountiful close-up photogenic scenes as the mostly level old fire road weaves through an enchanting forest of white spruce and jack pine. The tide pools and sand patterns waiting at the end of the trail during the minus low tide may tempt you to rush straight to the shoreline, but take some time to explore the evergreen branches draped with old man's beard lichen as well as an array of picturesque mosses along the beginning part of the forested path.

Before setting out on the easy-going, 1.4-mile (2.3-km) round-trip trail, stuff your **macro** and **telephoto lens** into your camera bag to prepare to record a magical world of details. **Extension tubes** can help magnify the little wonders you find. Sunny mid-day light often results in extreme contrast in images, so also bring along a **reflector**, **diffuser**, and/or **flash** to balance the highlights and shadows unless a blanket of clouds persist overhead.

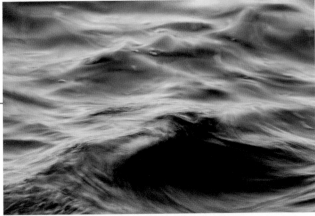

Waves reflect sunset light in the Atlantic Ocean. Canon 5DMII, 100-400mm at 400mm, ISO 400, f/13 at 1/8th sec.

Directions

As you walk towards the strengthening sounds of the ocean, peer to the right to view a cobble beach where a broad diversity of speckled granite intermixes with darker volcanic rocks. Where the end of the tree-lined peninsula juts out into the Atlantic Ocean, one of the largest stands of shrubby beach roses in the park appears (which bloom during July and August). The Cranberry Isles come into view in the distance as you approach Bennet Cove on the eastern side of the small cape, where pockets of tide pools teem with abundant aquatic life during receding waters. Brightly-colored starfish and spiny sea urchins turn up in the intertidal zone during the lowest of low tides, while even a normal low tide exposes rockweed, barnacles, and other marine life.

Keen observers might also spot remnants of lost fishing gear like mangled lobster pots, ropes, foam buoys, and other household items washed up in a previous high tide. Feel free to study through your lens, but keep in mind it is illegal to remove these manmade relics—as well as natural objects—from the park.

The abundance of details will no doubt keep your shutter finger working throughout the day, but keep an eye on the sky (and your telephoto lens handy) in case one of the area's bald eagles decides to take flight. To ensure you snap a perfect exposure of the regal bird at the decisive moment, anticipate where the action might take place and then take test shots to confirm the appropriate exposure settings for the existing conditions. Setting a faster ISO speed (like ISO 400) and a wide aperture (such as f/5.6 or f/8) will keep your shutter speeds fast enough to freeze moving wings.

High winds often barrel through the exposed point. While a **tripod** may sound like a logical piece of equipment to bring, handholding your camera with a faster ISO speed setting, and enabling the vibration reduction or image stabilization feature, may result in sharper photographs in these blustery conditions.

From the intersection of Main Street and West Street in Bar Harbor, travel south on Main Street for 0.3 miles (0.5 km). Turn right onto Mount Desert Street (which turns into Route 233/Eagle Lake Road). Drive 6.3 miles (10.1 km) and turn right onto Route 198 (also referred to as Sound Drive and Route 3) when you reach the T-intersection. Continue traveling about 1.4 miles (2.3 km). Turn left onto Route 102/Main Street and proceed another 8.6 miles (13.8 km). Turn left onto Route 102A and then travel 1.6 miles (2.6 km) before turning left to follow Route 102A. Drive 1.1 miles (1.8 km) to the signed Wonderland Trailhead parking lot. The trail begins on the southeast end of the paved parking area.

Seawall Picnic Area

Discover geological gems, intertidal life, and sea ducks from beach

TIME OF YEAR	TIME OF DAY	TIDE	HIKE
Year-round	*Sunrise to late morning*	*Minus low or high*	*Easy*

TOP: Low tide exposes dark volcanic rock along the coastline at Seawall. Canon 5DMII, 16-35mm at 16mm, ISO 50, f/22 at 13 sec., four-stop graduated neutral density filter.
OPPOSITE: Ice covers seaweed in the intertidal zone revealed at low tides. Canon 5DMII, 100mm macro, ISO 100, f/22 at 1.3 sec., reflector, diffuser.

Located near the southernmost point on MDI, this spot takes its name from the natural seawall of rocks visible to the east of the picnic area. For ages, large storm waves have folded high over the natural embankment, depositing boulders of all shapes and sizes on shore. Despite the relatively flat surrounding terrain, when incoming high tides coincide with squally weather, Seawall makes a great place to watch Mother Nature at work.

In sharp contrast to the characteristic granite cliffs along much of the Acadian coastline, here the gently sloping volcanic landscape casually slipping into the open ocean offers a fresh look for those seeking broad scenic compositions at sunrise. A row of towering spruce trees separates the rocky coast from the forest and serves as an effective leading line while using a **wide-angle lens**. When including ample sky, add a **graduated neutral density filter** over your lens to maintain consistent exposure across your composition.

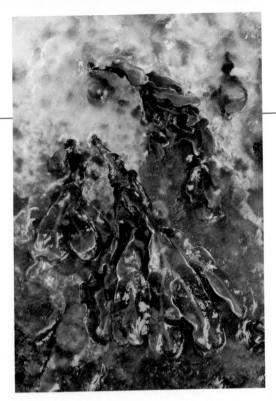

Directions

From the intersection of Main Street and West Street in Bar Harbor, travel south on Main Street for 0.3 miles (0.5 km). Turn right onto Mount Desert Street (which turns into Route 233/Eagle Lake Road). Drive 6.3 miles (10.1 km) and turn right onto Route 198 (also referred to as Sound Drive and Route 3) when you reach the T-intersection. Continue traveling about 1.4 miles (2.3 km). Turn left onto Route 102/Main Street and proceed another 7 miles (11.3 km). Turn left onto Route 102A/Seawall Road (follow the signs to the Seawall Campground) and then travel 3.1 miles (5 km). Turn left into the Seawall Picnic Area (the campground is directly across the street on the right).

Although a **polarizer** will also increase the apparent saturation in the sky and the water, watch for uneven polarization (when one part of the sky turns noticeably darker than the rest) in the area of the sky sitting at an angle of 90-degrees from the sun. Also referred to as banding, this unsightly effect commonly occurs when using wide focal lengths since the angle of view exceeds the effective angle of polarization. To resolve, either turn the filter at slight increments until the variation disappears or change to a **normal focal length lens**.

Keep an eye out to sea, particularly during the winter months, when sea ducks flock to the calm waters. A **telephoto lens**, **teleconverter**, **flash**, and **Flash X-tender™** will help record a common eider paddling nonchalantly by, a bufflehead or red-breasted merganser flaunting its striking plumage, or a cormorant showing off its fishing skills.

As the tide recedes, momentary tide pools appear between boulders slathered with rockweed, barnacles, and periwinkles to reveal a magical, colorful display at minus low tide. A **macro lens** proves most useful in studying the finer details of captivating rock textures and intertidal zone life. If you decide to shoot beyond the Golden Hour of sweet, warm sunrise light, aim a gold reflector into the shadows of your scene to create an attractive light within your composition. In sunny conditions, a diffuser positioned overhead will provide even illumination similar to what you would find on a cloudy day.

After exhausting your opportunities along this rocky shore, walk about 0.25 miles (0.4 km) to the east and cross the street to the Seawall Pond to extend your photo outing.

Low sweet blueberry turns a showy red along the eastern granite coastline of the Schoodic Peninsula. Canon 5DMII, 16-35mm at 16mm, ISO 100, f/13 at 0.8 sec., three-stop graduated neutral density filter.

Schoodic Peninsula

Schoodic Peninsula

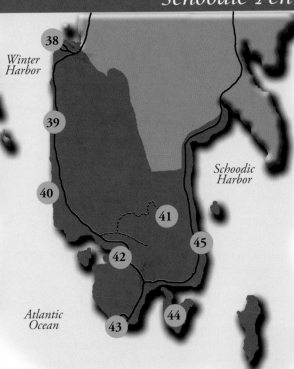

Winter Harbor

Schoodic Harbor

Atlantic Ocean

38 Frazer Point Picnic Area ... 152

39 Schoodic Drive (West) 158

40 Ravens Nest 160

41 Schoodic Head 164

42 West Pond Cove 166

43 Schoodic Point 172

44 Little Moose Island 178

45 Schoodic Drive (East) 182

Key:
————— = Major road
– – – – = Dirt/gravel road

Colorful pre-sunrise light along the east side of the Schoodic Peninsula. Canon 5DMII, 16-35mm at 16mm, ISO 200, f/13 at 0.3 sec., four-stop graduated neutral density filter.

Schoodic Peninsula Introduction

Often called "the quiet side of Acadia," the National Park Service estimates that only about 10% of Acadia National Park visitors make it out to experience the Schoodic Peninsula. Solitude and serenity along one of the park's most unspoiled, dramatic coastlines rewards those who make the 44-mile (70.8-km) drive from downtown Bar Harbor on MDI.

Although a new campground (called Schoodic Woods) is currently in the planning stages on the north side of Acadia, no lodging, camping, dining, or other services exist within the Schoodic Peninsula's park boundaries. As such, many visitors base themselves out of Bar Harbor and simply make a day-trip to the only part of the park residing on the mainland. However, the nearby small towns of Winter Harbor, Birch Harbor, and Prospect Harbor offer limited, but convenient, lodging and dining options to those photographers wishing spend extended time exploring this area. Like MDI, many restaurants and other tourist-based services shut down during the winter months.

If you choose to drive a vehicle from late June to early September, first stop by the Schoodic Peninsula Visitor Center before entering the park. Located en route at 10 Newman Street in Winter Harbor, it is the perfect place to pick up informational brochures and delicious homemade fudge for your ride.

After turning onto Moore Road and driving 1.4 miles (2.3 km) to the park entrance, the visitor's first introduction to the Schoodic Peninsula comes at the Frazer Point Picnic Area. The park does not collect an entrance fee to visit this part of Acadia.

From here, the 5.6-mile (9-km) one-way road meanders along granite-lined beaches and spruce-fir forests on this 2,300-plus-acre (931-hectares) gorgeous piece of secluded land. A quick side-trip on a dirt road whisks you up to the 440-foot (134.2-m) headland called Schoodic Head. Another short diversion from the loop road leads to Schoodic Point, where crashing waves, sea ducks, and intriguing geology await. Before rejoining the main road, stop by the Schoodic Education

The rising sun transforms the barnacle-encrusted granite rocks into a glowing spectacle on the Schoodic Peninsula's east side. Canon 5DMII, 16-35mm at 16mm, ISO 100, f/16 at 2 sec., two-stop graduated neutral density filter.

A clearing winter snowstorm leaves behind a blanket of white along Arey Cove. Canon 5DMII, 24-105mm at 28mm, ISO 100, f/16 at 1/20th sec., polarizer.

and Research Center (SERC) to visit the small welcome center at the historic Rockefeller Building. Upon exiting the park on the equally scenic eastern side, visitors will need to drive an additional 5.2 miles (8.4 km) to return to Frazer Point, making the entire loop around the peninsula a memorable 10.8-mile (17.4-km) endeavor.

A convenient alternative to driving, the Bar Harbor-Winter Harbor Ferry provides passenger ferry services from—you guessed it—Bar Harbor to Winter Harbor seven days a week from late June to late September. To check the current schedule and rates for this water taxi, visit **downeastwindjammer.com/cruises/bar-harbor-ferry**.

Upon your arrival at the Winter Harbor Marina, the seasonal and free-of-charge Island Explorer shuttle bus drives visitors to and from Schoodic Point. Bring a bike to freely cycle the entire loop at a more leisurely pace. Watch your time, though, so you successfully catch the ferry back to Bar Harbor!

A lone pine tree grows on the rocky coastline near Blueberry Hill parking area. Canon 5DMII, 24-105mm at 55mm, ISO 100, f/9 at 2 sec., two-stop graduated neutral density filter.

Frazer Point Picnic Area

Serene harbor, wooden pier, and granite ledges offer Schoodic introduction

TIME OF YEAR	TIME OF DAY	TIDE	HIKE
Year-round	Sunset	Mid to high	Easy

A fiery winter sky erupts over Frazer Point in February. Canon 5DMII, 16-35mm at 16mm, ISO 50, f/22 at 13 sec., four-stop graduated neutral density filter.

$\mathcal{T}$he name "Frazer Point" honors one of the first recorded non-Native American settlers to this area, Thomas Frazer, an African-American who operated a salt works nearby in the late 1700s. A perceptive eye can pick out the stone structural remains embedded in the grass in the parking loop's center.

A visitor's first introduction to the Schoodic Peninsula comes immediately after crossing the Mosquito Harbor Bridge. Substantial tidal waterfalls flowing from freshwater Frazer Creek collide with the saltwater in Mosquito Harbor during the changing water levels. Thankfully, its name is not an indication of the amount of pesky mosquitoes here, as a lack of standing water and the consistent ocean breeze typically keep them at bay much of the year.

Grab a **wide-angle** or **normal lens**, **polarizer**, **graduated neutral density filter**, **tripod**, and **cable release** and then head to the north side of the picnic area. An elongated wooden pier extends into the serene cove and creates a logical leading line in either a horizontal or a vertical orientation. Although shooting from one side or the other creates a dynamic line across

your frame, do not hesitate to break the compositional rules by centering the walkway in your photo. Tightly compose and scan the edges of your frame when pointing your camera to the north to ensure the homes and buildings of Winter Harbor across the water do not inadvertently appear in your photo.

If photographing natural scenes of the Schoodic coastline suits your fancy, then instead mosey towards the western shoreline. As you progress down the shoreline, multi-hued, speckled granite benches with boulders resting on top provide not only excellent foreground for broad landscapes, but also endless subject matter for more intimate studies of patterns and shapes with a **macro** or **telephoto lens**.

The protected harbor and relatively flat terrain means the ocean's waters rarely crash into the coastline featured here. Instead, the waves casually roll into the gently-sloped beach, much as they do at Pretty Marsh Picnic Area (see page 136) on MDI. As such, use a slow ISO speed and a **neutral density filter** to slow your shutter speed enough to record the motion of this slow-moving surf.

Because of the point's west-facing orientation, photographers will experience the setting sun draping shaping sidelight across the rocky terrain throughout the entire year. However, around both the winter and summer solstices, when the sun's azimuth falls at its most extreme angles, use a **lens shade**, your hand, or a hat to protect your lens from lens flare. The Birch Harbor and Buck Cove mountains (which are not located within the park's boundary), as well as healthy stands of evergreen and deciduous trees, keep this spot in shadow for much of the morning.

Directions

From the intersection of Route 186 and Main Street in Winter Harbor, travel east on Route 186 for 0.5 miles (0.8 km). Turn right onto Moore Road at the signed entrance to Acadia National Park. Drive an additional 1.6 miles (2.6 km) and then turn right into the Frazer Point Picnic Area.

Winter encases rockweed along the shore in ice. Canon 5DMII, 100mm macro, ISO 100, f/22 at 0.8 sec.

Fish Sandwiches

"The more I learn, the more I realize how much I don't know."
~Albert Einstein

$\mathcal{A}$s I was driving through Winter Harbor on a chilly November morning, an unusually large collection of buoys artfully arranged and tacked to the side of a cedar-shingled brown house piqued my interest. Hoping to photograph the scene but not necessarily trespass on private property, I pulled over and then cautiously sauntered across the grassy yard for a closer look.

Three or four snaps later, I knew I needed to respectfully seek permission from the owner to continue exploring all this vibrant scene had to offer. As I made my way towards the front of the house, a clatter emerged from the garage. Immediately thereafter, a gentleman with a friendly face shuffled into his driveway among his parked cars.

"Excuse me, sir?" I called out to him while walking slowly towards him.

"Oh yes, hello. How are you?" he gently responded.

"I'm wonderful. How are you?"

After exchanging pleasantries, I inquired, "Say, would you mind if I photographed the side wall of your house? I'm from Arizona and I have never seen anything like it!"

He smiled and replied, "Oh no, of course not. In fact, lots of photographers come by to photograph them."

As he began walking towards the decorated side of the wooden structure with me as his shadow, he continued, "I can tell you where each one came from."

Standing in front of the fishing remnants of all shapes and sizes, he launched into a thorough history lesson of where he had located each buoy. After a few minutes, he then introduced himself as Wes Shaw, the Winter Harbor Harbormaster.

After several minutes more of casual conversation, he asked, "Say, I'm planning to sail over to Bar Harbor to check on things in Frenchman Bay and to get a fish sandwich. Would you like to come with me? I could show and tell you more about the area."

Without hesitation, I replied enthusiastically, "Certainly!"

"Meet me at the town dock in a half hour."

"Deal!"

As he disappeared into his home and I returned to my parked car, I realized I did not have the first clue as to where the town dock resided. Giddy with excitement, though, I traveled up and down all of the roads I knew in Winter Harbor to find out. Unsuccessful in finding our meeting place, I drove up to

TOP: Harbor seals rest along a rocky outcropping revealed at low tide in Frenchman Bay. Canon 5D, 100-400mm at 400mm, ISO 125, f/5.6 at 1/400th sec.
OPPOSITE: Colorful buoys on the side of Wes Shaw's garage in Winter Harbor. Canon 5D, 24-105mm at 40mm, ISO 125, f/4 at 1/50th sec., polarizer.

the Winter Harbor 5 & 10 Cent Store. I poked my head into shop to ask the owner, Peter Drinkwater, "Where is the town dock? I'm to meet Wes there in a half hour."

As Peter outlined clear directions, it occurred to me that I was about to get on a boat with someone I had spoken with for merely 10 minutes. I felt more comfortable that someone I knew had an idea of what I was about to do—travel across the bay to Bar Harbor with a complete stranger to get a fish sandwich for lunch.

Within a few short minutes, I arrived at the dock ahead of schedule. I collected my warm clothes and my camera gear before heading to the edge of the pier. About 12 feet (3.7 m) below, a C-Dory called "C-Nile" swayed in the outgoing tide along a small wooden dock. Wes peeked his head out from the small craft and waved. In my excitement, I was early for our appointment, but Wes had beaten me there. I climbed down the slippery, seaweed-covered wooden ladder to join him.

Wes' intriguing lessons started the second I loaded my gear onto the C-Nile. While he addressed his final preparations, he shared the history of his prized craft. Once we pulled away from the Winter Harbor dock, Wes started our foray by explaining the stacks of lobster crates on top of floating docks nearby. Then, as we motored past the Mark Harbor Light (also known as the Winter Harbor Light), he shared the celebrated history and the extent of the recent renovations the current owners had made. Afterwards, he sailed along the Schoodic Peninsula's jagged western coastline to point out a prominent perch called the Ravens Nest (see page 123). When he turned the C-Nile westward towards Bar Harbor, he expressed curiosity in how an osprey had oddly made a nest atop the channel marker this season. I felt like I had just opened the local's copy of the encyclopedia!

Crossing the calm waters of Frenchman Bay, he knew exactly where the harbor seals enjoyed a nap and swim during low tide. No sea creatures appeared on a small rocky ledge in

Fish Sandwiches (continued)

the middle of the bay at this moment, but Wes said with some confidence, "Perhaps on the way back, they'll be hanging around there. We'll check on the way back."

After navigating beyond the handful of tiny islands offshore from Grindstone Neck and into the open waters of Frenchman Bay, Wes started to enlighten me about his time in the area. While we continued motoring across the calm waters, he began enlightening me with his stories about his own days past. Pride swelled in his eyes and his already jovial smile enlarged when he spoke of his experiences with his beloved company, the MDI Water Taxi and Launch Service.

Although he sold the charter business in 2006, he spent 30 years taxiing celebrities from their palatial "cottages" in Northeast and Southwest harbors to various places and events. He spoke fondly of his times smoking cigarettes on the dock with Liz Taylor. He relayed how he helped Ted Kennedy Jr. acquire a new prosthetic leg. He talked about motoring Martha Stewart to dinner just days before allegations of insider trading hit the airwaves. He reminisced—with a chuckle—about watching Walter Cronkite get refused service at a lobster pound because it had closed early. His tales were as plentiful—and in some cases, as colorful!—as the buoys hanging on the side of his house.

I hung onto every word Wes shared as we toured around the bay for two hours. When we arrived at the pier in Bar Harbor, they greeted Wes like an icon. Everyone knew him!

I commented, "Wes, this isn't the first time you've traveled to Bar Harbor for a fish sandwich, is it?"

The unpretentious Harbor Master responded, "Oh no, I've done this many times. I like to pick up fish sandwiches after I've checked on things in the bay."

We strolled the short distance from the dock to Galyn's, where we ordered two fish sandwiches to go from the bar upstairs and then brought them back to enjoy on his boat.

Wes sharing one of his favorite stories aboard the C-Nile in Bar Harbor. Canon 5D, 24-105mm at 24mm, ISO 160, f/5.6 at 1/100 sec.

A fully loaded fishing boat in Bar Harbor. Canon 5D, 100-400mm at 260mm, ISO 125, f/5.6 at 1/400th sec., polarizer.

Immediately, I pulled my camera out of my backpack and began photographing our meal. "What are you taking a picture of?" Wes asked with curiosity.

I replied, "I am photographing you and the fish sandwich so I can remember this forever! You may do this all the time, but I've never hopped in a boat and traveled across the ocean just to get a fish sandwich before! What a hoot!"

We shared more laughs and continued to enjoy our lunch as the boat rocked to the rolling waves at the dock.

On the way back, as Wes promised, we stopped at the seal hangout. Lo and behold, the expanded rocky outcropping revealed at low tide was littered with resting and frolicking harbor seals. Occasionally, one or two would inquisitively glance at the boat only to quickly ignore us and resume its play in the gentle surf. Wes graciously positioned the C-Nile such that I could photograph the animals with a telephoto lens aimed into the sun to achieve backlighting.

Before day turned to night, Wes steered the C-Nile back to the Winter Harbor dock. I brought home many images from our memorable afternoon adventure across Frenchman Bay, but I was more grateful for the experience and time spent with a new friend. It was Wes—by sharing his rich collection of stories and in-depth knowledge—who thankfully showed me that I had just begun to scratch the surface of Acadia and its surroundings. It only made me want to learn more.

Four years after our quest for fish sandwiches, I delightfully learned that Wes had started a new touring company, where he now shares his passion for sailing, unbelievable stories, and local knowledge with a broader audience. For more information about his tours, visit **winterharborwatertaxiandtours.com**.

Schoodic Drive (West)

Unprecedented sunset views of Schoodic's pristine granite coastline

TIME OF YEAR	TIME OF DAY	TIDE	HIKE
Year-round	Sunset; night	Mid to high	Easy

An ephemeral waterfall caused by the passing storm falls onto a cobble beach along the west side of Schoodic Drive. Canon 5DMII, 24-105mm at 35mm, ISO 100, f/22 at 0.3 sec., polarizer.

Schoodic Drive goes by many names, including Schoodic Loop Road, Big Moose Road, Maine Scenic Byway, and Schoodic National Scenic Byway (**www.schoodicbyway.org**). Maps also referred to it as Moore Road, which honors the original property owner and first builder of this scenic thoroughfare, John G. Moore. No matter what you call it, one can sum up the experience of photographing along this loop at sunset with just one word: amazing!

The Civilian Conservation Corps established a presence on the peninsula under Franklin D. Roosevelt's New Deal program in the 1930s to support the construction of the U. S. Navy communications station at the southern tip of the Schoodic Peninsula (when John D. Rockefeller Jr. constructed MDI's Park Loop Road). Today, the paved 6-mile (9.7-km) loop circles some of the most pristine woodland and coastline found within this national park.

The western section offers intimate views of the restored Mark Island Light (also referred to as the Winter Harbor Light) and Frenchman Bay with MDI in the distance along an untouched granite coastline so characteristic of Acadia. Since the road becomes one-way after Frazer Point Picnic Area, consider allocating extra time to scout each of the pullouts first and then follow Schoodic Drive back around to your favorite locations.

To photograph the striking 150-year old (but now inactive) Mark Island Light from the various pullouts, use a telephoto lens with a wide-aperture (such as f/5.6 or f/8). Keep your shutter speed at least as fast as "1/focal length of your lens" (e.g., if using a 400 mm lens, the shutter speed should be 1/400th of a second or faster) or use a tripod instead to prevent the camera from shaking during foggy or low-lighting conditions.

Along the entire length of the wooded shoreline, rock outcroppings isolated by high tides turn into prominent seaweed-adorning stones at low tides. During the winter months, sometimes the tide change is not significant enough to melt the accumulated snow perched on top of these boulders, making the granite clusters look like oversized cupcakes topped with thick white icing.

Because of its isolation from large cities with artificial lights, the western Schoodic Peninsula shoreline is one of the best locations in the park to photograph the Milky Way and star trails during a clear night sky. Consult the Photographer's Ephemeris (www.photoephemeris.com) to determine which days during your visit will provide either a moonless night or a quickly-setting crescent moon. However, before setting out on an astrophotography shoot here, scout the area in daylight hours and bring a headlamp or flashlight to light your way in the dark.

A wide-angle lens that allows an f/2.8 or f/4 aperture setting works best to record the cosmos. To photograph moving stars, set your camera to Bulb mode and use a lower ISO speed setting like ISO 100 or 200. Then, trigger the shutter remotely using a locking cable release for at least a one- to two-hour exposure (if not longer). Alternatively, to snap frozen stars or the Milky Way floating above the landscape, keep your shutter speeds faster (e.g., 30 seconds or less) by increasing your ISO speed setting to ISO 1600 or 3200 with a wide aperture.

Directions

From the intersection of Route 186 and Main Street in Winter Harbor, travel east on Route 186 for 0.5 miles (0.8 km). Turn right onto Moore Road at the signed entrance to Acadia National Park. After driving 1.8 miles (2.9 km), a number of paved and dirt pullouts exist on the right side of the road for parking.

A granite boulder hosts frozen rockweed during the winter. Canon 5DMII, 100mm macro, ISO 100, f/16 at 2.5 sec.

Ravens Nest

Soaring, aerial-like view of rugged cliffs and Frenchman Bay

TIME OF YEAR	TIME OF DAY	TIDE	HIKE
April to November	*Sunset*	*Mid to high*	*Moderate*

TOP: *Rugged cliffs of the Ravens Nest greet crashing ocean waves. Canon 5DMII, 16-35mm at 35mm, ISO 100, f/11 at 0.8 sec., polarizer, two-stop graduated neutral density filter.*
OPPOSITE: *The setting sun drops behind Cadillac Mountain on Mount Desert Island as viewed from the Ravens Nest area. Canon 5DMII, 16-35mm at 16mm, ISO 100, f/18 at 2.5 sec., four-stop graduated neutral density filter.*

*L*ocated on the rugged western shoreline of "the quiet side of Acadia," the Ravens Nest might be the park's best-kept secret and one of Schoodic Peninsula's most photogenic locations at sunset. Given Acadia's style for obvious, descriptive names, even a quick visit will help you understand from where the "Ravens Nest" label originated.

A short stroll along a faint social path reveals stunning aerial-like views as if you were a soaring bird peering down at steep, jagged granite cliffs dramatically dropping into the ever-changing tidal flows of the sea below. To the south, a small, rocky perch overlooks the striking rock formations, while the north end showcases a sheer ravine plunging from the precipice.

A mid- to high tide fills your composition's middle ground with swirling and crashing waves while also keeping the fallen rocks visible enough to create a well-balanced arrangement.

Whether you utilize a **wide-angle lens** to include the sky or a **telephoto lens** to hone in on the detailed wave action, use a slower shutter speed (e.g., around 1/4th of a second) to create a sense of motion while recording silky textures in the water. The slow speeds, combined with the low light of sunset and possible windy conditions in this exposed location, necessitates the use of a tripod and cable release to keep the camera steady and your images tack sharp.

A **polarizer** will reduce the shine from the rocks and increase the saturation in both the land and sky. From May to August, though, watch for uneven polarization in your frame due to the position of the setting sun. No matter the timing of your visit, a graduated neutral density filter will hold back light in the sky to keep exposures balanced with the land.

As you wander around the Ravens Nest, protect the fragile ecosystem by staying on the existing paths. With no guardrails or fences present, be extremely cautious of your footing around the steep cliffs in any season, but especially when water or ice is present. Shutterbugs with a fear of heights might skip this location altogether.

Directions

From the intersection of Route 186 and Main Street in Winter Harbor, travel east on Route 186 for 0.5 miles (0.8 km). Turn right onto Moore Road at the signed entrance to Acadia National Park. Drive 3.1 miles (5 km) and park in the small, unmarked dirt pullout on the left side of the road. Walk across the road and follow the faint path, which begins on the southwest side of the road, no more than 100 yards (91.4 m) to the cliffs.

The setting sun bathes the rocky western shoreline near the Ravens Nest. Canon 5DMII, 16-35mm at 16mm, ISO 50, f/22 at 13 sec., four-stop graduated neutral density filter.

Schoodic Head

360-degree views from the summit of Schoodic's tallest mountain

TIME OF YEAR	TIME OF DAY	TIDE	HIKE
May to October	*Sunrise to late morning*	*N/A*	*Moderate*

Jacque Miniuk pauses to admire the view from a clearing along the East Trail near Schoodic Head. Canon 5DMII, 24-105mm at 28mm, ISO 400, f/13 at 1/60 sec., polarizer, two-stop graduated neutral density filter, flash at -1 TTL.

$\mathcal{A}$s the Civilian Conservation Corps assisted in building the United States Navy's new radio communications station on Big Moose Island near the southern tip of the Schoodic Peninsula, the same hardworking labor also constructed four hiking trails nearby: the Schoodic Head, East, Anvil, and Alder trails. All but the Alder Trail lead to the peninsula's highest point within the park, Schoodic Head, at 440 feet (134.1 m) elevation. Ambitious photographers will enjoy exploring these moderately difficult paths in their entirety, but those short on time can get a quick taste of what each offers by driving to the top on the maintained Schoodic Head Road.

A soaring vista across Frenchman Bay to Cadillac Mountain on MDI, a mere 5 miles (8.1 km) away as the crow flies, greets visitors on the west side of the parking area. The surrounding foliage stays in shadow as the sun's first light of the day slowly illuminates the mountainous terrain of the distant isle, tree-topped islands, and the Mark Island Lighthouse. To add depth

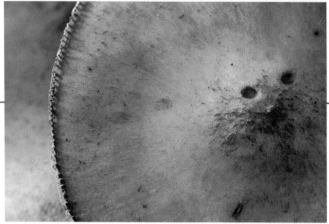

Macro detail of a mushroom head found along the Schoodic Head Trail. Canon 5DMII, 100mm macro, ISO 100, f/8 at 1.6 sec., flash at -2 TTL.

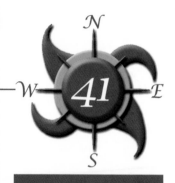

Directions

From the intersection of Route 186 and Main Street in Winter Harbor, travel east on Route 186 for 0.5 miles (0.8 km). Turn right onto Moore Road at the signed entrance to Acadia National Park. Drive 3.8 miles (6.1 km) and then turn left at the unmarked, dirt Schoodic Head Road. Continue 0.2 miles (0.3 km) until the road splits. Veer left at the split onto an unmarked dirt road and drive an additional 0.8 miles (1.3 km) until the road ends at the parking area (RVs are not permitted on this stretch). Follow the East Trail, which begins on the east side of the parking area.

The Schoodic Head Road closes to motorized vehicles from December to mid-April.

and dimension to your composition, use these trees as a frame around your scene with a **wide-angle** or **normal length lens** paired with a polarizer. To ensure the foreground vegetation, as well as the distant landscapes, possess sharp detail in your final photo, use a smaller aperture (like f/16 or f/22) and set your focus point to the hyperfocal distance. Should you need slow shutter speeds, set your camera on a tripod to keep your images sharp.

An even better glimpse of this scene, as well as an expansive overlook to the east towards the fishing villages of Prospect Harbor and Corea, awaits atop open granite ledges a short five- to ten-minute stroll on the East Trail.

Although a healthy mix of spruce, fir, and Jack pines—which appear here at the southern-most extent of their growing habitat—obscures the view for much of the route, the path bustles with rich details best photographed through a **macro** or **telephoto lens**. Pincushion moss grows at the base of boulders encrusted with multi-colored patterns of lichen. Scattered delicate wildflowers bloom throughout the spring and summer. Fantastical bulbous mushrooms sprout under the canopy from late summer and into autumn. After discovering an intriguing subject, tame harsh contrasty light by using a **reflector** to add light into the shadows or a **diffuser** to create even light across your entire scene.

Even when clouds obscure the sun's rays, avoid recording flat, shapeless light on your chosen subject by using a technique called the "Reverse Boston Salute." As the silly name implies, raise your hand and drop your middle finger to your palm, leaving your other fingers raised to the sky. Turn your entire body in a 360-degree turn, carefully watching the magnitude of the shadow beneath your middle finger. Stop turning when the shadow appears the strongest. The sun's direction originates opposite of your finger. With this information in mind, position your camera to achieve visually appealing, shaping side or back light relative to your subject.

West Pond Cove

Fleeting ice formations transform serene cove into winter paradise

TIME OF YEAR	TIME OF DAY	TIDE	HIKE
December to March	*Late afternoon to sunset*	*Low to mid*	*Easy*

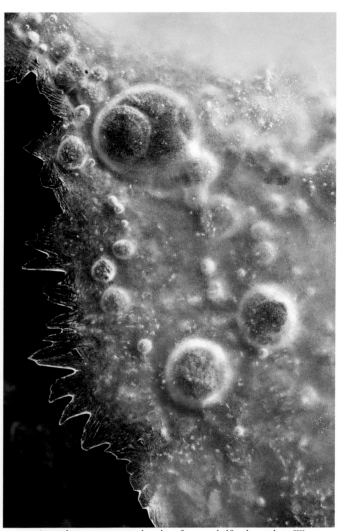

An explosive pattern on the edge of an ice shelf at low tide in West Pond Cove. Canon 5DMII, 100mm macro, ISO 100, f/20 at 0.6 sec., diffuser.

*T*he West Pond Cove exudes serenity throughout the year, but the spruce and fir-lined, protected inlet often remains overshadowed by grander, more striking, scenes along Schoodic Drive. Come winter, however, this tranquil bay transforms into a Mecca of fleeting ice formations, allowing photographers to record unparalleled, one-of-a-kind photographs.

When the sea waters chill after extended periods of bitterly cold weather, slick-looking grease ice forms in the slowly moving waters, followed by slush-like frazil, and then finally free-floating, circular pancake ice. In extremely frigid conditions, the high tide forms a thin layer of hexagonal ice patterns resembling the salt flat formations in Death Valley National Park's Badwater Basin. Similar to what occurs on the Mount Desert Narrows near Thompson Island (see page 48), as the tide recedes, the frozen layer lowers on top of the boulders. This leaves behind intriguing volcano-like shapes along the shore until the next high tide rolls in.

Because the scene constantly changes, arrive about 60 minutes before sunset with lenses ranging from **wide-angle** to **telephoto lenses**, as well as a **polarizer**, **graduated neutral density filter**, **tripod**, and **cable release** to explore the multitude of wintry photographic opportunities. Shoreline compositions

Directions

From the intersection of Route 186 and Main Street in Winter Harbor, travel east on Route 186 for 0.5 miles (0.8 km). Turn right onto Moore Road at the signed entrance to Acadia National Park. Drive 4.2 miles (6.8 km) and park in the paved pullout on the right side of the road.

through a **macro lens** reveal magical frosty patterns and shapes.

After you snap the shutter, if your images appear too blue (or subsequently you see a spike in your Blue channel on the far right side of your RGB histogram), warm your scene by setting your white balance to either the Cloudy or Shade setting to add a touch of orange to your photograph.

As the sun drops behind the forested Pond Island, sunbursts become a photogenic possibility. With your camera positioned to the west, remove all filters from the front of your lens and then set your camera to a small aperture (such as f/16 or f/22). Trigger the shutter as soon as the trees or clouds partially obscure the sun to render radiating rays.

Once the sun disappears, prepare your camera to record silhouettes as soon as the undersides of the clouds overhead illuminate. With your camera on spot meter, set your exposure meter to the "0" hash mark in your viewfinder or live LCD display while pointing your lens towards the sky. This setting will grab the gorgeous rich colors in the sky while underexposing the land, making the foreground appear black. A correctly exposed histogram while using this technique will indicate few highlights, some mid-tones, and an abundance of shadows.

As you explore the area, watch your step on the ice. Do not venture far off the shore since the tidal flow beneath the ice remains active constantly, but out of view.

TOP: A thin layer of grease ice forms in supercooled ocean waters. Canon 5DMII, 24-105mm at 67mm, ISO 100, f/11 at 0.3 sec., polarizer.
RIGHT: A thin layer of pancake ice forms across the cove at high tide during frigid weather. Canon 5DMII, 16-35mm at 16mm, ISO 100, f/14 at 1/40th sec.

Season for Change

"No man ever steps in the same river twice, for it's not the same river and he's not the same man."

~Heraclitus

𝒰pon hearing my desire to visit Acadia time and time again, one of the questions people ask me most frequently is why I continue to return to the same park when there are so many other exciting places to see across the world. I will admit, it is the same question I asked myself when I applied for my third residency.

With no prior experience with the park, during my first residency, I set out to see all the popular places I had previously seen in other people's pictures—the iconic Boulder Beach, Cadillac Mountain, and Bass Harbor Head Lighthouse. Classic scenes such as these draw attention from visitors and photographers alike for good reason—they offer striking beauty. I wanted to see them with my own eyes, through my own lens, and attempt to put my own spin on these admired compositions in November when most people do not visit the park.

In sharp contrast, my second residency occurred in October, when the park bustles with "color chasers." I balanced my time between reworking the old classics and seeking out lesser-known locations. In both cases, the screaming autumn colors made the park's tableau glow every shade of red, orange, and yellow imaginable. The seasonal shift also made it very difficult to make a bad image so long as you had your camera turned on.

After each visit, I brought home more questions than answers and more ideas than photographs. As my understanding and emotional connection with the park increased, I wanted to record a more complete visual by exploring even more new locations on a more profound, creative level. I wanted to find the smaller, less obvious things that contributed to making the park so special.

When I considered applying for an unprecedented third Artist-in-Residency, I happened to come upon Heraclitus' quote: "No man ever steps in the same river twice, for it's not the same river and he's not the same man." In hopes I would have the chance to see how Acadia and I as an artist had changed from the previous years, I proceeded to submit my application. My fortunate third residency allowed me to rediscover the same park I loved so much in a new light and season—winter.

While ambling along the coastline throughout my four-week stay in January and February 2013, I still felt the same sense of awe I had experienced so many times before. However, I was not connecting well with grand landscape scenes. I still ventured out at sunrise, stood along Schoodic Drive's rugged eastern shoreline, pointed my camera south, set a small aperture, slapped a three-stop graduated neutral density filter across my lens, and voila! Within seconds of the first rays of the day, I would pocket very pleasant images of the gorgeous Acadian coastline. The morning process had become routine, my photographs safe, and my artistic voice quiet.

Only after I drove around the peninsula and casually meandered along the shaded western side would I see sights that stirred my soul! The various types of ice—frazil, grease, and pancake —collecting on the water's edge captivated me. Seeing this new fascination was not a matter of simply switching lenses or looking at other peoples' previous pictures. To find these special

OPPOSITE: Ice formations remaining after low tide beneath the stars at West Pond Cove. Canon 5DMII, 16-35mm at 16mm, ISO 1600, f/7.1 at 30 sec.

Season for Change (continued)

minute details, I had to follow my curiosity wherever it led me, knowing that if I expressed enthusiasm for a subject, I could make an emotionally charged image, which conveyed my own unique visual message.

Though I found focusing on the details enthralling, I found embracing my new voice exhausting. After three days of very successful photography outings under crystal clear blue skies—reproducible conditions I generally dislike when photographing broad scenes—I actually said aloud to myself, "This would be so much easier if I could just get a colorful sunrise or sunset."

I could not believe my own ears. But after the shock, it made perfect sense.

Making a pretty photograph on the Acadia coast—or other classic scenes like the Watchman in Zion National Park, Delicate Arch in Arches National Park, or Zabriskie Point in Death Valley National Park—is easy. Mother Nature has already painted the beautiful palette and hundreds upon thousands of people have already figured out the composition. "All" you have to do is show up, know how to operate your camera, and wait for a colorful sky. However, when it comes down to it, the repeatable photograph essentially represents the same documentary "trophy" shot other photographers have already snapped. Because of their remarkable beauty, I would encourage everyone to include these in their portfolio. However, I would also challenge you to look beyond them for your own artistic expression.

The dictionary defines the word "cliché" as "a trite, stereotyped expression…usually expressing a popular or common thought or idea, that has lost originality, ingenuity, and impact by long overuse." As an artist, this is not how I want people to describe my photographic work or style. Is this how you want others to describe your photography? I doubt it.

Requiring more time, effort, and emotional involvement, I was determined to find a different creative expression I could call my own during my winter stay. The evening before Winter Storm Nemo stopped by, the Maine coast experienced remarkably frigid, but clear and calm weather conditions. I felt I had two options for my imminent sunset outing. One, I could photograph the "sure-thing" at Schoodic Point (see page 172), where I knew I could make great landscape-style images of waves crashing against the granite ledges with Cadillac Mountain as my scenic backdrop (something I had done at least 10 times over the course of my visits here). Or two, I could visit to less-known, less-flashy West Pond Cove (see page 166), where I could marvel over the bizarre ice formations at low tide with very little preconceived notions of what kind of photograph I might end up with at the end of the evening.

I chose option number two. The coast certainly made me feel alive, but the ice formations caused my soul to sing louder than it had sung before in the park. I had to listen to this.

When I arrived at the small bay, I started making images based solely on what was catching my eye. For about an hour, I photographed various perspectives of the ice, but did not necessarily create an image that represented the way I felt about my wonder. I did not let the lack of success bother me. No expectations meant I did not have to hit it out of the ballpark; I merely had to stand at the plate and keep swinging.

As the sun touch the horizon at the end of the day, I fell in love with a composition of the thin ice shelf collapsed into shapes I affectionately called "ice volcanoes." The voices in my head started up, "Dang! If I would have only found this scene 30 minutes earlier, I could have photographed it in direct light!"

Instead of focusing on what I could no longer control, I focused on the opportunities that lie ahead, "Now wait a second. These formations are otherworldly. What if I stayed here for another hour until the stars started to come out to show another world?"

As I chased fleeting ice during the course of my winter stint, I had learned quickly that if I saw a scene I liked, I had to shoot it right then and there. There was no waiting for "ideal" light. There were no second chances. Unlike stationary lighthouses and boulders, the ice melts, tides change, and snow covers the ice creating unreproducible moments and advantageously, photographs.

I quickly developed a technical visualization for the photo I wanted to create with the opportunity I had. I pulled out my fast wide-angle lens and set it to a wider aperture to allow enough light to enter the lens during the nighttime exposure. I also set a high ISO speed to keep my shutter speed fast enough such that the emerging stars appeared frozen overhead. I settled on a 30-second exposure at an ISO speed of 1600 and an aperture setting of f/7.1. (For full frame sensors, one can calculate the approximate number

A thin sheet of ice collapses on shoreline boulders, creating ice formations resembling mini-volcanoes. Canon 5DMII, 16-35mm at 35mm, ISO 100, f/20 at 1/4 sec.

of seconds in which the stars will appear to move in a photograph as 600/focal length of lens. For example, in order to freeze the stars with my 16mm lens, I needed to use a shutter speed equal to 37.5 seconds or faster.)

In addition to technical settings, I considered the current lighting conditions. No moon meant little light on the landscape. Little light meant a lack of distinguishable features and shapes in the landscape. No distinguishable features meant I needed to bring my own artificial light to create shape and draw attention to the intriguing ice mounds in the foreground. Once I defined my vision, I crossed my fingers the tide did not rise high enough on shore to erase the scene like an Etch-a-Sketch® drawing before I could make an image!

That evening's session proved that winter was truly a season a change for me. I realized I had previously relied on Mother Nature too heavily to provide the creative "juice" and had not been bringing enough of my own. Nothing excites me more than starting or ending the day with a miraculous fiery sky. I also fully appreciate all the opportunities nature has to offer —even clear blue skies. However, the natural settings are not enough always to complete an image; it is merely the start. By tapping into our individual backgrounds and passions, we create a distinctive expression that represents us as unique individuals. Since our interests grow and change over time as we gain knowledge and collect ideas, it also means we will never step in the same river no matter how many times we visit it.

Schoodic Point

Crashing waves and ample sea ducks where land meets the sea

TIME OF YEAR	TIME OF DAY	TIDE	HIKE
Year-round	*Sunrise and sunset*	*Mid to high, incoming*	*Easy*

The setting sun momentarily peeks out behind summer storm clouds to illuminate the granite rocks on Schoodic Point. Canon 5DMII, 16-35mm at 16mm, ISO 200, f/13 at 0.3 sec., four-stop graduated neutral density filter.

*I*nitially, the Schoodic Peninsula puts up a convincing facade. As the historic loop road gracefully hugs the rocky coastline and gently weaves beneath the crowns of evergreens, visitors may begin to truly feel the serene, peaceful ambiance "the quiet side of Acadia" offers. That is, until they reach Schoodic Point.

After stepping onto the sloping, house-sized pink granite slabs marbled with dark, volcanic diabase dikes, visitors will immediately sense the raw power from the rhythmic pounding of frothy surf unleashing against the land. Because of the Atlantic Ocean's unobstructed path to the spruce-lined, southernmost tip of the peninsula, Schoodic Point serves as one of the premiere places in the park to watch energized waves pummel the coast during incoming high tides and storms. However, stay a safe distance away from the cliff edge, as enormous rogue waves have swept unsuspecting people into the ocean here.

Bring a **wide-angle** to **normal-length lens**, **polarizer**, and **graduated neutral density filter** to shoot scenic photographs

of the promontory at sunrise or sunset. Also, pack a **telephoto lens** to record colorful silhouettes once the sun drops behind rounded Cadillac Mountain, which is visible to the west in the distance across Frenchman Bay. Remember to remove all your filters from your lens when shooting towards the sun.

Unrelenting high winds frequent the exposed peninsula tip, so while a **tripod** and **cable release** may sound like a logical choice, handholding your camera (with your image stabilization or vibration reduction feature enabled), paired with a fast shutter speed, may result in sharper images in breezy conditions. Before moving on to another composition, use your camera's image playback mode to check your image for sharpness (use the zoom function to hone in on the photo in detail). Reshoot the scene if the focus in your photo appears soft. You may need to increase your ISO speed to a faster setting, especially during cloudy or low lighting conditions around sunset.

When calm seas prevail, the protected Arey Cove to the east of the headland offers a first-class setting to observe sea-faring animals with a telephoto lens, **teleconverter**, **flash**, and **Flash X-tender™**. Year-round, gulls, common eiders, red-breasted mergansers, black guillemots, and scoters paddle along the shore while an occasional bald eagle scouts the area from the sky. In winter, harlequin ducks, common goldeneyes, common loons, great cormorants, horned and red-necked grebes, and buffleheads join the party. Harbor seals sometimes nap on the rockweed-covered rocks during low tide.

Should you have some extra time while visiting, stop by the Schoodic Education and Research Center campus to visit the small welcome center and to photograph the gorgeous Rockefeller Building, which Grosvenor Atterbury designed to mimic the style of the carriage road gatehouses located on MDI.

Directions

From the intersection of Route 186 and Main Street in Winter Harbor, travel east on Route 186 for 0.5 miles (0.8 km). Turn right onto Moore Road at the signed entrance to Acadia National Park. Drive 4.6 miles (7.4 km) and then veer right at the fork towards Schoodic Point. Continue 0.4 miles (0.6 km) until the road ends at the paved parking area.

In 2013, Winter Storm Nemo caused blustery conditions on the exposed Schoodic Point. Canon 5DMII, 100-400mm at 285mm, ISO 400, f/9 at 1/800th sec.

Nemo Leaves its Mark

"I am not afraid of storms, for I am learning to sail my ship."
~Louisa May Alcott

*T*he forecasters called the blizzard that hit the Northeast in early February 2013 many things, including the "storm of the century," "the worst blizzard since 1978," and even "Winter Storm Nemo." I was familiar with hurricanes receiving names, but winter storms getting labeled was a relatively new convention for me. According to their website, the Weather Channel decided to name significant winter storms for the 2012-2013 season to raise awareness.

While known by many as the cute fish character in the movie, *Finding Nemo*, the word "nemo" means remote. Remote I was on the Schoodic Peninsula in Acadia National Park during my winter residency. And essentially alone, as most workers returned to their homes by mid-afternoon, heeding the officials' blizzard and coastal flooding warnings. Before heading out himself, my neighbor stopped by on Thursday evening to ensure I had enough food and water to last me through Sunday and to advise that I stock up on any last minute supplies on Friday morning before staying put through the storm.

I woke at 4 a.m. on Friday morning, hoping to photograph Thunder Hole on MDI (see page 76) booming two hours prior to high tide in conjunction with the sunrise at 6:40 a.m. (which occurred on a single occasion during my residency—February 8—so I had only this one chance to photograph it). Dark, threatening clouds swirled overhead as I arrived at Ocean Drive. The ocean stood eerily still. Thunder Hole displayed not so much of even a spray, but rather an occasional small spit hinting at its capabilities, but certainly not living up to its name. No doubt, I was watching the proverbial calm before the storm.

Once the light snow flakes began to drop from the sky, I packed my gear and headed back to the Schoodic Peninsula. Heeding the locals and forecasters recommendations, I stopped at the market to pick up a jug of water, a loaf of bread, and peanut butter en route as emergency provisions.

While ushering my groceries into my apartment, park officials called to suggest that the ocean waves from Friday evening's and Saturday morning's high tide might cover the outbound road near Little Moose Island (see page 178). They had additional concerns about the inbound road flooding as well. I was wisely advised, "Plan to not drive at those times."

The problem was not simply the occurrence of the high tides or the incoming blizzard (which originated from two inland storms colliding over Boston). It was that the peak of the storm was forecasted to hit at precisely the same time two spring tides would occur (one on Friday night at 10.9 feet [3.3 m] and one on Saturday morning at 12.2 feet [3.7 m]) under a nearly new moon. Add another 4-foot-plus (1.2-m) storm surge and you have the recipe for elevated, killer waves. The severe coastal flooding, if occurred as predicted, would transform the Schoodic Peninsula into a temporary island with a population of one—me. From my perspective, this storm had all the makings of a thrilling experience! Rather than feel scared, I could not have been more excited to witness my first blizzard.

At the suite, as delicate flurries continued to dance outside, I fell into a ritual of monitoring the TV and internet news outlets as well as the weather-related apps on my iPhone. When will the storm arrive? How bad will it get? What will it look like?

As day turned to night, the news channels began reporting how large amounts of snow were pummeling Boston and New York and causing widespread power outages. Before retiring

Pines persist in high winds and swirling snow from the February 2013 nor'easter (called Winter Storm Nemo) on Schoodic Point. Canon 5DMII, 100-400mm at 170mm, ISO 400, f/9 at 1/800th sec.

to bed, I prepared for the worst-case scenario by piling all my warm winter clothes, my down sleeping bag (rated to 0-degrees Fahrenheit or -18-degrees Celsius), a stack of hand warmers, and two flashlights stocked with fresh batteries next to my bed.

I awoke in the middle of the night to blustery winds furiously rattling the building's windows and wooden frame. Unrelenting gusts continued throughout the night. By 8 a.m., a 3-foot (0.9-m) snow drift blocked my apartment's door. Nevertheless, I still had power.

Sipping my hot tea and enjoying my warm oatmeal breakfast, I peered outside the dining room window, captivated by the howling wind carelessly flinging cotton-ball puffs of snow every which way. A little itch nagged inside of me. I could not just sit and watch the blizzard. I needed to be IN the blizzard.

The voice of reason spoke softly, "Do you really want to feel uncomfortably cold and wind-blown? It's warm and cozy right where you are sitting!" I grabbed my telephoto lens and made a few images of the swaying trees out the window. After three snaps, I could not take it anymore. I had to be a part of it—sorry, voice of reason—and not just a comfortable bystander.

After all, the people who came before us weathered each storm without the benefit of today's amenities. The Wabanaki Indians who wandered the Acadian lands before the European settlers arrived, did not have television, radios, or iPhones to warn of impending doom. They also did not have an apartment heated to 72 degrees F (22.2 degrees C) where they could warm themselves. In their world, a blizzard was a blizzard. They connected with the natural rhythms and cycles in order to survive, in ways we as a modern society have long forgotten. As we enjoy our conveniences, our disconnection with our natural world grows.

That said, I choose to rely on modern survival solutions to venture into the outdoors safely. I dressed in three layers of winter clothes, such that the only part of me exposed to the elements were my eyes (in hindsight, I wish I had brought ski goggles). I stuffed hand warmers into my gloves, boots, and winter hat. I packed my fully-charged cell phone, my enabled SPOT™ tracking device, two Clif® Bars, and water. I promised myself that if, during

Nemo Leaves its Mark (continued)

my walk on Schoodic Drive towards Schoodic Point, waves even remotely threatened to cover the road, I must turn around immediately.

Considering the unforgettable photographic moments I was sure to encounter, I desperately wanted to take my whole camera bag along with me. Then I had visualizations of my gear blowing away in the high winds and snow filling the insides of my camera as I attempted to change lenses. Listening to the voice of reason this time, I instead popped a fresh battery and memory card into a single camera fitted with my 100-400mm telephoto lens. I outfitted my slimmed-down set-up with my rain cover to protect it from the blowing snow.

Fighting estimated 20- to 30-mile per hour (32.2- to 48.3-km/h) sustained winds and conservatively 50-mile per hour (80.5-km/h) gusts, I arrived at Schoodic Point just in time to watch the high, high tide at 9:30 a.m. Monster waves pounded the granite ledges along the rugged shoreline, cracking like thunder when the crest collapsed over itself. Watching the waves' magnitude and power left me with a mix of wonder and terror.

Seeing several worthy compositions through the haze of swirling snow, but unable to keep the camera still enough to see through the viewfinder, I photographed along the headland essentially blind. Snowflakes shot into my exposed eyes, causing them to close involuntarily. When I could see, I could barely make out the histogram on my camera's LCD.

In hopes of creating a wind block to protect me and my gear, I tried to sit down next to a large granite boulder. Just as I made the squatting motion, a whirling squall knocked me flat onto the rocks. Taking a moment to confirm I had not broken any bones or camera equipment, I pushed myself up and laughed. If you are going to visit Mother Nature's house, you play by her rules. She has no mercy for the inattentive and unsuspecting. For that wake-up call, I felt thankful.

Winter Storm Nemo blew out as fast as it blew in, but only after leaving its mark. The exposed Mount Desert Light, which resides offshore approximately 25 nautical miles (40.2 km) south of Schoodic Point, recorded astonishing 89 miles per hour (143 km/h) wind gusts. In less than 24 hours, Portland, Maine received 31.9 inches (81 cm) of snow, making Winter Storm Nemo the greatest snowstorm this area had seen since January 1979.

Perhaps the biggest mark the storm left, though, was on me. Observing and experiencing the raw and wild force of nature—during the worst conditions I have ever photographed in—made me feel so alive.

OPPOSITE: Snow flurries from Winter Storm Nemo began on Friday, February 8, 2013. Before hunkering down on the Schoodic Peninsula to weather the storm, I could not resist stopping near Frazer Point to photograph the cotton-like puffs of snow falling from the sky onto the bare trees along Mosquito Harbor. Canon 5DMII, 100-400mm at 320mm, ISO 500, f/10 at 1/60th sec.

Little Moose Island

Sea birds and rugged cliffs among sub-alpine landscape on remote isle

TIME OF YEAR	TIME OF DAY	TIDE	HIKE
Year-round	*Sunrise and sunset*	*Low*	*Moderate*

TOP: *The rising sun warms the tundra-like landscape near the southern end of the island. Canon 5DMII, 24-105mm at 24mm, ISO 100, f/16 at 5 sec., polarizer, three-stop graduated neutral density filter.*
OPPOSITE: *Mussels cluster together at low tide in East Pond Cove. Canon 5DMII, 24-105mm at 105mm, ISO 200, f/16 at 0.5 sec., polarizer.*

*I*f the Schoodic Peninsula has earned the nickname, "the quiet side of Acadia," then Little Moose Island deserves the title, "the quiet side of the quiet side of Acadia." The primitive haven offers granite ledges and cliffs, crescent-shaped cobble beaches, spruce-fir forest, a stand of jack pines, and a rare maritime shrubland—a glimpse of some of Acadia's most striking natural features packed onto one little 54-acre (21.9 hectare) isle. A trip here is like escaping to a remote hideaway where solitude and unsurpassed beauty awaits, but only for four hours at a time.

From two hours before low tide until two hours after low tide, a briefly exposed land bridge allows passage for intrepid photographers. This may sound like a generous window, but shutterbugs may find themselves running short on time, given the large number of photographic opportunities. As you plan your adventure here, consult the tide charts as well as the Photographer's Ephemeris (**www.photoephemeris.com**) to determine when low tide and sunrise and/or sunset coincide. Then, before you make the crossing, set your watch or mobile device's alarm to go off at least 30 minutes before the end of this time frame to ensure your safe return. If you set out before the sun rises or stay after the sun sets, wear a **headlamp** or carry a **flashlight** to help illuminate your path in the dark.

At the beginning of your stroll across the approximately 300-foot (91.4-m) temporary passageway, the rockweed-covered boulders interspersed with tide pools teem with aquatic animals like barnacles, periwinkles, snails, and crabs, especially during a minus low tide. You could easily fill a memory card or two using a **macro** and/or **telephoto lens**, **extension tubes**, **reflector**, and diffuser without ever reaching the island. Watch your step on the slick rocks though.

Once on the isle, take a short stroll along the northeastern cobble shoreline towards East Pond Cove, which provides a safe refuge for shorebirds where seagulls, common loons, and common mergansers loiter. Isolate a flying bird against the distant Schoodic Island using a wide aperture on a telephoto lens, **teleconverter**, **flash**, and **Flash X-tender**™.

To explore the rugged southwestern side, rock hop over the granite benches due south of the crossing point. Then, walk to the far southern end of the crescent-shaped cobble beach to meet with a distinct social trail heading up the rocks. A myriad of informal footpaths crisscross through an exposed sub-alpine landscape similar to what you find at the higher elevations of Cadillac and other Acadian mountains. Because of the harsh growing conditions and extremely fragile environment, do not venture from these existing walkways.

Jagged cliffs come into view quickly on the west side, as does Schoodic Point (see page 172) and the rest of the eastern shoreline of Big Moose Island across Arey Cove. Bring a **wide-angle** or **normal lens**, **polarizer**, **graduated neutral density filter**, **tripod**, and **cable release** to photograph the sweeping view at sunset. Position your camera low to the ground and close to the lichen-covered rocks to lead your viewers into an exaggerated, expansive perspective. Though the isle does not see much color in autumn, wildflowers like shrub rose, blue flag, bunchberry dogwood, and roseroot can add a splash of vibrancy to your foreground as they sprout in June and July.

Continue following the trail through the heath scattered with photogenic stands of jack pines and around the rocky southern tip to reach a cobble beach on the southeast side. Referred to as "Boulder Beach," the rounded rocks are smaller—but no less photogenic, especially at sunrise—than those found on MDI's more popular Boulder Beach (see page 86).

As you wander, you are bound to see a multitude of leftover treasures washed up by the sea. Enjoy, ponder, and photograph, but do not remove, as it is illegal to remove any manmade (or natural) remnants from the park.

Directions

From the intersection of Route 186 and Main Street in Winter Harbor, travel east on Route 186 for 0.5 miles (0.8 km). Turn right onto Moore Road at the signed entrance to Acadia National Park. Drive 4.6 miles (7.4 km) and then stay left/straight towards Winter Harbor when the road forks. Continue 0.5 miles (0.8 km) and turn right into the signed, paved Blueberry Hill Parking Lot. Park here and then walk westward on Moore Road for 0.3 miles (0.5 km) until you reach the unmarked access point on the south side of the road.

Chasing Light on Little Moose Island

"Wherever there is light, one can photograph."

~Alfred Stieglitz

$\mathcal{M}$y parents—who had not visited Acadia before—joined me at the coastal park during the third week of my first residency. I eagerly played the tour guide role, enthusiastically showing them the classic sights and sharing my collected knowledge from my short time in the area. Based on my previous wanderings, the one special off-the beaten-path place I especially wanted them to experience was Little Moose Island (see page 178).

When I explained to my folks that we could only cross onto the small isle within a four-hour window around the low tide, my dad exclaimed with a combination of surprise and delight, "Can you really walk to an island?"

In the two weeks prior to my parents' arrival, I had walked across the exposed rocky bar twice: once with my husband, Craig, and once alone. In both cases, I had conscientiously timed my journey to coincide with either the sunrise or sunset to tap into the most favorable lighting conditions for landscape photography. However, during my parents' stay, low tide occurred in the middle of either the day or the night. Since I preferred they actually see the surroundings on the isolated island, I chose to lead them on the hike during daylight.

Although the lighting is not always ideal for landscape photography, the lengthy time in between sunrise and sunset supplies ample—albeit different— opportunities to record memorable experiences, moving stories, and finer details. While sometimes I have the fortunate chance to revisit a location on multiple occasions to chase the best light, often times fleeting moments do not allow for a second chance later. More frequently, I challenge myself to photograph a subject or an idea that instantaneously strikes my fancy in the very best light I can find at the time. Since those short-lived occasions can—and often do—happen at any time, I tend to pack all my photography gear no matter the time of day. (Besides, Murphy's Law states that the equipment you leave behind will be the exact tool you will need to follow through on your vision.)

With this philosophy in mind, I toted my fully loaded, heavy backpack and tripod in hopes of finding smaller treasures during my adventure to Little Moose Island with my parents even if our adventure began at 10 a.m. under mostly cloudy skies. From the minute we ventured from the mainland to the isle across the slick, barnacle- and rockweed-covered boulders, we wandered and wondered about our temporary peek at the ocean's normally hidden secrets. We identified and learned more about the intriguing sights by consulting our field guide.

After observing the different marine subjects, I pulled out my macro lens—my "go-to" piece of equipment during mid-day hours—to study seemingly-still sea creatures like periwinkles, dog whelks, and limpets. I evaluated my results on the back of my camera's LCD screen, only to see blurry parts of my photos. I checked my exposure settings to ensure I had a shutter speed fast enough to handhold my camera. Then I snapped again, only to see softness in my frame again! Something did not make sense. Putting the camera aside, I carefully observed the small critters attached to the rocks. They were moving (albeit extraordinarily slowly)! I increased my ISO speed and shutter speed accordingly.

We continued exploring the cobble beaches along East Pond Cove. Among the typical collection of shells, mussels, rockweed, sea urchin skeletons, and dismembered crab shells, the small cobble beach was also littered with an array of fishing remnants. Chewed buoys, crushed

Tangled fishing remnants rest along the shore on Little Moose Island. Canon 5DMII, 24-105mm at 24mm, ISO 100, f/8 at 1/50 sec., polarizer, flash set to -1 TTL.

lobster pots, torn rubber gloves, and tangled ropes along the fringes of this quiet island granted a brief glimpse into the violent churn of the sea. Like two little kids in a candy store, my parents discovered one debris discovery after another, making their way down the beach with finger and arms pointing in all directions and excitedly announcing their latest find.

I knelt next to an unusually large collection of debris, where the twisted mess appeared entrenched in the granite rock. Where did it come from? What had it been? To whom did it belong? To me, each piece possessed a different tale and represented the unfulfilled aspirations anglers had as the call of the sea took hold.

Anxious to record this story, I switched from my macro lens to my wide-angle lens—a piece of equipment I most often reserve for sweeping views at sunrise and sunset. Tapping into the broader perspective my 16-35mm lens afforded me, I could showcase my subject—"the twisted mess appearing entrenched in the granite rock"—not just one small detail of the clutter.

The overcast, threatening conditions not only provided deeper color saturation across my scene, but also served as a fitting backdrop for my primary subject. I quickly noticed the green tones in the lobster traps blended with the forest in the distance, so I dropped my tripod as low to the ground as I could (such that I ended up laying flat on the rocks). Then, to make the jumbled pile stand out even more so from the background, I added a pop of flash during the exposure—mimicking the sun's light and direction as if it had it peeked out from behind the clouds. By increasing my shutter speed, I intentionally darkened the ambient light to create a stormier mood.

After exploring the immediate area for a few more minutes, our watch alarm rang. Our window of opportunity to return safely to the mainland would disappear in 45 minutes. Within about six hour's time, high tide would pull the scattering of fishing remnants along the shore back into its grasp and erase my story forever.

Schoodic Drive (East)

Sunrise vistas of craggy cliffs and cobble beaches

TIME OF YEAR	TIME OF DAY	TIDE	HIKE
Year-round	Sunrise; night	Any	Easy

Dawn's first light kisses the granite rocks along the eastern section of Schoodic Drive. Canon 5DMII, 16-35mm at 17mm, ISO 200, f/16 at 1/10th sec., three-stop graduated neutral density filter.

*T*he extensive tree-lined Acadian coastline along the eastern section of Schoodic Drive is every bit as impressive as the western segment (see page 158). However, the best time to photograph the craggy cliffs intermixed with cobble beaches along the east-facing side of the Schoodic Peninsula is not at sunset, but rather when the day's first sun rays radiate above the horizon and bathe the entire shoreline in rich, warm sidelight.

The Blueberry Hill Parking Area provides visitors a first glimpse of the natural beauty that lies ahead. With a **wide-angle lens**, **polarizer**, and **graduated neutral density filter**, head to the rocky beach where Little Moose Island to the south and Schoodic Island to the southeast act as scenic backdrops to waves dancing in between jumbo rocks in the foreground.

During the summer, fragrant and vibrant beach rose blooms add a splash of color along the shoreline. In autumn, the same plant bears rose hips, which resemble miniature crab apples. A **macro lens**, paired with **extension tubes**, can help record the finer details of both the blossom

Mystical Atlantic sea smoke rises offshore on the east side of the Schoodic Peninsula. Canon 5DMII, 100-400mm at 400mm, ISO 100, f/36 at 4 sec., polarizer.

and the fruit. Hold a **diffuser** over your scene if Mother Nature does not produce an overcast sky.

As you explore the other unnamed pullouts along this drive, the soaring vistas intermingled with easily accessible, gently sloping, cobble beaches supply endless landscapes and macro compositions in all seasons. Receding waves leave long elegant foamy streaks between the clapping cobblestones. Stunted picturesque pitch pine trees pose with character along the granite ledges. Delicate mosses like peat, white, and hair cap blanket the forest floor, and create a striking visual combination when the surrounding low sweet blueberry turns lipstick red.

Rolling Island to the east slightly delays the sunrise from April through September, but the sun rising over the open ocean from October to March can result in beautiful sunbursts. Point your camera towards the sun while using a small aperture (like f/16 and f/22) and remember to remove all filters from your lens before photographing.

During long durations of especially cold weather (well below freezing), the rare Atlantic sea smoke effortlessly glides above the water's surface. This ethereal fog occurs when cold air from the land flows over warmer ocean water temperatures. Since it typically appears at a fair distance offshore, hone in on the fog with a **telephoto lens** coupled with a **teleconverter**.

The water-hugging haze moves fast! Freeze the motion of both the clouds and the waves with a faster shutter speed (such as 1/50th of a second or faster). To create a blurred, mystical effect instead, try a slower shutter speed (such as 1/4th of a second or slower). Consider using a **tripod** and **cable release** to keep your camera free from shaking during longer exposures.

Since the road becomes one-way after Frazer Point Picnic Area, consider allocating extra time the day prior to your morning outing to scout each of the pullouts first to find your favorite locations.

Directions

From the intersection of Route 186 and Main Street in Winter Harbor, travel east on Route 186 for 0.5 miles (0.8 km). Turn right onto Moore Road at the signed entrance to Acadia National Park. Drive 4.6 miles (7.4 km) and then stay left/straight towards Winter Harbor when the road forks. Continue 0.5 miles (0.8 km) and turn right into the signed, paved Blueberry Hill Parking Lot. An additional paved pullout exists along the one-way Moore Road 150 yards (137 m) beyond the Blueberry Hill turnoff. Three more pullouts of special interest are an additional 0.3 miles (0.5 km), 0.7 miles (1.1 km), and 1.4 miles (2.3 km) along Moore Road.

Striated granite along the Western Head Trail makes for interesting foreground at sunset. Canon 5DMII, 16-35mm at 16mm, ISO 100, f/16 at 5 sec., three-stop graduated neutral density filter.

Isle au Haut

Isle au Haut

46 Eben's Head Trail 186

47 Duck Harbor 184

48 Western Head Trail 188

49 Cliff Trail 194

50 Long Pond 196

Atlantic
Ocean

Isle au Haut
Bay

46

47

48

49

50

Key:

———— = Major road

– – – – = Dirt/gravel road

Maple trees flaunt their vibrant autumnal colors at Long Pond. Canon 5DMII, 100-400mm at 160mm, ISO 100, f/11 at 8 sec., polarizer.

Isle au Haut Introduction

*P*hotographers who enjoy experiencing the natural beauty on both MDI and the Schoodic Peninsula, but crave an even more raw, remote, and off-the-beaten path adventure than even "the quiet side of Acadia" provides will thoroughly enjoy a trip to Isle au Haut.

Deemed "High Island" (or "Isle au Haut" in French) by Samuel Champlain during his explorations of the area in 1604, this 6-mile (9.7 km) long by 2-mile (3.2 km) wide island offers intrepid travelers the chance to see Acadia in its most pristine form. As with MDI to the northeast, Acadia National Park's boundary spans only a portion of the small island (approximately 2,728 acres, or 1,104 hectares, residing predominantly in the central and southern sections of the island). A tiny year-round population (the 2010 United States census suggested 73 residents) and relatively few visitors even during the summer months all but guarantee a memorable outing where you will not compete for space with other photographers.

However, getting to this solitude and serenity requires significant advanced planning and extra effort. Located approximately 15 miles (24.1 km) southwest of MDI as the crow flies, visitors to the most popular part of Acadia must first drive 58.3 miles (93.8 km) from Bar Harbor to the quaint town of Stonington on Deer Isle. From here, visitors board a first-come, first-serve, passenger-only mail boat and travel 40 to 45 minutes across the island-dotted Merchant Row

to reach Isle au Haut. Overnight parking at the dock is available for a fee.

Although ferry service runs year-round to Point Lookout (private dock) and the Town Landing, from June 15 to September 15, the Isle au Haut Ferry Company boat service brings you directly to Duck Harbor, which is a short 0.25-mile (0.4-km) stroll to the campground. Outside of that time frame, vacationers disembark at the Town Landing, which requires a 5-mile (8.1 km) walk along the island road to reach Duck Harbor Campground.

While the mail boat does not limit the amount of suitcases, camera gear, and boxes of food you bring on board, as a courtesy to other passengers, pack efficiently and light. Handcarts at the Stonington dock can help you load your luggage, but you must carry your belongings from the Town Landing or the Duck Harbor dock yourself. Because the daily schedule changes throughout the year, visit the Isle au Haut Ferry Company's website at **www.isleauhaut.com** to assist in planning your travels.

Wooden planks lead the way on the Median Ridge Trail. Canon 5DMII, 16-35mm at 16mm, ISO 100, f/18 at 4 sec., polarizer.

Duck Harbor at dusk. Canon 5DMII, 24-105mm at 75mm, ISO 100, f/14 at 30 sec.

Though a single day spent on the island will not disappoint, those wishing to capture sunrise or sunset light will inevitably miss the optimal times for landscape-style photography during a day trip. Because of the required advanced planning and effort involved for even a short stay, I recommend staying at least three days or longer.

The Keeper's House Inn (**www.keepershouse.com**) offers bed and breakfast accommodations from mid-May to early October. Also, numerous vacation homes with varying modern amenities are available for rent year-round. Some rentals include bikes (which are permitted on paved and unpaved roads, but not the island's trails) and/or a car to use during your stay.

For a more primitive experience, the National Park operates the Duck Harbor Campground, which features five designated sites with lean-to shelters. The park requires advanced reservations for camping (available from May 15 through October 15) on their website at **www.nps.gov/acad/planyourvisit/duckharbor.htm**.

Those staying at the campground or in a private rental house should consider stopping at a grocery store on the mainland or in Stonington to stock up on food prior to boarding the mail boat. The Island Store (**www.theislandstore.net**) near the Town Landing provides an impressive, but still limited, spread of fruits, vegetables, dry goods, and other necessities. During the summer months, stop by The Lobster Lady's (**www.mainelobsterlady.com**) food truck to taste fresh local seafood. Afterwards, give your sweet tooth a thrill at Black Dinah's Chocolatiers and Café (**www.blackdinahchocolatiers.com**) with their fresh baked goods and divine homemade chocolates.

Once you are ready to explore, the 12-mile (19.3-km) loop road (paved on much of the northern part of the island, but a rough, single-lane dirt road throughout the park) enables access to 18 miles (29 km) of hiking trails that crisscross the island and park. Unspoiled spruce forests, mountain summits, bogs, marshes, a freshwater pond, and some of the most rugged coastline contained within all of Acadia await!

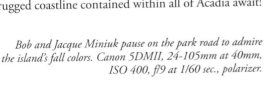

Bob and Jacque Miniuk pause on the park road to admire the island's fall colors. Canon 5DMII, 24-105mm at 40mm, ISO 400, f/9 at 1/60 sec., polarizer.

Eben's Head Trail

Prominent granite outcropping provides endless shoreline vistas

TIME OF YEAR	TIME OF DAY	TIDE	HIKE
May to October	*Late afternoon to sunset*	*Mid to high*	*Moderate*

TOP: *The sun's final rays illuminate the rocky shoreline along the Eben's Head Trail. Canon 5DMII, 24-105mm at 35mm, ISO 200, f/18 at 1.6 sec., two-stop graduated neutral density filter.*
OPPOSITE: *A tranquil coastline view along the trail at dusk. Canon 5DMII, 100-400mm at 135mm, ISO 200, f/13 at 20 sec.*

*N*ot a single spot along the remarkable Isle au Haut coastline will disappoint even the most discriminating coastline-lover. Eben's Head Trail is no exception, and a short stroll from the campground puts you in a perfect location to record rich, warm sunset light falling on the conifer-lined granite ledges along the isle's pristine, rugged shore.

Venture out to the trail an hour or two prior to sunset to first scout the area around Eben's Head, which is a prominent, dome-shaped granite outcropping located on the southern end of the trail. A quick scramble to the top promises endless vistas to the north towards the unnamed crescent-shaped cobble beach and Shark Point. Equally spectacular views appear to the south across Duck Harbor and towards the primitive campground as well. Regardless of which direction you point your camera, a **normal lens** fitted with a **polarizer** will help you capture

these lesser-known, yet incredibly picturesque coastal scenes.

The cobble beach to the north of Eben's Head provides endless smaller studies of the sea. Study the intriguing patterns and shapes of rockweed clinging to large boulders, waves dancing among polished granite cobble, and tide pools teeming with tiny creatures through a **macro** or **telephoto lens**. If the sun's light appears too harsh and direct, utilize a **reflector** and **diffuser** to tame the contrast. If backlighting illuminates your smaller scene, ensure the diffuser adequately covers your entire composition but does not appear inadvertently within your frame.

Follow the blue blazes around the cobble beach for approximately 0.3 additional miles (0.5 km) for an even more expansive view of the coastline in both directions. Although a normal and telephoto lens will come in handy to isolate waves crashing against the rock formations, a **wide-angle lens** will allow close-by rocks as foreground. Remember to pack a polarizer to darken the sky and water reflections as well as a **graduated neutral density filter** to hold back light in the sky as the sun sets.

After rain, fog, and high tide, the exposed tree roots along the trail and the rocks along the coastline become very slick. Wear hiking shoes with solid treads and watch your footing as you explore this area.

Directions

From the Duck Harbor Campground, follow the unpaved Western Head Road (closed to motor vehicles) to the east and eventually north for 0.3 miles (0.5 km) until you reach the unpaved island road. Turn left and follow the dirt track for an additional 0.3 miles (0.5 km). The Eben's Head Trail begins on the southwest side of the road.

Looking for Answers

"There's more than one right answer."

~Dewitt Jones

Gaelic Storm—a Celtic band which makes toe-tapping, knee-slapping music I enjoy tremendously—produced a song titled, "Don't Go for the One." The lyrics tell of a gentleman going to buy snails to impress his houseguests, but gets talked into having a single beer at the bar. One brew becomes two, three, four, and what was supposed to been a quick chat turns into an all-night event. As the title and chorus hilariously suggests, one should not expect to enjoy only one beverage with your friends.

While it may seem like a stretch, this philosophy can apply to photography as well. Don't go for the one photograph!

Very rarely am I fortunate enough to get everything to come together perfectly in a first frame. Even after I have spent ample time observing, analyzing, and visualizing an intriguing subject to define a clear vision, more often than not, I will also explore the scene through recording a series of frames with my camera.

Assuming the lighting conditions are not changing quickly, I contemplate an abundance of "what if" scenarios to determine how I will accomplish recording my visual message before snapping the shutter. What if I only included this section of the scene? What if I positioned my camera lower to the ground? What if I used side light instead of backlight? What if, what if, what if? I continue tapping into this iterative evaluative process as I begin photographing, as it helps me refine what my eye is seeing and how to share that through a photograph.

Not only does this process enable me to achieve my creative vision, but it also helps me fully appreciate the subject from a variety of perspectives and find the many right answers a scene possesses, as Dewitt Jones' quote suggests. If I have spent the time and money to travel 3,000 miles (4,828 km) from Arizona, hopped on a passenger-only ferry to the remote Isle au Haut, biked 6 miles (9.7 km) along a bumpy, single track dirt road, and then walked a mile (1.6 km) uphill with a heavy camera backpack to get to a location, you can be sure I am not going to snap only one photo and head home. Instead, I want to challenge myself to see how many right answers I can discover.

On the first day of our visit to Isle au Haut, my parents and I ventured to the Eben's Head Trail (see page 188) well before sunset to allow extra time for wandering and discovering along the unfamiliar trail. After a short meander through the forest, we emerged on the rocky coast and scrambled to the top of Eben's Head, where a breathtaking 180-degree panoramic view of the isle's western shoreline and open waters of Isle au Haut Bay greeted us. We noticed the receding tide leaving behind small tide pools on the volcanic ledges surrounding the cobble beach directly north of our perch. Eager for a closer look at these fleeting windows into the typically hidden ocean world, we hiked the short distance to the seashore.

After only a few seconds of exploring, the fine, hair-like seaweed floating in the tide pools fascinated me. A few steps ahead on the black boulders, my mom, Jacque, spotted a slightly larger saltwater puddle and called to me, "Hey Colleen, you have to see these bubbles!"

When I gazed into her find, I did not just see tangles of seaweed and floating bubbles. The

OPPOSITE: Though this was the first frame I snapped, the scene fascinated me with additional compositions. Canon 5DMII, 100mm macro, ISO 100, f/18 at 4 sec.

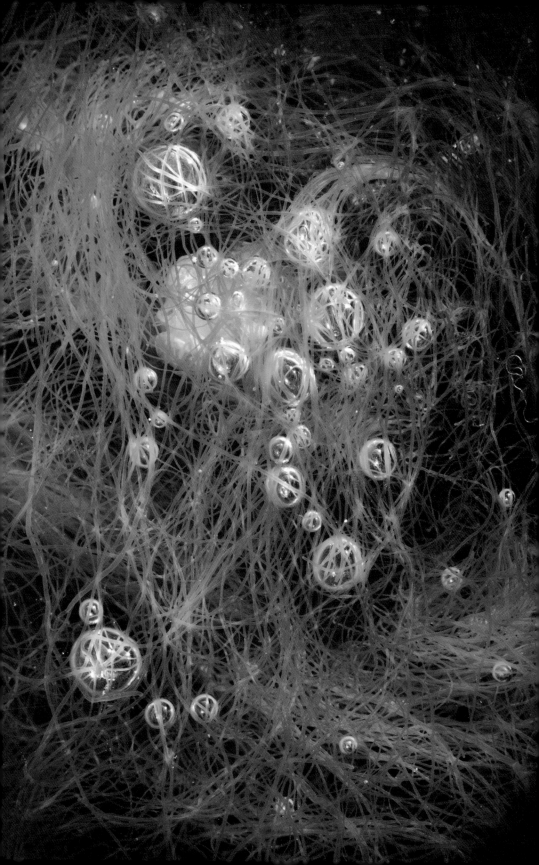

Looking for Answers (continued)

scene immediately transported me to outer space, where planets swirled in a distant galaxy. I knew I had to create an image of precisely that subject!

I walked around the small pool to begin the visualization process. First, I noticed how the backlight from the late afternoon created a dark backdrop in the deep pool. Then, I settled on a vertical orientation based on the bubbles' arrangement. I knew I needed to keep my lens (positioned to look down upon the scene) parallel to the surface of the water so that the face of the bubbles and the top layer of seaweed remained in focus. A small aperture on my 100mm macro lens would provide the depth of field necessary for my tight composition. I needed to remember to twirl my polarizer to get just enough reflected light on the water, but not so much that it overshadowed the primary scene.

With this vision in mind, after diligently setting up my composition and exposure, I snapped the frame and immediately reviewed the image on the back of my camera's LCD. Shockingly, on the first try, I managed to record an image that matched my vision—a right answer!

Despite being pleased with my first snap, I continued exploring the scene for 45 more minutes. After a number of frames, I picked out an odd reddish tint occurring across the image. It was the reflection of my red jacket! I experimented keeping the extra color in the frame by hovering over the scene. I also eliminated it by stepping a short distance away from the scene and triggering the shutter with a cable release. Contrasting with the rich greens and blues, the additional color made the scene look even more other-worldly—a second right answer!

I tried turning the camera to the left slightly and then to the right slightly, utilizing a Dutch tilt, to play with the composition as the bubbles appeared, disappeared, and then reappeared, changing the visual balance entirely from image to image - more right answers!

Then, I used extension tubes to allow me to get a closer perspective. I felt the broader perspective better conveyed my initial notion of "planets swirling in a distant galaxy," but I enjoyed the results of this more intimate view—another right answer!

During the process, I felt my photographic message and my confidence strengthening with each additional frame. Heeding Gaelic Storm's advice, had I gone for "the one," I would have missed the chance to see all the possibilities this magical scene had in store.

OPPOSITE: Close-up of a smaller grouping of tide pool bubbles. Canon 5DMII, 100mm macro with two 12mm extension tubes stacked, ISO 100, f/18 at 4 sec.

Duck Harbor

Classic granite ledges and cobble beaches with convenient access

TIME OF YEAR	TIME OF DAY	TIDE	HIKE
May to October	*Late afternoon to sunset*	*Low to mid*	*Easy*

Low tide (at approximately 3.5 feet [1.1 m]) reveals ample off-shore boulders and ephemeral waterfalls as the gentle waves roll onto the beach. Canon 5DMII, 16-35mm at 17mm, ISO 50, f/20 at 0.6 sec., three-stop graduated neutral density filter.

*O*f all the photogenic locations on Isle au Haut, only one allows you to photograph a stunning sunset along the coast and make it back to camp in time for dinner at a reasonable hour: Duck Harbor. Located a hop, skip, and a jump from the campground with the same name, the speckled granite ledges and cobble beaches summon shutterbugs to record classic Maine coastal landscapes and a protective harbor with little effort.

Although the campground is in close proximity, pack your camera bag with a **wide-angle**, **normal**, **macro**, and **telephoto lenses**, **polarizer**, **graduated neutral density filter**, **tripod**, and **cable release** to make the most of your outing from late afternoon through sunset.

If feasible, time your visit to coincide with a low to mid-tide (6 feet [1.8m] or below). At this desirable water level, clusters of offshore rocks intermingling with waves, exposed colorful and circular lichen on rock faces, and washed-up fishing remnants offer ample compositions through a macro or telephoto lens. As you set up your frame, ensure side or backlight

illuminates your smaller subject to convey a sense of dimension. If needed, take a step or two to the right or left around your center of interest to avoid recording flat front light.

As the sun lowers to the horizon, switch to wider-angle lens to photograph Eben's Head across the harbor to the north and the crescent curve of the cobble beach to the south. Save for stormy weather, the waves effortlessly roll onto the gently sloped beaches here. To render a silky appearance to the water, set as slow of a shutter speed as possible. Use a slow ISO speed and a neutral density filter to reduce your exposure time even more so.

After the sun's final rays illuminate your scene, point your camera towards the open view of the ocean to create striking silhouettes. No matter your lens choice, remove all filters from the front of your lens and expose such that the landscape appears black and the sky records adequate mid-tones (i.e., the histogram will show an abundance of pixels on the left-hand side but limited pixels on the right-hand side with some mid-tones appearing in between). To enhance the color of the clouds, consider setting your white balance to Cloudy or Shade.

As with the entire Acadian coastline, the rocks become very slippery when wet, so watch your footing as you explore the beach. Wear water shoes with good traction, especially if you plan to get close to the water's edge. Finally, even though a somewhat constant, light coastal breeze keeps mosquitoes at bay, bring bug spray during calm, windless conditions.

Directions

From the dock at the Duck Harbor Campground, follow the social trail to the west towards the coastline.

Vibrant crustose lichen on a granite boulder in Duck Harbor. Canon 5DMII, 100mm macro, ISO 100, f/20 at 1.6 sec., polarizer.

Western Head Trail

Unusual striated granite rocks among western shoreline

TIME OF YEAR	**TIME OF DAY**	**TIDE**	**HIKE**
May to October	*Late afternoon to sunset*	*Any*	*Moderate*

Intriguing striations in the granite ledges along the Western Head Trail. Canon 5DMII, 16-35mm at 16mm, ISO 100, f/16 at 5 sec., three-stop graduated neutral density filter.

Like the Eben's Head Trail (page 188) and Duck Harbor (page 194), the Western Head Trail promises shutterbugs a productive photographic outing along Isle au Haut's spectacular unspoiled western coastline. However, beyond the classic Maine coastal scenes you would expect to find, this location offers the chance to photograph a gorgeous and unusual outcropping of striated granite rocks along the shore.

Although the hike is short and only moderately difficult, allow yourself extra time as exposed tree roots, rotting logs, boulders, and narrow wooden planks make the initial walk through the predominantly spruce forest slow going. Watch your step, especially after rain, and bring an extra hiking pole to help keep yourself steady.

As the sound of the ocean increases, the trail elevation increases and eventually crests on top of granite cliffs. Then, it weaves inland through the forest and traverses numerous crescent-shaped cobble coves. Pack a **macro lens**, **reflector**, and **diffuser** to photograph

smaller treasures like rockweed, shells, and patterns in polished rocks along this stretch of coast. Seabirds like seagulls, black guillemots, and common eider take refuge here, so also bring your **telephoto lens**, **teleconverter**, **flash**, and **Flash X-tender**™.

Approximately 0.5 miles (0.8 km) from the trailhead, the striated granite ledges come into view. Whether you face north or south (both offer equally expansive scenes), a **wide-angle** or **normal lens** positioned low to the rocks will allow you to include the lines in your foreground to lead a viewer into your composition. Set a small aperture (such as f/16 or f/22) and then focus on the appropriate hyperfocal distance for your camera, focal length of your lens, and aperture to maximize your depth of field.

This unique geological feature could keep you busy for hours, but you will find a plethora of additional subjects and landscapes as the trail continues along the

Directions

From the Duck Harbor Campground, follow the unpaved Western Head Road (closed to vehicles) to the south for 0.5 miles (0.8 km). The Western Head Trail begins on the west side of the road.

coastline for an additional 0.8 miles (1.3 km) to the southernmost tip of the isle. At low tide, the ocean recedes and reveals a small bar visitors can cross to reach the tiny offshore island called Western Ear. When the Western Head and Cliff trails meet, follow the short 0.1-mile (0.2-km) spur trail to the south to locate the bar.

No matter where you stop along the west-facing shoreline, keep a **polarizer** and **graduated neutral density filter** within reach as the sun drops below the horizon and turns the whitish-pink granite crags into a glowing orange spectacle.

Once you are done with your shoot here, use a **headlamp** or **flashlight** to help illuminate the trail as you walk back in the dark.

Rockweed clings to the side of a cliff face along the trail. Canon 5DMII, 24-105mm at 82mm, ISO 100, f/20 at 10 sec., polarizer.

Cliff Trail

Dramatic aerial-like panoramic vistas of the isle's eastern coastline

TIME OF YEAR	TIME OF DAY	TIDE	HIKE
May to October	*Sunrise to late morning*	*Mid to high, incoming*	*Strenuous*

*I*f you seek sweeping, aerial-like panoramic vistas of the rugged Isle au Haut coastline then look no further than the Cliff Trail, where grand overlooks await as soon as you climb the first set of steps. Arguably, this undulating trail also serves as one of the best places on the island to watch crashing waves during high tide or stormy weather.

The strenuous 0.6-mile (1-km) long trail (not including the walk along the Western Head Road) tightly follows the coastline's meandering tree-lined terrain. Similar to a roller coaster ride, the steep dirt trail ascends to prominent granite perches surveying the rugged cliffs, weaves through the forest draped in old man's beard lichen, and dips to reveal intimate views of coves and cobble beaches along the way. As you venture up and down the path, though, watch your footing over the exposed tree roots and the granite rocks, especially after wet weather when both become treacherously slick.

Begin walking the Western Head Road at least 30 to 45 minutes

Aerial-like views await along the strenuous Cliff Trail on the southwestern tip of Isle au Haut. Canon 5DMII, 16-35mm at 16mm, ISO 100, f/18 at 6 sec., four-stop graduated neutral density filter.

prior to civil twilight to catch glowing pre-dawn light and sunup along the Cliff Trail. Wear a **headlamp** or bring a **flashlight** to illuminate your path in the dark. If time permits, consider scouting the route the day prior to your outing.

Carrying a heavy pack stuffed with gear makes this trek even more challenging, so lighten your load by carrying only a **wide-angle** or **normal focal length lens**, **polarizer**, and **graduated neutral density filter**. Since much of the trail is exposed to the elements, also bring a **tripod** and cable release to keep your camera steady during the commonly windy conditions. Remember to turn off the vibration reduction or image stabilization feature on your camera or lens unless you decide to handhold your gear.

If you have extra room in your backpack and are feeling energetic, add a long **telephoto lens**, **teleconverter**, **flash**, and a **Flash X-tender**™ to your bag to isolate common eiders and harlequin ducks that frequent the area.

Directions

From the Duck Harbor Campground, follow the unpaved Western Head Road (closed to motor vehicles) to the south for 1.4 miles (2.3 km) until the road ends. The trailhead is located on the southwest side of the road.

A telephoto lens also comes in handy if you venture to the two cobble beaches along the trail, where studies of waves and rocks intermingling never gets old. Use a fast shutter speed (e.g., 1/100th of a second or faster) to freeze the raw power of a crashing wave. On the other hand, use a slow shutter speed (e.g., 1/4th second or slower) to blur the movement of the water against the shoreline. Reduce the exposure time even further by placing a **neutral density filter** over your lens.

If you would rather skip the demanding hike or if you have not filled your memory cards after your outing on the Cliff Trail, wander along the nearby Goat Trail no more than 0.3 miles (0.5 km) from the Western Head Road to explore additional seascapes on the cobble beaches tucked into Deep and Squeaker coves.

Crashing waves polish the partially-submerged rocks along the Cliff Trail. Canon 5DMII, 100-400mm at 170mm, ISO 50, f/22 at 0.6 sec., polarizer.

Long Pond

Reflections and symmetry in a serene, slender pond

TIME OF YEAR	TIME OF DAY	TIDE	HIKE
May to October	*Sunrise to late morning*	*N/A*	*Easy*

Fog, mirror-like reflections, and a colorful sky make for a memorable morning at Long Pond. Canon 5DMII, 16-35mm at 16mm, ISO 100, f/16 at 6 sec., four-stop graduated neutral density filter.

*L*ike Long Pond and Little Long Pond (which, on the maps, goes by Long Pond as well) on MDI to the northeast, Long Pond on Isle au Haut offers tranquility and ample photographic opportunities. The 3-mile (4.8-km) moderately strenuous Long Pond Trail kisses the far northwestern shoreline within the Acadia National Park boundary, but the easiest access and most photogenic views reside at the southern end of this scenic, tree-lined pond outside of the park along the island's main road.

Arrive on the gravel beach at least 45 minutes prior to sunrise to record the colorful pre-dawn light softly illuminating the maple trees, evergreens, ferns, and granite rocks along the water's edge. A **wide-angle** to **normal focal length lens** enables the inclusion of both foreground and background in your frame to convey a sense of depth. To minimize the water in between your near and far subjects, drop your **tripod** lower to the ground. Alternatively, to maximize the middle ground, raise your gear. Swimming is permitted here, so if you wish to get even closer to partially submerged rushes and boulders in the foreground, wear water shoes and roll up your pants to wade comfortably.

On calm days, mirror-like reflections of the V-shaped horizon create a striking visual symmetry. To record this balance, break the Rule of Thirds and place the converging shorelines in the middle of your frame. Pair your lens choice with a **polarizer** to enhance the reflection in the water and darken the sky's tonality. If Mother Nature graciously puts on a vibrant cloud show in the sky overhead, then position a **graduated neutral density filter** over your lens to achieve a well-balanced exposure across your frame.

If windy conditions prevail, slow your shutter speed (e.g., 1/4th of a second or slower) to smooth the movement of the undulating waves during your longer exposure. However, also experiment with faster shutter speeds (e.g., 1/50th of a second or faster) to record the ever-changing patterns and shapes occurring in the reflections. If needed, increase your ISO speed to enable faster shutter speeds in the morning's lower light levels.

Once you have exhausted landscape-style opportunities with your wider lenses, explore and isolate the multitude of water reflections using a **telephoto lens** coupled with a polarizer.

The north-south orientation ensures abundant appealing side light in the morning throughout the year. However, around the summer solstice, when the sun reaches its most northern azimuth, the angle of the sun creates back-sidelight across the lake. Around this time frame, protect your lens from the sun's reflection by using a sun shade or holding your hand over your lens.

Directions

From the Duck Harbor Campground, follow the unpaved Western Head Road (closed to motor vehicles) to the east and eventually north for 0.3 miles (0.5 km) until you reach the unpaved island road. Turn right and follow the dirt track for an additional 2.2 miles (3.5 km).

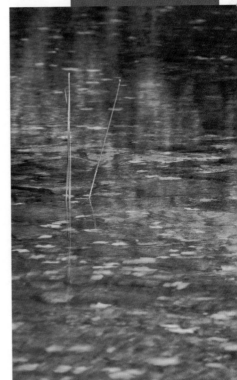

Rushes among reflections of a maple tree along the shoreline. Canon 5DMII, 100-400mm at 400mm, ISO 100, f/13 at 1/4 sec., polarizer.

Colorful sunset vistas from the Cadillac Mountain South Ridge Trail. Canon 5D, 24-105mm at 24mm, ISO 100, f/14 at 8 sec., four-stop graduated neutral density filter.

Appendix

Additional Resources

Abrell, Dianne, *Carriage Roads of Acadia: A Pocket Guide* (Rockport, Maine: Down East Books, 3rd edition, 2011)

Acadia National Park Motorist Guide: Park Loop Road (Bar Harbor, Maine: Acadia Publishing Company, reprint 1997)

Butcher, Russell D., *Field Guide to Acadia National Park, Maine* (Lanham, Maryland: Taylor Trade Publishing, revised edition, 2005)

Dorr, George B., *The Story of Acadia National Park* (Bar Harbor, Maine: Acadia Publishing Company, 4th printing, 2005)

Kaiser, James, *Acadia, The Complete Guide* (Chicago, Illinois: Destination Press, 3rd edition, 2010)

Nangle, Hilary, *Acadia National Park* (Moon Handbooks) (Berkeley, California: Avalon Travel Publishing, 4th edition, 2012)

National Geographic Maps (firm), *Acadia National Park, Maine, USA: Trails Illustrated Map* (Evergreen, Colorado: National Geographic Maps, 2002)

Roberts, Ann, *Mr. Rockefeller's Roads: The Untold Story of Acadia's Carriage Roads* (Rockport, Maine: Down East Books, 2nd edition, 2012)

Fog in Frenchman Bay surrounds the Mark Island Lighthouse. Canon 5DMII, 100-400mm at 135mm, ISO 125, f/6.3 at 1/200th sec., polarizer.

Shoot Calendar

#	Location	Pg.	Jan	Feb	Mar	Apr	May	Jun	Jul
1	Thompson Island	48	✔	✔	✔				
2	Bar Island	50					✔	✔	✔
3	Bar Harbor Shore Path	54	✔	✔	✔	✔	✔	✔	✔
4	Compass Harbor Trail	56	✔	✔	✔	✔	✔	✔	✔
5	Great Meadow	58					✔		
6	The Tarn	60						✔	✔
7	Sieur de Monts	62	✔	✔	✔	✔	✔	✔	✔
8	Jesup Path	66	✔	✔	✔	✔	✔	✔	✔
9	Beaver Dam Pond	68							
10	Sand Beach	70	✔	✔	✔	✔	✔	✔	✔
11	Great Head	72				✔	✔	✔	✔
12	Newport Cove Overlook	74	✔	✔	✔				
13	Thunder Hole	76	✔	✔	✔	✔	✔	✔	✔
14	Monument Cove	78	✔	✔					
15	Gorham Mountain Trail	84				✔	✔	✔	✔
16	Boulder Beach	86	✔	✔	✔	✔	✔	✔	✔
17	Otter Cliff	88	✔	✔	✔	✔	✔	✔	✔
18	Otter Point & Cove	94				✔	✔	✔	✔
19	Little Hunters Beach	96				✔	✔	✔	✔
20	Day Mountain	98						✔	✔
21	Hunters Beach	100				✔	✔	✔	✔
22	Little Long Pond	102	✔	✔	✔	✔	✔	✔	✔
23	Asticou Azalea Garden	106					✔	✔	✔
24	Waterfall Bridge	108					✔	✔	✔
25	Eagle Lake	110	✔	✔	✔	✔	✔	✔	✔

Mount Desert Island

Aug	Sep	Oct	Nov	Dec	Time of Day	Tide	Hike
				✔	Sunrise and sunset	Low	E
✔	✔	✔			Sunrise and sunset	Low	M
✔	✔	✔	✔	✔	Sunrise to late morning	Any	E
✔	✔	✔	✔	✔	Sunrise	Low to mid	E
	✔				Late morning to early afternoon	N/A	E
✔	✔	✔			Early morning	N/A	E
✔	✔	✔	✔	✔	Sunrise to early afternoon	N/A	E
✔	✔	✔	✔	✔	Sunrise to early afternoon	N/A	E
	✔				Early morning to early afternoon	N/A	E
✔	✔	✔	✔	✔	Late morning to early afternoon	Any	E
✔	✔				Sunrise to early morning	Any	M
		✔	✔	✔	Sunrise	Mid to high, incoming	M
✔	✔	✔	✔	✔	Sunrise	Two hours before high	E
		✔	✔	✔	Sunrise	Mid to high	E
✔	✔	✔	✔		Sunrise	N/A	S
✔	✔	✔	✔	✔	Sunrise	Low to mid, outgoing	M
✔	✔	✔	✔	✔	Sunrise	Any	M
✔	✔	✔	✔		Late afternoon to sunset	Minus low or high	E
✔	✔	✔	✔		Sunrise to early afternoon	Low to mid	M
✔	✔	✔			Late afternoon to sunset	N/A	E/S
✔	✔	✔	✔		Late morning to early afternoon	Low to mid	M
✔	✔	✔	✔	✔	Sunrise to early morning	N/A	E
✔	✔	✔			Early morning to late afternoon	N/A	E
✔	✔	✔			Early to late afternoon	N/A	M
✔	✔	✔	✔	✔	Sunrise and sunset	N/A	E

	#	Location	Pg.	Jan	Feb	Mar	Apr	May	Jun	Jul
Mount Desert Island	26	Duck Brook Bridge	112	✔	✔	✔	✔	✔	✔	✔
	27	Cadillac Mountain	114				✔	✔	✔	✔
	28	Bubble Pond	124					✔	✔	✔
	29	Bubble Rock Trail	126					✔	✔	✔
	30	Jordan Pond Shore Path	128	✔	✔	✔	✔	✔	✔	✔
	31	Jordan Stream	130	✔	✔	✔	✔	✔	✔	✔
	32	Deer Brook Bridge & Waterfall	132					✔	✔	✔
	33	Pretty Marsh Picnic Area	136					✔	✔	✔
	34	Bass Harbor Head Lighthouse	138	✔	✔	✔				
	35	Ship Harbor Trail	142	✔	✔	✔	✔	✔	✔	✔
	36	Wonderland Trail	144	✔	✔	✔	✔	✔	✔	✔
	37	Seawall Picnic Area	146	✔	✔	✔	✔	✔	✔	✔
Schoodic Peninsula	38	Frazer Point Picnic Area	152	✔	✔	✔	✔	✔	✔	✔
	39	Schoodic Drive (West)	158	✔	✔	✔	✔	✔	✔	✔
	40	Ravens Nest	160				✔	✔	✔	✔
	41	Schoodic Head	164					✔	✔	✔
	42	West Pond Cove	166	✔	✔	✔				
	43	Schoodic Point	172	✔	✔	✔	✔	✔	✔	✔
	44	Little Moose Island	178	✔	✔	✔	✔	✔	✔	✔
	45	Schoodic Drive (East)	182	✔	✔	✔	✔	✔	✔	✔
Isle au Haut	46	Eben's Head Trail	188					✔	✔	✔
	47	Duck Harbor	194					✔	✔	✔
	48	Western Head Trail	196					✔	✔	✔
	49	Cliff Trail	198					✔	✔	✔
	50	Long Pond	200					✔	✔	✔

Aug	Sep	Oct	Nov	Dec	Time of Day	Tide	Hike
✔	✔	✔	✔	✔	Late morning to early afternoon	N/A	M
✔	✔	✔	✔		Sunrise and sunset	N/A	E/M
✔	✔	✔			Late morning to early afternoon	N/A	E
✔	✔	✔			Late morning	N/A	S
✔	✔	✔	✔	✔	Early afternoon to sunset; night	N/A	M
✔	✔	✔	✔	✔	Early morning to early afternoon	N/A	M
✔	✔	✔			Early to late morning	N/A	M
✔	✔	✔			Sunset	Any	M
		✔	✔	✔	Sunset	Mid to high, incoming	M
✔	✔	✔	✔	✔	Late afternoon to sunset	Minus low or high	M
✔	✔	✔	✔	✔	Late morning to early afternoon	Minus low	M
✔	✔	✔	✔	✔	Sunrise to late morning	Minus low or high	E
✔	✔	✔	✔	✔	Sunset	Mid to high	E
✔	✔	✔	✔	✔	Sunset; night	Mid to high	E
✔	✔	✔	✔		Sunset	Mid to high	M
✔	✔	✔			Sunrise to late morning	N/A	M
			✔		Late afternoon to sunset	Low to mid	E
✔	✔	✔	✔	✔	Sunrise and sunset	Mid to high, incoming	E
✔	✔	✔	✔	✔	Sunrise and sunset	Low	M
✔	✔	✔	✔	✔	Sunrise; night	Any	E
✔	✔	✔			Late afternoon to sunset	Mid to high	M
✔	✔	✔			Late afternoon to sunset	Low to mid	E
✔	✔	✔			Late afternoon to sunset	Any	M
✔	✔	✔			Sunrise to late morning	Mid to high, incoming	S
✔	✔	✔			Sunrise to late morning	N/A	E

Top Experiences

While I could argue all the locations featured in this book fall into the "can't miss" category, I recognize not everyone has the time to experience it all in a single trip. The two lists below offer a summary of the "best of the best" photographic spots within Acadia National Park.

Top 10 Classic Locations

If this is your first visit to Acadia National Park and/or you have limited time to explore the area, put the following 10 locations on your itinerary to see the classic spots that make this coastal park so special!

- #7: Sieur de Monts (pg. 62)
- #10: Sand Beach (pg. 70)
- #13: Thunder Hole (pg. 76)
- #16: Boulder Beach (pg. 86)
- #23: Asticou Azalea Garden (pg. 106)
- #25: Eagle Lake (pg. 110)
- #27: Cadillac Mountain (pg. 114)
- #29: Bubble Rock Trail (pg. 126)
- #30: Jordan Pond Shore Path (pg. 128)
- #34: Bass Harbor Head Lighthouse (pg. 138)

Top 10 Lesser-Known Locations

Photographers who have visited Acadia before may enjoy finding quieter, lesser-known places within the park. Here are 10 photogenic spots a little further off the beaten path:

- #2: Bar Island (pg. 50)
- #15: Gorham Mountain (pg. 84)
- #19: Little Hunters Beach (pg. 96)
- #20: Day Mountain (pg. 98)
- #22: Little Long Pond (pg. 102)
- #24: Waterfall Bridge (pg. 108)
- #40: Ravens Nest (pg. 160)
- #43: Schoodic Point (pg. 172)
- #44: Little Moose Island (pg. 178)
- #48: Western Head Trail (pg. 196)

OPPOSITE: An autumn storm rolls in at sunrise atop Gorham Mountain. Canon 5DMII, 16-35mm at 16mm, ISO 100, f/16 at 0.4 sec., four-stop graduated neutral density filter.

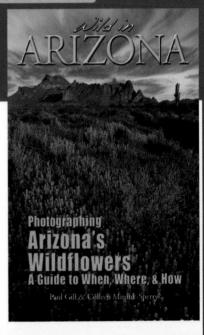

Additional Book Sponsors

In addition to the sponsors featured on the previous pages, I would like to extend my sincerest appreciation to the following companies and individuals for their generous contributions and support to enable this book project to come to fruition:

Winter Harbor 5 & 10
www.winterharbor5and10.com
349 Main Street
Winter Harbor, Maine 04693
Phone: (207) 963-7927
Email: wh5n10@myfairpoint.net

The Winter Harbor 5 & 10 is a true old fashioned 5 & 10 Cent Store. Our motto is "Everything from A to Z, Aspirin to Zippers." The store has been featured in the Smithsonian magazine as one of the last remaining 5&10's in the country. The store opened in 1972 and we—Pete and Sandy Drinkwater—purchased it in 1989. We will celebrate our 25th year in 2014. The store is also the home of Pete's real estate office, Realty of Maine.

We offer name brand household items, health and beauty aids, Ambassador greeting cards, sewing and craft supplies, hard-to-find gadgets, local souvenirs, UPS shipping, fax service, photocopying, and much more.

If you are in the Schoodic Area enjoying this book and taking pictures, we also have a digital photo developing machine that prints 3" x 5", 4" x 6", and 8" x 10" photos. We carry SD cards and flash drives.

Come browse our aisles and enjoy the old fashioned charm and friendly, personal service. We are open year-round, seven days a week from May to December (closed on Sundays in the winter).

Gary Fong, Inc.
www.garyfongestore.com
228 Park Avenue S.
Ste. 36122
New York, New York 10003
Phone: (800) 906-6447, extension 1
Email: support@garyfonginc.com

Since 1993, Gary Fong, Inc. has positioned itself as a leading developer and manufacturer of cutting-edge photography equipment designed to help photographers experience new levels of quality and creativity in their work. The top-selling legendary Lightsphere, recently updated with the Lightsphere Collapsible Speed Mount, is just one of a myriad of products that has enabled photographers to create studio-quality lighting effects, on-location, with very little equipment.

Not only is Gary Fong, Inc. known as a trusted source for quality and design in the photographic accessory category, but they are also pioneers of customer education with over 300 tutorial videos and 17,000 subscribers to the Gary Fong, Inc. YouTube channel at **www.youtube.com/user/GFIGARYFONG**.

Gary Fong, Inc. continues to invent new ways to meet its customers' changing needs, giving photographers of all experience levels the tools necessary to elevate their photography to the next level. For more information, visit **www.garyfongestore.com**.

Valued Individual Contributors

- **Jen Bookman**
- **Amy Minton**
- **Gwen Williams**
- **Rebecca Wilks**
- Ambika Balasubramaniyan
- John Benet
- Jonathan & Lisa Bitting
- Helen Glaenzer
- Thomas Hiscox
- Rob & Bianca Miniuk
- Robert & Jacqueline Miniuk
- Ken Natoli
- Matt Nickell
- Bev Secord
- Regina & Sterling Skouson
- Kerry Smith
- Rebecca Zaharias

Winter reflections in a pool of water near Blackwoods Campground. Canon 5D, 24-105mm at 40mm, ISO 100, f/18 at 1.6 sec., polarizer.

Index

*Note: A **bolded** number indicates a photo reference.*

Abbe Museum   65
Abstract   **43**, **53**, **73**, **75**, **109**, **113**, **119**, **139**, **145**, **165**, **183**, **191**, **193**, **195**, **199**
Acadia Birding Festival   19
Acadia National Park Headquarters   47
Acadia Night Sky Festival   20
Alder Trail   164
American kestrel   118
Anvil Trail   164
Aperture   27-31, 33-34, 38, 104, 118, 129, 159, 171
   definition   28
   small   28, 30, 42, 51-52, 89, 97, 115, 125, 165, 167-168, 183, 192, 197, *See also* depth of field
   wide   28, 42, 51-52, 59, 65, 129-130, 145, 159, 179, *See also* depth of field
Arey Cove   **151**, 173, 179, **219**
Arizona Highways Photography Workshops (AHPW)   5, 10, 80, 211, 224
Arrowhead   60
Artificial light   35, 37-39, 122, 159, 171, *See also* flash
Aspen   21, **58**, 73, 115, **127**, 132
Aster   64, 85
   New England   67, **143**
Asticou Azalea Garden   106-107, 208
Astrophotography   **121**, **123**, **169**, 171
   test shots   120, 122, 129, 145
Atlantic sea smoke   18, **183**
Atterbury, Grosvenor   14, 173
Azalea   106-107

Background   33-34, 37-38, 42, 49, 59, 64, 102, 125, 130, 171, 181, 200
   blur   59, 95
Balance Rock   54-**55**
Balanced Rock   **126**, *See also* Bubble Rock
Bald eagle   25, 68, 110-111, 118, 145, 173
Bangor International Airport   46
Bar Harbor   20-21, **46-47**, 50-51, 54-55, 65, 67, 89, 104, 110, 114, 118, 120, 122, 150-151, 154-157, 186
Bar Harbor Chamber of Commerce   47, 54, 119
Bar Harbor Inn   5, **50**-51, 210
Bar Harbor Shore Path   54-**55**, **217**
Bar Harbor-Winter Harbor Ferry   151
Bar Island   50-**51**, 208
Bar Island Trail   51
Barnacle   **27**, **71**, 95, 145, 147, 179-180

Bass Harbor   47, 138, 141
Bass Harbor Head Lighthouse   47, **138**, 140-**141**, 168, 208
Bates, Waldron   85
Beaver   25, 68
Beaver Dam Pond   **68-69**
Beaver Log park newspaper   47
Beech   21, **65**, 109, 111, 115, **130**
The Beehive   71, 73, **84**
Better Beamer flash extender   22, 39, *See also* Flash X-tender
Big Moose Island   164, 179
Birch   14, 21, **58**, 67, 73, 111, 113, 115, 132-**133**, 150
Black guillemot   173, 197
Blue flag iris   64, 67, **79**, 179
Blue Hill Overlook   118
Blue vetch   79
Blueberry, low sweet   **2-3**, **6**, **116-117**, 118, **148**, 183
Blueberry Hill   **151**, 179, 182-183
Boulder Beach   **36**, **44**, 47, 81, **86-87**, 168, 179, 208
Brook Trail   109
Bubble Pond   **124**-125
Bubble Pond Bridge   125
Bubble Rock   **126**-127
Bubble Rock Trail   126-127, 208
The Bubbles   111, 124, 126, **128**-129
Bufflehead   48, 147, 173
Bulb mode   28, 120, 129, 159
Bunchberry dogwood   79, **95**, 142, 179

Cadillac Cliff Trail   85
Cadillac-Dorr Trail   115
Cadillac Mountain   **1**, 10-11, **21**, 23, 47, 58, 60, 98, 110-111, **114-120**, 122, 124, 133, 140, **161**, 164, 168, 170, 173, 179, **202**, 208
Cadillac Mountain North Ridge Trail   114, 118
Cadillac Mountain South Ridge Trail   202
Cadillac Mountain Sunrise Club membership card   119
Cadillac Summit Loop Trail   114, 118
Camera mode   27, 30-31
   aperture priority (Av)   27, 30-31
   manual (M)   27, 31, 33, 38, 92
   program (P)   27
   shutter speed priority (Tv)   27
Camera's LCD screen   30, 67, 104, 120, 176, 180, 192

A stormy morning sky along the Bar Harbor Shore Path. Canon 5DMII, 100-400mm at 400mm, ISO 400, f/13 at 1.6 sec.

Campgrounds
  Blackwoods 46
  Duck Harbor 186-187, 195
  Schoodic Woods 150
  Seawall 46, 147
Carriage road 11, 14-16, 23, 25, 47, 98-99,
    108-109, 112-113, 130-135
Carriages of Acadia 98-99
Champlain, Samuel 14, 186
Champlain Mountain **50**-51, 58, 60-61, 68
Chokecherry 77, 79
Church, Frederic 14
Civilian Conservation Corps 95, 158, 164
Cliff Trail 197-**198**, 199
Cobblestone Bridge 130-131
Cole, Thomas 14
Compass Harbor 56
Compass Harbor Trail 56-57
Composition 26, 29, 34, 39, 41, 61, 64, 69, 75,
    79, 82, 87, 92, 101, 109, 120, 125, 127,
    129, 134, 140, 142, 146-147, 153, 165,
    170, 173, 176, 189, 192, 197, 201
  asymmetrical balance 41-42, 131
  break the rules 43
  horizon line 33, 41
  layers 42, 127, 192
  lines
    converging 41
    diagonal 33, 41-2
    leading **41**, 49, 87, 131, 143, 146, 197
    S-curves 41
    Z-curves 41
  mergers 43
  perspectives 42-43, 71, 104, 111, 134, 138,
      181, 190, 192
  Rule of Odds 42
  Rule of Space 42
  Rule of Thirds 40, 69, 201
  simplicity 39
  symmetrical balance 41-42
  symmetry 41, 69, 200-201
  viewer's eye 40-43
Continuous drive mode 52, 76
Contrast 35, 38, 75, 131, 189
Convergence, caused by wide-angle lens 138
Cormorant 48, 79, 147, 173
  double-crested 48
  great 173
Crab, green 95
Cranberry Island Formation 88
Cranberry Isles 98, 145

Day Mountain 47, 98-99, 208
Day Mountain Loop 99
Day Mountain Summit Trail 99
Deer Brook **132**-133
Deer Brook Bridge **132**
Depth of field 28-30, 33, 42-43, 57, 59, 125,
    192, 197
  hyperfocal distance 29, 125, 165, 197

Index (continued)

near-far technique 42
preview button 33
Depth of Field Master 29, 125
Diffuser 36-37, 65, 73, 77, 95, 101, 107, 113, 126, 131, 133, 142, 144, 147, 165, 179, 183, 189, 197
Dog whelk 180
Dorr, George B. 15, 51, 56-57, 62, 64-66, 68, 203
Dorr Mountain 58-60, 64, 67
Du Gua de Monts, Pierre 14, 62
Duck Brook **112-113**
Duck Brook Bridge 112
Duck Harbor 186-**187**, 188, **194**-196
Dutch tilt **40**-41, 55, 192

Eagle Lake **29**, 47, **110**-111, 118, 126-127, 208
Eagle Lake Bridge 110-111
East Pond Cove 179-180
East Trail **164**-165
Eben's Head 188-190, 195
Eben's Head Trail 188-191, 193, 196
Egg Rock 55
Egg Rock Lighthouse 56, 73, 104
Egret
   great 48
   snowy 48
Eider, common 18, 51, 71, 79, 147, 173, 197, 199
Eliot, Charles 15
Ellsworth Schist 54
Exposure 26-28, 30, 32-33, 35, 38, 51, 61, 79, 87, 97, 103-104, 113, 115, 120, 129, 137-138, 161, 181, 192, 195, 199
   add light 30, 165
   definition 27
   Exposure Value (EV) compensation 30-31
   highlights 30, 34-38, 61, 98, 113, 118, 144, 167
   nighttime 171
   open up 27
   overexposure 31, 33
   settings 27, 32-33, 43, 97, 120, 122, 129, 135, 145, 180
   stop down 27
   subtract light 30-31, 38
   underexposure 30, 49, 77
Extension tubes 59, 144, 179, 182, 192

F-stop 28, *See also* aperture
Fabbri, Lieutenant Alessandro 94

Fabbri Picnic Area 94
Falcon 65
   peregrine 19, 25, 65, 118
Father of Acadia 57, 65, *See also* Dorr, George B.
Fern **19**, 67, 75, 113, 200
File format 26
Filters 31-33, 43, 51, 89, 115, 167, 173, 183, 195
   graduated neutral density 33-36, 51, 55, 57, 61, 73, 75-76, 79, 85, 87, 95, 97, 99, 103, 111, 113, 115, 127-128, 137, 139, 143, 146, 152, 161, 166, 168, 172, 179, 182, 189, 194-195, 197, 199, 201
   neutral density 32-34, 60, 71, 79, 87, 89, 97, 109, 113, 131, 133, 137, 139, 153, 199
   polarizer 31-32, 49, 51, 55, 57, 59-60, 67, 69, 71, 73, 75-76, 78, 85, 87, 89, 95, 97, 99, 101, 103, 107-109, 111, 113, 115, 125, 127-128, 131, 133, 137-8, 143, 147, 152, 161, 165-166, 172, 179, 182, 188-189, 192, 194, 197, 199, 201
      uneven polarization 32, 147, 161
   split neutral density 33, *See also* graduated neutral density
   ultraviolet (UV) 31
   warming 31-32
Flash 37-**39**, 71, 128, 142, 144, 147, 173, 179, 197, 199
   camera-to-subject distance 29
   Flash Exposure Compensation (FEC) 38
   inverse-square law 38
   lighting in layers 38
   manual mode 38
   off-camera 37
   on-camera 37-39, 51, 59, 65, 77, 79
   ring flash/light 37-8
   Through-the-Lens (TTL) 38
   twin lights 38
Flash X-tender™ 22, 39, 51, 59, 65, 71, 79, 128, 136, 147, 173, 179, 197, 199
Flowers 42, **56**, **58-59**, **61**, 64, **106-107**, 119, *See also* wildflowers
Flycatcher 65, 68
Focus 28-29, 39-40, 42, 51, 55, 57, 95, 101, 125, 129-130, 173, 192, 197
Fog, photographing in **20**-21, 55, 96, 102-103, **118**-119, **124**, **126**-127, **183**, **203**
Foreground 33, 38, 42, 49, 69, 75, 88, 120, 125, 127, 129, 139, 143, 167, 171, 179, 182, 189, 197, 200-201

Frazer, Thomas   152
Frazer Point Picnic Area   150-153, 158, 177, 183
Frenchman Bay   **1**, 15, 51, **55-56**, 73, **84**-85,
    94, 105, **114-115**, 118, 120, 154-**155**, 156-
    158, 160-**161**, **162**-164, 173, **203**
Friends of Acadia   16
Frog   103
Frostbite   24

Gary Fong   5, 214
  Lightsphere   38
  Puffer Pop-Up Flash Diffuser   38
Glacial erratic   10, 54-**55**, **126**
Goat Trail   199
Goldeneye, common   18, 48, 173
Goldenrod   67, **85**
Google™ Earth, Sunlight feature   34-35, 140
Gorham Mountain   47, 71, **84**-85, 208-**209**
Gorham Mountain Trail   84-85
Grass, bayonet   60
Great blue heron   48, 68, 103, 111
Great Fire of 1947   21, 66-67, 85, 111, 132
Great Head   70-**72**, 73-74
Great Meadow   20, **58**, 60, 62, 67

Grebes
  horned   173
  red-necked   173
Green Mountain Railway   110
Hadlock Brook Loop Carriage Road   108-109,
    135
Hadlock Falls   **108**-109
Hancock County/Bar Harbor Airport   46, 104
Hancock County Trustees of Public Reservations
    15, 64, 68
Harbor seal   25, **155**, 173
Harlequin duck   173, 199
Hawk   21
  sharp-shinned   118
Hawk Watch program   21, 118
Haze, reduce   31-32
Hemlock Bridge   108, **134**
High Dynamic Range (HDR)   34, 36, 75, 79,
    97, 131, 139
Highlight Alert   31, 33
Histogram   30-31, 33, 38, 55, 115, 118, 122,
    129, 176, 195
Hoodman Corporation   5, 212
Hoodman Hoodloupe   22

Intriguing ice patterns surround a lone rock in Arey Cove on the Schoodic Peninsula. Canon 5DMII, 100-400mm at 275mm, ISO 400, f/16 at 1/5th sec., polarizer.

Index (continued)

Huguenot Head   51, 58, 60, 68
Hunters Beach   100-**101**
Hunters Brook   **100**
Hunt's Photo & Video   5, 22, 211
Hypothermia   24

Ice   12, **18**-19, 24-**25**, **48-49**, **57**, **75**, **81**, **83**-84,
   87, 99, 103, 109, **113**, 126-127, 130, **147**,
   151, **152-153**, **159**, 161, **166-167**, 168,
   169, 170-**171**, **219**
   frazil   168
   grease   166-**167**
   pancake   **18**, **49**, 166-**167**
Ice fishing   110-111
Image stabilization   73, 107, 119, 145, 173, 199,
   See also vibration reduction
Island Explorer park shuttle   46, 151
Isle au Haut   **12**, 16, 20, 184, **186**-190, **194**,
   196, **198**, **200**, **222**
Isle au Haut Bay   **188-190**, **194**, **196**
Isle au Haut Ferry Company   186, *See also* mail
   boat
ISO speed   27-28, 30-31, 38, 65, 92, 104, 129,
   137, 143, 145, 153, 159, 171, 173, 180,
   195, 201
   definition   27
   faster   27, 30-31, 129, 145
   slower   30-31

Jesup Path   **19**, 64, **66-67**
Jordan-Bubble Ponds Loop Carriage Road   124,
   132-133, **135**
Jordan Pond   11, 47, 126-**128**, 129-130, 132-
   133
Jordan Pond Gatehouse   10, **14**
Jordan Pond House   47, 129, 131
Jordan Pond Shore Path   **128**-129, 208
Jordan Stream   130-**131**, 132
Jordan Stream Bridge   132
Jordan Stream Loop Carriage Road   130
JPEG   26-27, 30

L'Acadie   10, 15
Lady's slipper orchid   64
Lafayette National Park   15
Landpools   **52**, *See also* skypools
Laurel   107
   sheep   **63**, 85, 113, 119
Lens
   focal length   29, 38, 104, 107, 147, 197
   macro   51, 55, 59, 61, 64, 71, 73, 77, 95, 97,

   101, 107, 109, 113, 125-126, 130, 132,
   142, 144, 147, 153, 165, 167, 179-182,
   189, 192, 194, 196
   normal   49, 51, 57, 59, 61, 73, 75, 78, 87-88,
   95, 97, 100, 111, 115, 125, 127-128, 131-
   133, 136, 138, 143, 147, 152, 165, 172,
   179, 188-189, 194, 197, 199-200
   telephoto   49, 51, 55, 57, 59, 61, 64-65, 67-
   69, 71, 75-76, 79, 85, 89, 92, 96, 99, 101,
   103, 107-109, 111, 113, 115, 118, 125,
   128, 130, 132-133, 136, 140, 142, 144-
   145, 147, 153, 157, 159, 161, 165-166,
   173, 175-176, 179, 183, 189, 194, 197,
   199, 201
   wide-angle   32, 49, 51, 55, 59, 61, 64, 67, 69,
   73, 75-76, 85, 89, 92, 97, 103, 108, 111,
   113, 125, 127-129, 131-133, 135, 138,
   146, 152, 159, 161, 166, 171-172, 179,
   181-182, 189, 194, 197, 200
Lens flare, prevent   34, 69, 89, 99, 113, 139,
   153
Lens hood   24, 34, *See also* lens shade
Lens shade   89, 99, 113, 139, 153, *See also* lens
   hood
Lichen   109, 113, 130, 144, 165, 179, 194-195,
   198
Light
   back   34-**35**, 37, 64, 69, **93-94**, **97**, 113, **156-**
   157, 165, 189-190, **192**, 194
   The Blue Hour   35-**36**
   diffused   36, **101**, 103, 107, **113**
   front   34, 37, 139, 195
   The Golden Hour   35-36, 95, 147
   mid-day   36, 71, 107, 127, 144
   reflected   36
   shade   36, **64**, 131
   side   **34**, 37, 64, 69, **87**, **165**, 190, **194**, 201
   sweet light   35
   top   34
Lily pads   61, 102-**103**
Limpet   95, 180
Little Harbor Brook Bridge   132
Little Hunters Beach   11, 47, **96-97**, 100-101,
   208
Little Long Pond   25, **102**-103, 200, 208
   Little Moose Island   23, 174, **178**-180,
   181-182, 208
Live View   42, 97
Long Pond, Mount Desert Island   102, 110
Lond Pond, Isle au Haut   **185**, **200-201**
Long Pond Trail   200

Loon, common   18, 48, 71, 111, 128, 173, 179
Lupine   51, **56**-57, **58**-59, **61**
Mail boat   186-187
Manfrotto   5, 212
Maple Spring Trail   108-109
Maple   21, 56-**57**, 59, **66-67**, **102**, 107-109, **111**, 113, 115, **125**, **129**, 132-133, **185-186**, 200
The Margaret Todd   **50**
Mark Island Lighthouse   155, 158-159, 164, **203**, *See also* Winter Harbor Light
Median Ridge Trail   **186**
Merchant Cove   **222**
Merganser   79
   common   128, 179
   red-breasted   48, 71, 147, 173
Meter, spot   33, 118, 167
Mid-tones   30, 37, 167, 195
Middle ground   42, 103, 111, 160, 200
Milky Way   11, **121**-122, 159
Monument Cove   **41**, **78-79**, **81**
Moore, John G.   15, 158
Moore Road   150, 158, 179, *See also* Schoodic Drive
Morgan, J.P.   72
Moss   **13**, 96, 113, 137, 144, 165, 183
Motion
   blur   **26**, 28, 30, 60, **77**, 79, **97**, **101**, **108-**109, **112-113**, 129, **132-133**, **143**, 153, **199**, 201, *See also* shutter speed, slow
   freeze   27-28, 30, 39, 67, 87, 92-**93**, 97, 103-104, 129, 143, 145, 171, 183, 199, *See also* shutter speed, fast
Mount Desert Island (MDI)   10, 12, 14-16, **46-48**, **50**, 64, 68, 81, 94, 102, 104-**105**, 118, 126, 138, 140, 146, 150, 153, 158, 164, 173-174, 179, 186, 200
Mount Desert Narrows   **48-49**, 166
Mountain cranberry   85
Mushroom   **40**, 113, **137**, **165**
Mussel   **179**-180

National Park pass   47
National Register of Historic Places   16, 65, 138
Nature Center   64-65, 67
Newport Cove   **70**, 73-**74**, 76, 81, 122-**123**
Newport Cove Overlook   **74**
Northeast Harbor   47, **105**-106, 108, 156
Norumbega Mountain   109

Oak   21, 113

Ocean Drive   41, 52-53, 74-77, 79-83, 86-90, 93-94, 122-123, 174, *See also* Park Loop Road
Ocean Path   **25**, 75, 78, 87-88, 95
Old Farm   56
Oldfield cinquefoil   113
Olmstead, Frank   15
Orientation
   horizontal   42, 57, 75, 89, 113, 133, 152
   vertical   42, 57, 75, 115, 133, 137, 152
Osprey   103, 111, 155
Otter Cliff   16, **41**, **74**-76, 84-**85**, 86-91, 92, 95, 122-**123**
Otter Point and Cove   **94**-95
Oxeye daisy   58-**59**, 79, 113

Panoramas, how to photograph   115
Park Loop Road   16, 18, 47, 58, 81, 94-95, 110, 125, *See also* Ocean Drive
Pemetic Mountain   **110**-111, 124, 127-128, 133
Penobscot Mountain   **102**, 127-128, 133
Periwinkle   95, 147, 179-180
The Photographer's Ephemeris   34, 50, 122, 140, 159, 178
Pickerelweed   60
Pitcher plant   64
Playback mode   43, 67, 173
Pond lily   103
Porcupine Islands   **1**, **55**, **114-115**, 118
Portland International Jetport   46
Post-processing software   31, 34, 87, 138
Pretty Marsh   **136**-137, 153
Pretty Marsh Harbor   **136**-137
Prospect Harbor   150, 165

Rain cover   77, 87, 119, 131, 176
Ravens Nest   **121**-122, 155, **160-163**, 208
RAW file   26-27, 30
Reflection, water   32, 41, 52-**53**, **60**, **68-69**, 101-103, 107, 124-125, **133**, **137**, 139, **185**, 189, 192, 200-**201**
Reflector   37, 65, 73, 77, 95, 107, 113, 126, 133, 142, 144, 165, 179, 189, 196
Reverse Boston Salute   165
Rhododendron   106-**107**
Rhodora   58, 142
Rockefeller family   102
Rockefeller Jr., John D.   15-16, 94, 98, 106, 108, 110, 112, 125, 130-134, 158
Rockefeller's Teeth   15
Roosevelt, Franklin D.   158
Rose, rugosa (beach)   77, 79, 145, 179, 182

Index (continued)

Roseroot 179

Rush **60**-61, 125, **201**

Sand Beach 11, **27**, **70-71**, 72-73, 85, 95, 208

Sandpiper. purple 18

Sargent Mountain 111

Saturation, increase color 32, 67, 69, 97, 115, 131, 133, 161, 181

Savage, Charles K. 106

Scenic Flights of Acadia 5, **46**, 104-**105**, 210

Schoodic Drive (East) **2**, **11**, **17**, **148-50**, 168, **182**

Schoodic Drive (West) **18**, **26**, **158-159**

Schoodic Education Adventure (SEA) 5, 7, 10

Schoodic Education and Research Center (SERC) 5, 16, 150-151, 173

Schoodic Harbor 150, **182-183**

Schoodic Head **150**, **164**-165

Schoodic Head Trail 165

Schoodic Peninsula **2**, **6**, **11**-12, 15-**17**, 20, 55-56, 73, 80, 94, 98, 104-105, 120, 122, 129, **149**-52, 155, **158-60**, **164**, **172**, 174, 178, **182**, 186, **219**

Schoodic Point 10, 16, 81, 94, 150-151, 170, **172-173**, **175**-176, 179, 208

Scoter 173

Sea duck 21, 39, 51, 146, 150

Sea urchin 25, **39**, 70, 95, 142, 145

Seagull 25, **137**, 173, 179, 197

Seal Harbor 98

Seawall Picnic Area **146-147**

Seawall Pond 33, 147

Sedges 10, **62**, 67

Self-timer 101, 127

Shadows 30, 34-38, 49, 61, 65, 73, 77, 79, 109, 122, 133, 138-139, 144, 147, 153, 164-165, 167

Shatter Zone 96, 100

Ship Harbor Trail **142-143**

Shutter speed 27-28, 30-31, 38, 104, 111, 113, 145, 159

  definition 28

  fast 28, 30, 51-**52**, 65, 87, 97, 103, 129, 136, 143, 173, 183, 199, 201

  slow 28, 30, 32, 51, 55, 60-61, 69, 76-**77**, 79,

Morning light skims across boulders and rockweed revealed by low tide at Merchant Cove on Isle au Haut. Canon 5DMII, 16 to 35mm at 16mm, ISO 100, f/16 at 1/6 sec., two-stop graduated neutral density filter.

85, 87, 89, 96-**97**, **100-101**, **108**-109, **113**, **132**-134, **143**, 153, 161, 165, **183**, **199**, 201
Sieur de Monts   10, 58, **62-65**, 67, 208
Sieur de Monts National Monument   15, 64, 68
Silhouette, photographing   118-**119**, **167**, 173, **187**, 195, **217**
Skypools   52-**53**, 69, **137**, *See also* landpools
Snow, photographing   49
Somes Sound   16, 104-**105**
Southwest Harbor   47, 156
Star trails   122-**123**, 128-129, 159, *See also* astrophotography
Starfish   25, 95, 142, 145
Stonington   186-187
Subject, primary   40-42, 95, 181
Sumac   21, 73
Summer solstice   19-20, 153, 201
Sun shade   69, 201, *See also* lens shade
Sun star   51-**53**, *See also* sunburst
Sunburst   11, 89, **90-91**, **97**, 139, **167**, 183, *See also* sun star

The Tarn   60-61, 67
Teleconverter   51, 59, 65, 79, 103, 111, 118, 147, 173, 179, 183, 197, 199
Thompson Island   **23**, 47, **48-49**, 81, 166
Thompson Island Visitor Center   47, 49
Thunder Hole   47, 76-77, 81, 174, 208
Tide pools   25, 36, 94-95, 101, 142, 189-**91**, **193**
Tide
  charts for Maine   13, 24, 50
  high   24, 73, 75-77, 82, 95, 139, **141**, 143, 145-146, 160, 166, 172, 174, 176, 181, 198
  incoming   49-50, 87, **138**
  low   13, 24, **48**, **50-51**, 75, 95-96, 101, 139, 141-**142**, 144-145, **146**-147, 155, 157, 159, 170, 173, 178-180, **194**, 197, **222**
  mid   75, 139, 160, 194
  minus low definition   95
  outgoing   87, 155
  spring   77, 174
Tilt-shift lens   138
Tongue switch   135
Town Landing, Isle au Haut   186-187
Tripod   24, 37, 42, 49, 51, 55, 59, 61, 67, 73, 77-78, 85, 87, 89, 95-96, 99, 101, 103, 107-108, 111, 113, 115, 119, 127-128, 131, 133, 137-138, 145, 152, 159, 161, 165-166, 173, 179-181, 183, 194, 199-200
Twilight   120, 122, 128

astronomical   35-36, 122, 129
civil   35-36, 137, 199
nautical   35-36

United States naval radio station   16, 94

Vibration reduction   73, 107, 119, 145, 173, 199, *See also* image stabilization
Vision   13, 40, 43, 122, 135, 171, 180, 190, 192
Visitor center   47
Visualization   120, 135, 140-141, 171, 190

Wabanaki   10, 14, 65, 175
Warbler   19, 65
Water lily   60, 102, 107
Waterfall Bridge   43, 108-109, 208
Waterfall   75, **100**, **108**-109, **112-113**, 130, **131-132**, **158**
West Pond Cove   18, **166-167**, **169**, 170-171
Western Ear   197
Western Head Road   198-199
Western Head Trail   **12**, **184**, **196-197**, 208
White balance   31-32, 49, 167, 195
  Auto White Balance (AWB)   31
  cloudy   31-32, 167, 195
  definition   31
  shade   31-32, 167, 195
  sunny   31, 49
  tungsten   31, 49
The Wild Gardens of Acadia   62-**63**, 64
Wildflowers   12, 19-20, 23, 27, 36, 39, 58-59, 60-**63**, 71, 73, **79**, **85**, **95**, 101, 106-**107**, 142-**143**, 144, 165, 179, *See also* flowers
Wildlife   12, 22-**23**, 25, **27**, 39, 42, 47, 58-59, 68, 102, 110, **137**, **144**, **155**
Wimberley   5, 213
Wimberley Plamp   22, 37, 59, 119
Wimberley tripod head   22
Wind, photographing in   19, 22, 24, 59, 61, 69, 73, 76, 82, 85, 105, 119-120, 143, 145, 161, **173**, **175**-176, 199, 201
Winter Harbor   150-151, 153-154, 157
Winter Harbor 5 & 10   5, 155, 214
Winter Harbor Light   155, 158, *See also* Mark Island Lighthouse
Witch Hole Pond Loop Carriage Road   **40**, 113
Wonderland Trail   **5**, **144-145**
Woodpecker   19, 65, 136
Working the scene   43, 135

About the Author

Photo by Jacque Miniuk

As an award-winning internationally-published outdoor photographer and writer, **Colleen J. Miniuk-Sperry** supports a wide range of assignments for editorial, fine art, and stock clients, specializing in nature, outdoor recreation, conservation, and travel. Her publication credits include *National Geographic* calendars, *Arizona Highways* magazine, calendars, and books, *Outdoor Photographer, AAA Highroads, AAA Via, InsideOutside Southwest, Sonora Es,* Smith-Southwestern calendars, and a broad variety of other publications.

Colleen has been honored to serve as an Artist-in-Residence three times with Acadia National Park in November 2009, October 2010, and January/February 2013.

In late 2011, she co-authored and published the guide book, *Wild in Arizona: Photographing Arizona's Wildflowers, A Guide to When, Where, & How* (**www.wildinarizona.com**). In its first year, the book won seven international book awards, including the International Book Awards "Best Nature Photography Book" and the USA Book Awards "Best Travel/Travel Guide."

Colleen enjoys leading photography workshops for the Arizona Highways Photography Workshops, Arizona Wildlife Federation, The Nature Conservancy, Through Each Others Eyes, and numerous private clients, where she has become known for her instruction-intensive style, inquisitive storytelling approach, and enthusiasm for exploration.

She is an Associate of Through Each Others Eyes (TEOE), where she has participated in cultural photographic exchanges and international exhibitions with Japan, Mexico, and Canada. She is also an active member and Board Member in the Outdoor Writers Association of America (OWAA), where she has won numerous Excellence in Craft awards for her photography, book, and blog, as well as the prestigious 2010 President's Choice Award and the 2013 People's Choice Award.

Armed with a Bachelor of Business Administration degree from the University of Michigan-Ann Arbor, Colleen Miniuk-Sperry moved to Phoenix in 1997 to begin a 10-year project management career at Intel Corporation. Initially as an outlet to corporate life, she began making photographs of the Western United States landscapes in late 2001. Then, she left Intel in early 2007 to pursue a full-time career in photography and writing.

Originally hailing from Ohio, Arkansas, and Illinois, Colleen currently resides in Chandler, Arizona with her husband, Craig, and her cat, Nolan.

To see more of her work, learn more about her workshops and online photography classes, and sign up for her newsletter, visit her website at **www.cms-photo.com**. Also, to read her blog, visit **www.youcansleepwhenyouredead.com**.